Principles, Analysis, and Application of
Effortless Combat Throws

by Tim Cartmell
Beckett Media
4635 McEwen Road, Dallas TX 75244

***Principles, Analysis, and Application
of Effortless Combat Throws***

Copyright © 2013 by Beckett Media
ISBN 0-86568-176-7
All Right Reserved

Published by Beckett Media
4635 McEwen Road, Dallas TX 75244

Printed in the United States of America

Cover Photo by Todd Everhart
Illustrations by Ron Crandall

Table of Contents

Part Two

Chapter 3 - Analysis and Applications   51

Appendix   A-1

Foreword

This work is the result of over twenty years study in the martial arts. It has been my very good fortune to have studied under a number of remarkable men. Although the ideas and techniques presented here are a synthesis of what I have learned and represent my own understanding of the way things work, there is something of each of my teachers in all that I offer. And anything that I have discovered "on my own" would not have been possible without the foundations of those who taught me and those who taught them. Although space prevents me from listing all who were kind enough to share their knowledge with me, I would like to briefly mention the teachers who have had a major influence on my art, and express my heartfelt gratitude.

Ted Sias, Kung Fu San Soo Master. Ted taught me how to fight, when not to fight and has been one of the major positive influences on my life. The skills and values I acquired during my twelve years of study under Master Sias have unfailingly proven to be most valuable resources.

Jimmy H. Woo, Grandmaster of Kung Fu San Soo. I was fortunate enough to be able to study under Grandmaster Woo directly for several years before I moved to the Orient. It is a tribute to his consummate fighting skill and ability as a teacher that he has thousands of descendants carrying on his art.

Hsu Hong Chi and Hsu Chen Wang of Taipei, Taiwan. Master Hsu was gracious enough to accept me as his student and teach me Hsing Yi Ch'uan. After his passing, his son Hsu Chen Wang took me under his wing and I continued training with him for several years thereafter.

Ch'en Tso Chen of Taiwan. Master Ch'en was an indoor disciple of Hsu Hsi Tao founder Huang Lao Yang (Hsu Hsi Tao is an esoteric, internal version of the White Crane). He is also a senior student of the famous Hsing Yi, T'ai Chi Ch'uan master Ts'ao Lian Fang of Shanghai. I learned much about the development and use of "internal" power during the five years I studied with Master Ch'en.

Lin Ah Lung of Taipei, Taiwan. I studied the Yang and Chen styles of T'ai Chi Ch'uan with Master Lin for several years. He opened my eyes to the incredible potential of extreme softness and the technical "hows" of T'ai Chi Ch'uan as a combat art.

Kao Liu Te of Taiwan. Master Kao taught me Yi Ch'uan and related arts. His emphasis on naturalness and simplicity in practice coupled with his amazing martial skill left a deep impression on my art.

Hsu Fu Chin of Taiwan. Master Hsu learned Chen style T'ai Chi Ch'uan from a member of the Chen clan while serving as a spy during the Second World War. He taught me the Old Frame and Cannon Fist forms.

Luo Te Hsiu of Taipei, Taiwan. Master Luo is an extremely open and knowledgeable teacher and one who understands the essence of the Internal styles both as combat arts and methods of self cultivation. Besides being one of the most powerful fighters I have ever met, he is a fine gentleman. With Master Lou I studied Kao Style Pa Kua Chang and the Chen Pan Ling style of T'ai Chi Ch'uan.

Sun Jian Yun of Beijing and Sun Bao An of Tian Jin, China. Sun Jian Yun is the daughter of Sun Lu Tang, one of the most famous and able Chinese boxers of all time. I studied Sun style Pa Kua Chang and the Pa Kua sword with Master Sun and her student Liu Yan Lung. I also studied Sun style T'ai Chi Ch'uan and the T'ai Chi sword with Sun Lu Tang's grandson, Sun Bao An. The Sun's were very open and generous in their instruction and it was an honor indeed to be able to study with a "Living National Treasure."

Liang Ke Ch'uan of Beijing, China. I was able to study with Hsing Yi Ch'uan master Liang for brief periods over the last few years. He is the veteran of war time hand to hand combat, personal challenges and street fights too numerous to count. In addition to his formidable fighting prowess he is a living example of an indomitable human spirit.

Don Angier, Headmaster of Yanagi Ryu Aiki Ju Jitsu. Soke Angier has spent his valuable time meeting with me on several occasions to answer my questions and share the principles of his amazing art.

Joe Moreira, 6th degree Black Belt Brazilian Jiu Jitsu, 4th degree Black Belt Judo; Marc Eccard, Senior Student of Rickson Gracie; Nelson Montiera, Black Belt Brazilian Jiu Jitsu; Ted Stickle and Gustavo Moreira. With these fine teachers I've had the invaluable opportunity to study the grappling and ground fighting techniques of Jiu Jitsu.

Thanks to my family for their patience and support.

I'd like to thank Rick Jeffrey and Glen Rosenzweig, Terry Spaulding, and Todd Everhart for their friendship, help and support.

Thanks to Dan Miller for his encouragement and support.

I'd also like to thank William Breazeal for proofreading this work.

Finally, many thanks to my students for teaching me at least as much as I ever taught them.

vi

Part One
Chapter One

Types of Throws and Basic Principles

Introduction

I would like to briefly introduce the concepts covered in this work and talk about the advantages of throwing in a fight. It should first be mentioned that none of the techniques included in this book require any brute strength or the slightest amount of tension. Truly, the effectiveness of many of the throws will be greatly reduced or completely lost by the inappropriate use of force (usually too much). We seek to maintain a natural, balanced posture and total relaxation. This point cannot be overemphasized. Throwing an opponent should be as easy as walking about or swinging the arms in space, as in a form. Applying the actual technique should require no more effort than moving through the form of the throw without another present.

Adhering to the axiom which holds the sum to be greater than the parts, our goal is to generate power as a loose, relaxed and flexible unit. This type of coherent force is often referred to as "whole body power." As a general rule of thumb, if you can feel where your power is coming from (which part), you are using too much strength and are performing the technique inefficiently. Rather than using strength, we will generate power by allowing our bodies to compress and our limbs to swing freely. As gravity and momentum are providing the power, we should never experience the feeling of "exertion," whether practicing alone or during the application of the techniques on another.

A successful throw is executed in three phases (which flow together in a smooth continuum in actual application), the set-up, the throw itself and the follow up (always mental, and often both mental and physical). The key to throwing an opponent without effort is an appropriate set-up or entry. Keeping in mind the best technique in the world is useless unless one has the chance to apply it, we will go into great detail describing the correct method of setting up and entering the throws. Although the possible variations in technique are potentially unlimited, all are based on a relatively small number of basic principles.

As the principles are what make the individual techniques "work," all of the throws and variations will be analyzed in relation to those principles which apply. The techniques are based on using correct angles, momentum, the opponent's inherent structural weaknesses, space/time, gravity, rhythm, leverage and our inherent natural strengths to our advantage, which allows us to circumvent the opponent's strength and effect a throw without effort. In addition, the principles and mechanics covered may be applied to the throwing methods of any particular system.

With an understanding of principles comes the potential for creativity. I strongly recommend the student pay the greatest attention to the principles illustrated and not to the immediate results of the technique, especially during the early stages of training. "Cheating" or forcing a throw may provide temporary gratification, but the net result will be bad habits and inefficient technique. Once the student has the "feeling" of the throws and develops an understanding of the underlying principles through conscientious practice, the foundations of realistic and useful throwing skills will be laid, and one will have a point of reference from which any technique may be analyzed and adjusted.

What are some of the advantages of training in the throwing arts and throwing an adversary during a fight? First, with regards to training, throws may be practiced exactly as they are to be applied "for real." There is no need to wear restrictive protective padding or "pull" blows as in training the striking arts. Partners training in the throwing arts may enter and throw just as they would in a fight; familiarity with the techniques, mats and breakfall skills protect the partners from injury. This type of training provides an accurate indicator of the students level of skill and aids in building realistic confidence. The element of surprise, the absence of mats and unfamiliarity with breakfalls will transform a technique safely learned in practice into an efficient combat technique in a real confrontation. Second, throws

2

can be devastating. Opponent's will usually fare better being struck with a fist on one small area than being struck with the ground over most of their body. Even if the opponent is not completely incapacitated after the fall, the throw will usually stun the attacker long enough for you to follow up decisively or escape. Third, proficiency at throwing may be the only hope a smaller combatant has of overcoming the larger and stronger. A smaller person may throw a larger opponent he or she would almost certainly be unable to defeat trading punches (the sloppy punch of a heavyweight will still pack considerably more whallop than the best blow a lightweight could ever hope to throw). Proficiency in the throwing arts can help balance the scales of physics much more in favor of the smaller and lighter contender than skill in the striking arts alone. Throws can be used in conjunction with the striking arts to end the fight more quickly, thus decreasing the risk of injury and period of vulnerability to additional attackers. Fourth, most fights quickly end up in the grappling range. The ability to throw at this juncture may be the last line of defense between you and ground fighting. If not schooled in ground fighting techniques, you may be at a great disadvantage wrestling with stronger or heavier attackers, as well as being more vulnerable to multiple opponents (and if you know how to grapple on the ground, an appropriate throw may allow you to immediately dominate your adversary as soon as he lands). Finally, the skills developed through practice in the throwing arts will enhance other types of martial abilities and will make one a better all around martial artist. It is my sincere hope that the information included here will expedite the training of the beginning student and that the advanced student will find the material useful in clarifying already familiar concepts and in teaching others.

Types of Throws

Let's begin by organizing all throws into three basic categories. Traditionally, throws are usually labeled according to the type of technique applied (i.e. hip throws, sacrifice throws, joint techniques, flips, sweeps etc.), in other words, how the thrower makes the other fall. In contrast, we will organize throws in relation to the movement the person being thrown makes through space before hitting the ground, that is, throws will be categorized from the point of view of the person being thrown and not the partner doing the throwing. From this point of view, all throws may be placed into one of three broad categories, namely, circles, arcs and spirals.

Arc Throws

Throws which involve arcs cause the opponent's head to move in an arcing plane to the front, side or rear with one or both feet remaining stationary. Examples of arcing throws are "clothesline" takedowns, the O-Soto-Gari (Major Reaping Throw) of Judo or the Shiho Nage (Four Directions Throw) of Aikido.

Circle Throws

Simply put, circular throws are those which cause the opponent to rotate either forward or backward around a central axis (his or her own hips) with the feet moving approximately 360 degrees. Examples of circular throws are hip throws, the Fireman's Carry of Western wrestling, and the Tomoe Nage (foot in stomach sacrifice throw) of Judo.

Spiral Throws

Spirals cause the opponent's upper body to twist either forward or backward as it moves downward with their feet either leaving the ground (as in a circular throw) or remaining relatively stationary (as in an arcing throw). Examples of Spiralling throws are the head twisting throws of Ba Gua Zhang, the Japanese Whizzer of Western wrestling or the Kotegaeshi of Aikido. Although there are potentially additional spatial patterns through which an opponent may be thrown, all of the practical throws of every school can be organized into these three categories or a combination thereof. I organize techniques this way as I feel it clarifies the desired result and serves as a point of reference from which subsequent principles may be derived, much simplifying a seemingly complex art.

A simple method of determining to which category (arc, circle, or spiral) a specific technique belongs would be to imagine the thrower to be invisible; instead of looking at how the technique was done, look at what happened to the one being thrown. Did the person falling revolve in the air (make a circle), tip over (in an arc), or twist (in a spiral) as he or she fell? Again, we are not categorizing throws by specific techniques but rather by the results of the technique. For example, if the opponent flips over in the air, no matter the technique applied (sacrifice throw, hip throw, reaping throw...), that technique falls under the category of circle throws. Once you understand the dynamics of the trajectory the opponent should make during a throw (a circle, arc or spiral), you can invent an almost endless variety of techniques to achieve the desired result.

It is important to shift the point of view from "doing" a specific technique on a person to "causing" the opponent to move through a pattern in space. The latter orientation will allow for much greater flexibility and spontaneity in applying techniques which is essential when actually trying to throw an uncooperative opponent. Once the principles and basic mechanics of the throws are mastered, one will find there are no "set" techniques and that you must work with and not against the opponent during the throw. Based on the dynamics of the opponent's (or your) attack, how you are able to set up the technique, the opponent's reactions and the subsequent flow of events, you will move with the opponent, join centers then lead them into the throw. These things and not a specific technique that you "want" to do determine which type of throw may be applied.

In the Analysis of the Throws and Practical Application sections, the throws and techniques are presented by type: arcs, circles, or spirals. Please study carefully the section on principles and the chapters on Body Use and Analysis of the Throws before attempting the techniques themselves. The very foundation of the techniques are the basic principles of body use and application; these principles form the heart of the method, the individual techniques are only visible expressions of them. Remember that principles are universal whereas techniques are limited to specific situations. Principles are what make techniques work. And once you know how something works, you know how to fix it, modify it or create something new. In the Appendix at the end of the book I have included some observations of and ideas about martial principles in general, and comments on classical tenets in particular. I hope this section will help clarify the ideas included in this work and will present a more complete and non-mysterious explanation of the basic principles.

Basic Principles

This section is perhaps the most important in the book. All of the subsequent entries and techniques will refer back to the principles presented here. These principles are the very heart and soul of the Art. It would be best to study this section until you have a good intuitive grasp of the concepts included here before moving on to the Body Use Exercises and the throws themselves. Remember, the principles are what make the throws work.

The concepts covered in this section cover the basic principles of applying the throws on another. Principles of body use are covered in the next chapter.

PRINCIPLE ONE:
NON-OPPOSITION OF FORCE

This is perhaps the most basic rule we will follow. The ideal is to never directly oppose the force of the opponent with our own force. In a direct confrontation of power against power, the contender with the greatest strength will invariably win. This is naturally the case between untrained individuals and while it may be martial, it is not martial "art." The practical worth of a technique should be considered in light of its potential universal applicability or lack thereof. If a technique is only useful against the smaller and weaker it should be recognized as such and the individual needs to take honest stock of his or her own potential strength. The techniques included here all fall under the category of potential universal applicability, meaning with the proper set-up, they will work on anyone, regardless of differences in strength. But as stated above, the best technique is useless unless one has the opportunity to apply it, another way of stating the proper set-up must precede the throw. Even if our strength is equal to the opponent's, if we use force against force we will alert him to our intentions of impending attack and the opponent will reflexively pull back and go on the defensive, making the application of a technique all the more difficult. Therefore, we seek to never oppose force with force in order to create the possibility for an effortless throw.

Non-Opposition of Force: Methods

1) Maintain Safe Distance:
There exists a minimum distance between you and your opponent which must be maintained if you hope to avoid the opponent's attack, connect with him and lead him into a throw without effort. I refer to this space as "Safe Distance." If you allow another to stand within the minimum bounds of Safe Distance, it is physically impossible to prevent him from striking you if he moves quickly and directly. This is true because of the minimum amount of time it takes to process the information of the attack mentally then react to

it physically. Reaction to stimuli requires a certain basic minimum interval of time; if the opponent is too close and launches a swift attack, your brain will not be able to respond quickly enough to allow for efficient defensive action. Although training will sharpen reflexes and decrease response time, once you allow the opponent inside Safe Distance his initiating the attack will preclude any hope of defense, even with trained reflexes. Since fast punches thrown in rapid succession will move so quickly the brain will be unable to respond with an effective defense, our defensive strategy should be based on dealing with the very source of the opponent's power, his torso, and not on his hands and feet. While the hand may be quicker than the eye, the torso is not. Safe Distance is the amount of space which forces the opponent to either lean his torso forward (to punch or grab), backward (to kick) or move his whole body forward with a step in order to be able to reach his target (us).

Standing at Safe Distance from our opponent, if he does not move his body (torso), his hands and feet will be unable to reach us. So as long as an opponent stays outside Safe Distance, he may make any manner of aggressive motion, verbal threat or mean faces and we remain completely safe. But as soon as he breaches Safe Distance we must react. After training you will be able to intuitively judge Safe Distance and will automatically adjust your position relative to the opponent in order to maintain it. The great benefit of this ability is that no matter how fast the opponent or skillful the attack, you will always have ample time to respond and gain an advantageous position. This is an example of using time and space to our advantage. The combatant who utilizes time/space as an ally has a decided advantage over the one who does not.

The ability to recognize and maintain Safe Distance alone will enable you to avoid getting "sucker punched" and will afford you the opportunity to deal with an opponent you may be hard pressed to beat once he lands the first unexpected blow. Although it is true one will not always have the option of starting a fight from Safe Distance, and there are other ways of dealing with close range attacks without using force against force, maintaining Safe Distance whenever possible

between you and another or others perceived as a potential threat makes time/space your ally and best initial line of defense.

2) Move Off the Line of Attack:

No matter which form a particular attack takes, the main thrust of force moves along a single line. Whether the attack takes the form of a blow with the hand, a kick, a grab or a rushing tackle, the primary objective in defense is to avoid the entire flow of momentum and not to deal exclusively with the attacking weapon itself (this concept is analogous to the bullfighter avoiding the rush of the bull's entire body rather than trying to block the bull's horn. And just like a bullfighter, we want to avoid the attacker's center of power, his body, not only his fist or foot). As the hand is quicker than the eye, it is futile and dangerous to stand in the opponent's attack line and attempt to ward off individual blows; this type of defensive strategy will inevitably result in the use of force against force, and if the opponent is strong and fast, will most likely also result in your being struck. Whenever possible, we will move off the line of attack (sometimes this is not an option, as when you are pinned against a wall or on the ground), blend with the opponent's momentum, join centers and lead him into a throw.

Since attacking momentum moves at us along a straight line from the attacker's centerline, there are only two directions we should not go, we should neither move directly toward nor directly away from the opponent's centerline as it generates force in our direction. Obviously, if you move straight forward or straight backward along a straight line, you will never be off it. Moving directly forward results in a head on collision which is the most extreme case of force against force. And while moving straight back may allow you to avoid the opponent's initial attack, you are directly in line for the next attack, and the opponent will be able to run forward faster than you could hope to run backward. Therefore, whether moving in early or avoiding the opponent's power until his momentum is spent, we will always seek to move at an angle off the line of attack and will avoid moving either straight forward or directly backward.

3) Intercept Early/Avoid Late:

During an attack, there are two points at which you may apply force without clashing directly with the force of the opponent. The first is when the opponent's intent is committed to an aggressive action but his body has just begun to move. The second is after the opponent has delivered his attack and is at the end of his momentum (his energy is spent). As an example of intercepting early, imagine your adversary has cocked his fist behind himself in preparation for a big roundhouse punch. If you move in immediately, before the punch has a chance to build up any momentum, and press your palm against the opponent's biceps, he will be unable to complete the punch and very likely will be repelled backwards as he pushes himself off of your palm. If your own body is lined up correctly, it will take very little effort to hold the opponent back or repel him in his awkward position. This same principle may be applied to counter-striking, or achieving an advantageous position simply by changing your angle in relation to the opponent just as he begins to punch. It is important to distinguish this type of defensive entry from your attacking the opponent first; in this case, the opponent's intent is committed to attacking you and he has begun to move (you may, of course, attack the opponent first, but that is a different case).

If you do not have the opportunity to intercept early, in order to avoid clashing with the opponent's power at its peak, you must wait until the attacking momentum reaches its end and begins to slow. With proper timing and positioning, it is possible to join with the opponent at this time and lead him into a throw without resistance. For example, if an opponent steps in to shove your chest with both hands and you move to the side turning your body out of the way, you will avoid his force altogether; as the opponent's push reaches the end of its momentum it will be relatively easy to reach out and grab his hand, as it will be close to stationary at this point. You may choose to follow the opponent's momentum in as he retracts the blow and use that force against him, or you may add a small force in the same general direction of the opponent's attack, pulling him off balance. From here, the opponent may again be led into a throw without struggle.

Attacking force is weakest in the early stage before momentum has a chance to develop and after the momentum is spent. Attempting to connect with or stop a blow between these two points will most likely result in a clash of force against force and should be avoided. Imagine a large and heavy bookcase which tips over and falls to the ground. If we are standing in the path of its fall and are able to reach up and check the tipping bookcase early, just as it begins to fall, we may stop its downward momentum with a very small resistant force. It will be a simple matter to stop the bookcase's momentum before it has a chance to build. Once the bookcase begins to build momentum, our only safe option is to jump out of the way and allow it to fall harmlessly to the ground. In effect, if we are standing beneath a falling bookcase and wish to avoid injury, we must either intercept its momentum early, or avoid its momentum altogether once it is fully in motion. We need to time our movements to those of the opponent, entering and connecting by either intercepting early or avoiding the incoming force until it is spent, thereby leading the opponent into a throw without opposition.

PRINCIPLE TWO: CONNECT AND JOIN CENTERS

The next step in throwing an opponent without struggle is to connect with him physically and join centers. The purpose of joining centers is to become "one body," so that throwing the opponent becomes as easy as moving your own body or, as in the case of a sacrifice throw, "falling down" yourself. As long as you and the opponent move as two separate entities (have two separate centers) there will inevitably be opposition and struggle. It is very important to follow the opponent's momentum initially and time your movement to it until you can take over the flow and lead the opponent where you will. The vital consideration here is that the opponent is the "leader" at this stage, you need to follow (actively not passively) his actions until you literally "take over." Rather than viewing a confrontation as an opponent "attacking" you with whom you must "fight," it may be more helpful to view the same situation as a partner presenting various opportunities for cooperative action which result in his eventual downfall. Move with single minded focus on the idea that the opponent will go down, and he will do most of the work himself, you are only there to guide him. Also bear in mind that until you have caught the opponent in your own flow of momentum which he is obliged to follow, he is entirely free to change as he wishes. Consequently, we will seek only to follow and make a connection at this stage of the throw.

Connect and Join Centers: Methods

1) Blend the Motions of the Torso:

In Principle One we introduced the concept of coordinating our response to the movement of the opponent's torso primarily, and to the movement of his limbs secondarily. We literally move our body (torso) when the opponent moves his inside our Safe Distance. In addition to moving off the line of attack at an appropriate angle, we also need to coordinate our body motion to that of the opponent. As we are moving in a more or less linear direction off the line of attack, we also need to rotate our torsos relative to the opponent's in order to create an overall harmonious flow of momentum around the two bodies. This is necessary because our goal here is to connect with the opponent so we may join centers. The center referred to is the hip and pelvis area, the physical center of the body. This region is the seat of power and by controlling this area, we may control the opponent's entire body.

You may rotate your body either right or left depending on the direction of the opponent's incoming force and your position relative to him as he attacks. For example, if the opponent steps in with a right straight punch and you are to his right (outside), you will turn your body to your right as you connect with him outside his right arm. Your torso will rotate to your right as the opponent's rotates to his left; since you are outside his right arm the motions of your torsos will blend as two sprocket-like gears, the motion of one turning left causes the other to rotate in the opposite direction. Conversely, if you were standing a little to the opponent's left as he threw a right hook punch at the left side of your head,

your torso will rotate to your left as you connect. In this instance both your and the opponent's torso will be rotating to the left respectively. This causes a blending of motion as if you were one body spinning around a central axis. In both cases there is a harmonious blending of motion as you coordinate the rotational movement of your body to that of your opponent. As stated above, it is very difficult to try and time your movements to the opponent's hands or feet as they move too quickly to allow for a sufficient and appropriate response. The key to blending with the opponent and making a connection from which to set up a throw lies in coordinating our response to the movement of the other's torso. Once you have coordinated your movement and the rotation of your torso with that of the opponent, you have, in effect, joined centers even if you have not yet physically touched the opponent.

2) Connect Where There is No Relative Motion:

Up to this point you have moved off the line of attack and have coordinated the movement of your torso with that of the opponent. Almost simultaneously you need to make an actual physical connection somewhere on the opponent's body. The ideal place to connect is where there is no relative motion between the part of your body you seek to make the connection with (usually your hand) and the place on the opponent's body that is "still" in relation to it. We are all familiar with the fact that if driving in a car at the same speed and in the same direction as another car in the lane beside us, we do not perceive the car to be "moving" in relation to ourselves. Even if both vehicles were moving at 100 miles per hour, it would be a simple task to reach out and shake hands with a passenger in the other car as he or she would be sitting still from our point of view. Similarly, if we hope to connect with an opponent without struggle or alerting him to our intentions, the best place to make such a connection is between points of no relative motion. This is made possible because we have already timed the movements of our source of power (our center) to that of our opponent (our cars are already going the same speed, so to speak). Our hands will now automatically also be moving in about the same direction and at approximately the same speed as our opponent's hands, creating a condition of no relative motion between them. Now we may reach out calmly and connect without struggle.

To emphasize once again, it is most important to remember that connecting smoothly without clashing with the opponent's force is made possible by coordinating your motion with that of the opponent. The key is to blend the movements of your respective torsos, creating the condition of no relative motion between you. This is completely different from standing your ground and trying to grab incoming punches out of the air. Remember, the hand is quicker than the eye, but the movement of the torso is not.

3) Connect Without Alarming the Opponent:
Once you have coordinated your movement with the opponent's, joined centers, and have created a condition of no relative motion between your respective bodies, you need to establish some type of connective hold. As stated in the section above, in most cases the hand is used to touch, grab or press some part of the opponent's body which is more or less "still" relative to it. As there is no relative motion at this point, it is possible to reach out and grasp the opponent here. It is very important to grasp the opponent lightly and without clashing with his force. For example, if you grip the opponent's wrist forcibly he will immediately react by pulling away and you will have ruined your opportunity to lead him into a throw without struggle. In addition, gripping forcefully will result in tension in your own body which the opponent may use to his advantage.

Our purpose in connecting physically with the opponent is to use the connection as a place to transfer the momentum of our own centers through to the opponent's center. In order to do this we have to "lead" rather than push or pull the opponent in the general direction he wants to move (the direction he is already going). Moving with the opponent and leading him through a gentle connection into our own flow of momentum will allow us to take control of the situation before the opponent realizes what is happening. Since we lead without offering resistance, the opponent cannot resist.

Sometimes it is necessary to strike the opponent to set up the throw. The above principle still applies.

After the strike you must move with the opponent's reaction while making a gentle connection and then lead him into the subsequent throw (for example, it would be uneconomical to kick an opponent in the groin and then attempt to arch him over backwards after he has doubled over from the kick). Bear in mind that after striking the opponent you must move in with a throw which allows you to flow with his reaction to the strike; it is extremely difficult and often dangerous to attempt to throw an opponent by "insisting" on a specific throw. Let the opponent's reactions decide for you which throw is appropriate, then connect with him gently so he is unaware of your intentions and therefore unable to resist.

PRINCIPLE THREE:
APPLY FORCE WHERE THE OPPONENT CANNOT RESIST

Now that you are moving with the opponent having joined centers and made a physical connection, the next stage is to lead without clashing with his force. The way to do this is to apply your force where the opponent cannot resist in preparation for the actual throw. Even though you now have joined centers and are moving with the opponent in the same general direction he was originally moving, if at any time you apply your force inappropriately, (so that the opponent is able to offer resistance), the potential occurs for him to defend and counterattack. Therefore, we want to apply force in such a manner that there is no opportunity for counterattack on the opponent's part. It is at this time that we create the conditions necessary for taking over the opponent's momentum in preparation for the throw. Up until this point we are still "dancing" with the opponent as two entities in the same flow of motion. Here we adjust our positions so the opponent will be incapable of resistance when we actually transfer our momentum into him. We will take the slack out of our connection with the opponent so that there is a "bridge" between us which serves as a direct and solid connection between our respective centers. The net effect will be that the slightest movement of our center will affect the center of the opponent. Now we

9

may transfer momentum and lead the opponent where we will.

Apply Force Where the Opponent Cannot Resist: Methods

1) Lead at the End of the Lever:

The laws of mechanics tell us that the longer the lever arm the easier it is to move a load. Applying this principle to the art of throwing we find that if we are using the opponent's limbs as handles or connections to his center, the further down the limb toward the terminus (hand or foot) that we apply our force the easier it will be to move the opponent. For example, if the opponent throws a straight punch and "locks out" his arm so it becomes like an unbendable iron bar, we will have a much easier time moving it left or right, up or down if we apply our force at the hand or wrist than if we push or pull on his upper arm. The same holds true for the leg. If a sweep is applied at the heel it will be much easier to move the opponent's foot than if the sweep is applied to the back of the thigh. the same principle holds true for the body as a whole. When moving the opponent's whole body as a unit, we can minimize effort by applying force as close as possible to the top of his head.

Even though we will not always be leading the opponent from nor invariably be applying pressure to his wrist, in techniques which involve the opponent's arm or leg as a lever, we will seek to control the terminus (near the hand or foot). When applying force at the end of a limb, we naturally move the entire limb around its proper axis, the shoulder or hip for the arm and leg respectively. Since arms rotate around the axis of the shoulder and legs swing from the axis of the hip, again we are conforming to the principle of avoidance of force against force and natural motion; we literally move the opponent's limbs the way they are naturally designed to go. Leading the opponent in concert with the inherent functional design of his anatomy allows us to position the opponent where we want him without alarming him as to our intent, as his kinesthetic sense does not register any threatening or unnatural pressures (until it is too late for him to resist).

2) Take Out the Slack:

In order to establish a direct connection with the opponent's center in preparation for the throw, it is necessary to take any "slack" out of the opponent's tissue between our point or points of contact and his torso (center). If we want to tow one car with another, the car in front will not influence (begin to pull) the car in the rear until all the slack has been taken out of the rope tied between them. Once all the slack is out of the rope, there is a direct connection between the "centers" of the respective cars and an efficient transference of momentum may take place. The same holds true of our physical connection with another whom we hope to throw. If there is any "play" in the opponent's tissue or limbs between our hold and his center, our force will be dissipated and the opponent will have time to react and counter. Therefore, we will not attempt to actually transfer our own momentum into the opponent or throw until the slack of our connection is taken out and the movement of our center's momentum will immediately have an effect on that of the opponent. In this case, there is no time lapse or energy loss between our movements and their effect on the opponent, leaving no time (and therefore no chance) to counter or escape.

In illustration, let us imagine that we have a hold on another's wrist and wish to pull our partner to the ground. If our partner's arm is bent (leaving slack in the limb) and we suddenly jerk downward, we may succeed in causing pain in his shoulder or a "whiplash" effect but before the pull has influenced his center, our partner will have reflexively pulled back his arm. If we continue pulling at this point we will certainly be forced to resort to power against power (since we are now pulling in opposite directions). In contrast, if we gently lead our partners arm from the end of its lever in the direction it wants to go until all the slack between our grip and the opponent's torso is removed (meaning our partner's arm has been gently stretched taut, just like the rope between the two cars in our example above), and we then suddenly apply force downward, our momentum will be transferred to the other immediately and completely and our partner will have no choice but to topple forward. This same principle can be applied in reverse to our own limbs when we want to push the opponent away from us; in this case, the slack is taken out of our limbs by compressing them into the opponent.

3) Make Use of the Opponent's Inherent Structural Weaknesses:

We seek to remain in our strongest state, relaxed and balanced and capable of fluid motion and spontaneous change. In order to use our strengths most efficiently, we need to avoid clashing with the opponent's power. The logical way to avoid using force against force and still achieve the desired result (throwing the opponent to the ground) is to apply our strength in the areas where the opponent is inherently weak. Inherent weaknesses refer to those which are inborn and universal (present regardless of size and strength). For example, because humans only have two legs, pushing or pulling the torso at a more or less perpendicular angle to the baseline (the line which runs between the two feet) will cause imbalance. This holds true regardless of size, weight, or type of stance taken. A few other examples of inherent structural weaknesses are the limits of the range of motion of the joints, the startle reflex, the inherent instability of postural misalignment, reaction time and the time it takes to overcome inertia.

Another example of an often exploited structural weakness which is not so much inherent in the static structure as created during motion involves using the opponent's energy (momentum) against himself. This is often referred to as the famous technique of "borrowing force." Application of this principle involves joining with the opponent's momentum and adding a little more in the same general direction of flow in order to move the opponent off balance. We "borrow" the opponent's force naturally as we move with the opponent, make a connection, join centers and lead him into a throw.

To sum up, we know that in order to throw the opponent without effort it is necessary to always circumvent his power, avoiding the direct confrontation of force. Therefore, we need to apply our own force where the opponent cannot resist. Once we are familiar with the various inherent structural weaknesses present in us all, we strive to make our own weaknesses unassailable while exploiting those of the opponent to our advantage.

PRINCIPLE FOUR: TRANSFER MOMENTUM THROUGH THE HOLD

Besides applying our force where the opponent cannot resist, we must also be aware of why certain forces are applied. The goal to be achieved more or less dictates the type, intensity and duration of whichever forces are appropriate to any given situation. Since our immediate goal is to break the opponent's posture and throw him to the ground, the manner in which we apply our force will be different than if our goal was to strike the opponent and cause local tissue damage. Of course, applying percussive force at this juncture is fine if we wish to cause pain and damage a certain area, and may potentially end the fight. But if our goal is to throw the opponent (for all the reasons mentioned in the Introduction) a ballistic force applied here will more than likely ruin our chances for an effortless throw. The reason lies in the fact that percussive force will accelerate the opponent away from you and destroy the absence of relative motion you have created, which also means your respective centers will separate. Unless you repeat the process of connecting and joining centers again (which can often be done almost immediately) you will most likely have to resort to brute force to effect a throw (or continue striking the opponent, which again is perfectly acceptable and in some cases the preferred alternative if a throw cannot be "set-up" correctly). Remember, the point here is not if it is better to throw an opponent than strike him down or vice-versa; the important consideration is once you have decided to throw an opponent and have made a connection and joined centers, percussive force should be avoided during the throw.

Once we have joined centers with the opponent and have established a hold, we want to transfer the momentum of our mass through the hold into the opponent's center, creating a reciprocal reaction in his body. In the above paragraph I have alluded to the fact that this transference of momentum is somehow different than a percussive strike. The key to a smooth transference of momentum from your body to his is to continue moving into the opponent at a natural rate of acceleration (as determined by your position and direction relative to gravity). Since you and the opponent have joined centers, you must apply your force in such a manner that he becomes an "appendage," with his center subordinate to yours. The transfer of force is smooth and unbroken. This gives the opponent no choice but to follow until his balance is broken and he falls. If you have succeeded in merging with the opponent and joining centers, and understand how to make use of inherent structural weaknesses (applying power where the opponent cannot resist), transferring momentum into him will be as effortless as transferring momentum from your center into your own arm; all you need to do is align your skeletal structure, relax completely and move your body.

Transfer Momentum Through the Hold: Methods

1) Match Rhythm:

Before we can actually transfer our momentum into the opponent without knocking him away or giving him a chance to escape, we must first match the rhythm of our overall body motion with that of the opponent's. Since our goal is to cause our own centers to become the center of rotation around which the opponent revolves, we will often be moving more slowly than him in real time in order to maintain the overall rhythm and absence of relative motion between our two centers. For example, person A and person B are standing on a large rotating disc (like a phonograph record) with person A close to the center of the disc facing outward and person B standing at the outside edge of the disc facing in toward the center. As the disc rotates, person B will be moving through space much faster than person A, but if they are looking at it each other it will appear to themselves as if they are standing still relative to one another (it will appear to person A as if person B is standing still and the background is spinning and vice-versa). There is an overall, smooth rhythm to the rotation, and although A and B are moving at different speeds there is at the same time no relative motion between them.

As much as possible we seek to move our own bodies as relaxed as possible, allowing our frame to compress and spring and our limbs to swing at

the speed of gravity (see Chapter Two: Body Use). Once connected to the opponent, the angle and direction from which we apply force will allow us to maintain our own relaxed rhythm while "imposing" it on the opponent's body. At this stage of the throw it is crucial to continue following the opponent as your respective momentums flow into one overall rhythm. Then you may "entice" him to follow you, subordinate to the momentum of your center. The important point to remember here is that flowing with and matching the rhythm of the opponent does not necessarily mean your centers are moving (rotating) at the same speed through space.

2) Move the Opponent as Part of You:

We have connected with the opponent, joined centers, matched our motion to flow in one rhythm and are applying force where he cannot resist. The opponent has no choice but to follow our lead. We now need to shift our focus from following the opponent to leading with complete command. The opponent has become an "appendage" of your body and just like your own arm or leg his motion is subordinate to the motion of your center. From this point on it should be as easy to break the opponent's balance and throw him as it is to swing your own arm or leg about or fall down yourself (in the case of sacrifice throws). The subsequent principles involving breaking the opponent's balance and causing him to fall are to help insure he has no avenue of escape or chance for counter and that you always maintain balance in case you need to follow up, escape, or deal with another attacker.

With practice you will come to "feel" when the opponent has become reliant upon you for balance and subordinate to your motion. At this point (and it will come a split second after initial contact with proficiency on your part) you must dominate the opponent's motion and breaking his balance, lead him into a throw. The longer you wait to break the opponent's balance and throw after he is caught up in your flow of momentum, the more chance he has of counter or escape. It is important to remember that our sole purpose in following the opponent and blending with him is to lead him into our own flow of momentum so we may take over and throw him where we will.

3) Lead From a "Safe Angle":

A final consideration as we transfer our momentum into the opponent is that we should always position ourselves at "safe angles" relative to him. Safe angles refer to positions from which the opponent has a difficult time counter-attacking as well as affording a safe avenue of "escape" for you if something should go wrong with the technique. For example, you want to unbalance the opponent by pulling him forward, so you step back and pull him straight toward yourself. The opponent loses his balance, but he pitches forward unexpectedly and crashes into you knocking you down and landing on top of you. You may have followed all of the above principles of joining centers and matching rhythm while leading the opponent into your flow of momentum. The problem in this example is that you were not at a "safe angle" relative to him as you broke his balance. A safer alternative may have been to do exactly what you did in the example above but step to the side simultaneously. In this case, if the opponent lunges forward he will sail past you and fall, leaving you upright and balanced.

When transferring momentum into the opponent in preparation for breaking his balance, take into consideration potential ways he may be able to counter as well as the direction of his momentum. Leading the opponent in such a way that his momentum is directed toward your center is the same as putting yourself back on the line of attack. When leading the opponent by one arm it is especially important to be aware of possible counter-attack from his free hand. Transfer your momentum through the hold or connection you have with the opponent with a smooth acceleration, neither so quickly that he is propelled away from you causing you to lose control of his center nor so slowly that he is allowed to regain his balance.

PRINCIPLE FIVE: BREAK THE OPPONENT'S POSTURE

Once the opponent is caught up in your flow of momentum and his center is subordinate to your own you need to break his posture. This "breaking" of the posture may or may not cause the opponent to physically lose his balance. For example, if your posture is broken you would not necessarily fall unless additional pressure was applied. Breaking someone's posture implies misaligning their skeletal frame in such a manner that subsequent slight pressure will bring them to the ground. One advantage of this method of setting the opponent up for the fall is that it will not alarm the opponent or cause him to struggle to regain balance. Anytime you attempt to force another off balance they will instinctively and immediately react to right themselves and this may translate into an all out struggle to throw the opponent down. Since breaking the posture involves misaligning the skeletal structure rather than forcing the other off balance, the opponent will fall before realizing he was in such a vulnerable position to begin with. Another result of breaking the opponent's posture is that you will very often cause him to be dependent upon you for his own balance. This means the opponent will in effect "lose" his balance but as you are supporting him, he will momentarily be unaware that he is in such a precarious position. All that is necessary to down the opponent at this point is to remove the support.

In Chapter Two we will go into great detail about the principles and methods of aligning the body. We seek to maintain our own alignment and use our bodies in the most efficient and powerful manner while working against the opponent's inherent weaknesses and causing his body to be misaligned. Another of our greatest allies is the knowledge of correct postural alignment and how to generate power from this base along with the application of this knowledge to misaligning the opponent's structure (if I understand in which positions I am strong I also naturally understand in which positions another will be weak). The potential power of even the strongest individual can be more or less negated if he or she has misaligned posture. For example, imagine you are facing off with an individual who is twice as heavy and three times as strong as yourself. If you fight "toe to toe" using force against force you will have little chance of overcoming your adversary. Now imagine that this same opponent has his feet tied together and his arms tied behind his back. In this case you could use only a small portion of your potential force and still throw the opponent without effort. This illustrates the advantages of breaking the opponent's posture (postural misalignment inhibits use of strength much like having the hands and feet tied) before attempting a throw and is one of the keys to effortless technique.

Break the Opponent's Posture: Methods

1) Divide Attention:

Since the mind directs body motion, dividing the opponent's attention will necessarily cause his power to fragment. People are most powerful when their minds and motions are focused on a single task. If you can cause another to lose concentrated focus on the task at hand by dividing their attention, their power will be dispersed as well, leaving them "weaker" and easier to set-up and throw.

This principle can be applied at various times during a technique. For example, you may strike at the opponent just as he is about to initiate an attack in order to disturb his focus and change his intent from an offensive to a defensive mode. You may attack his left side to draw attention away from his right where you actually plan to apply your technique. Causing pain with a strike or a joint lock will scatter the opponent's focus long enough for you to apply a finishing technique. You may disturb the opponent's visual field, momentarily disorienting him while you move in to throw. Finally, you may lead the opponent in such a pattern that he is disoriented in space and unable to stop you from breaking his posture and throwing him. The above are some of the possible methods that result in a dividing of the opponent's attention. All serve to weaken his unified strength (mental and physical) and make it easier to apply your technique.

2) Misalign the Hips and Shoulders:

In order to generate "whole body" power and use the body as a coherent unit it is necessary to maintain the proper alignment of the hips and shoulders (please see Chapter Two: Body Use). Conversely, if you want to severely inhibit your opponent's potential power and set him up for an effortless throw you may break his posture in one of two general ways. The first is to misalign his hips and shoulders. This misalignment occurs if the shoulders are either lifted (one or both shoulders lifted as if "shrugging"), tilted forward or backward without reciprocal compensatory adjustment in the waist and hips (the torso is bent forward or backward from the spine rather than from the hips) or if the shoulders rotate out of linear alignment with the hips (rotating the upper body without rotating the hips). Each of the above conditions destroys the alignment of the hips and shoulders and results in a "broken" posture. Note that in these situations the opponent has not necessarily lost his balance (and therefore will not be forced to react by struggling to regain it).

3) Misalign the Base:

The second method of breaking the opponent's posture is to misalign his base. "Base" refers to the hips and legs to the feet, and the area between the feet. In order to have a stable base the correct alignment of the hips, knees and ankles must be maintained and the center of gravity must remain within the area of the base. Misaligning the base will occur in several situations. First, if the hips are moved so that the center of gravity is above the outside perimeter of the base (the area between the two feet; see Chapter Two), the opponent will teeter on the edge of his physical balance. Second, if pressure is applied to either the lower leg, knee or thigh which causes the knee to move out of its correct linear alignment with the hip and ankle the base will be destabilized. Finally, if the stance taken is either too wide or too long the base will again be unstable. Once the opponent's posture is broken by any of the above methods (and they are often used in combination) he may be thrown with very slight additional pressure.

Up until this point we have still been "setting up" the actual throw which downs the opponent.

We first followed the opponent in order to create the conditions needed to lead him. Now we have led the opponent into such a position that he may be thrown with a slight continuation of the pressure inherent in our momentum. It is at this point in the technique that many options as to the actual type of throw to be applied are created. Although there are only a limited number of ways in which to set-up the opponent and break his posture there are are literally hundreds of ways to bring the opponent down with a "throw." It is important to remember that the set-up is the more difficult part of the technique. With a proper set-up the throw itself is relatively easy. It is a grave mistake to try to rush into the throw itself without properly setting it up or to practice throws without devoting adequate time to training the prerequisite and essential skills which make the throw possible.

PRINCIPLE SIX: CAUSE THE OPPONENT TO FALL

Now we come to the actual part of the technique which is recognized as the "throw" itself. If you have set the opponent up properly, causing him to fall should be the easiest part of the entire process. As stated above, while there are a limited number of ways to set-up the throw and break the opponent's posture, there are a great many variations in the basic methods which cause him to fall. The examples given in Chapter Three are only a small sample of the potential range of technique. The most important point to remember is that it is the set-up, including the methods of entry and joining with the opponent and breaking his posture, which require the most care in practice and which literally decide whether or not the opponent may be thrown.

The methods of causing the opponent to fall which are covered below are not separate from the methods used to break his balance and should be viewed as a continuation of that process. In fact, the entire technique from the moment you move to engage the opponent until he hits the ground should ideally be one smooth flow of events. Like the methods of breaking the opponent's posture,

the methods of causing him to fall are often used in sequence and combination. As with all the preceding steps, at this stage of the technique it is important not to use brute force. Even as the opponent falls if you try to accelerate him by using force you will more likely than not give the opponent pressure to resist against which will enable him to partially reduce the speed at which he hits the ground. Cause the opponent to fall without giving him anything to "hang on to," and the throw will have maximum effect.

Cause the Opponent to Fall: Methods

1) Coupling:

Coupling involves two forces of equal magnitude moving in parallel but opposite directions. These forces cause rotation around a central axis (an example is turning a key with your index finger and thumb). Coupling is very commonly used in all types of leverage and throwing techniques. For example, if you rotate the opponent's shoulders with a coupling motion by pulling one forward and pushing the other to the rear at an oblique angle, the opponent will fall in a spiral pattern. Another example is pushing the opponent's chest to his rear while sweeping his leg to the front. In the first example the coupling force rotates the opponent around his centerline (a vertical line which passes through the center of the body). In the second example the coupling force rotates the opponent around the horizontal axis of is waist/hip area (coupling always creates rotational movement around a central axis). The above two throws provide examples of horizontal rotation around a vertical axis and vertical rotation around a horizontal axis respectively.

Coupling may be used to break the opponent's posture and continued in the same momentum flow directly into the throw, or it may be used to break the opponent's posture in combination with a different method of causing the opponent to fall. Conversely, the opponent's posture may be broken with a separate method and then brought down with a coupling momentum. The momentum created through coupling may be applied to all three categories of throws; arcs, circles, and spirals.

2) Weight Dropping:

Weight dropping involves "attaching" yourself to the opponent then using the force generated by gravity on your mass to push or pull the opponent to the ground. You may allow your weight to "drop" a short distance then "catch" yourself again or you may literally drop yourself to the ground in the case of a sacrifice throw. The force of your weight dropping should act on the opponent such that it pushes or pulls his center of gravity to a point outside his base of support (pushing or pulling the opponent into his feet will have negligible effect). As always, momentum is transferred through the hold you have on the opponent's body to his center. Weight dropping may either be applied downward from a point above the opponent "pushing" your momentum through your point of contact into him or from below "pulling" the opponent's center outside its base. As with any other method, you must join centers and make the opponent's center subordinate to your own, break his posture and then proceed with the throw.

A sacrifice throw is the most obvious example of weight dropping. In this type of throw you set the opponent up appropriately then allow yourself to fall; the weight of your body pulls the opponent down with you. Another type of throw which utilizes weight dropping in a less obvious manner is a variation of an "arm pull." One example would be to grab the opponent's wrist and then extended the opponent's arm until his wrist is at a point outside his base. At this point if you suddenly let your body "drop" a few inches the momentum will suffice to yank the opponent off his feet and onto the ground. Variations in weight dropping may be used to knock the opponent off balance, shock him percussively or project him away from you.

3) Removal of Support:

Removal of support involves taking away from the opponent that which keeps him from falling down. This "support" generally is of one of two types. The first type of support is the opponent's own base, that is his legs and feet. Sweeping and tripping techniques are examples of basic ways to remove the supporting base of another by "sweeping" it out from under him. The second

type of support one may rely on to maintain upright posture involves "leaning" on another. For example, you unbalance your opponent and cause him to lean against your body. He now becomes dependent upon you for physical support. All that is required to cause the opponent to fall is to move your body out of the way. While the opponent is leaning against you dependent upon you for support he is, in effect, "falling" already, your mass delays his fall momentarily as you lead him into a position from which he will be unable to regain balance once the support is removed. Throws of this type are analogous to leaning against a door which you believed to be tightly shut, only to discover after you have committed your weight to it that the door was ajar as it opens to let you fall.

Throws which involve taking out the opponent's base are always done after breaking his posture or when his stance is overextended. Trying to sweep or trip someone in a stable posture may cause pain but will rarely cause the opponent to fall. You may also remove the opponent's support by physically invading the area of his base with your own hips and legs. These types of techniques "displace" the opponent's base with your own, causing him to fall.

4) Leverage:

Throws always make use of leverage, most often involving second class levers. First class levers have the fulcrum between the load (the object to be moved) and the point of application of force which moves the force arm. The see-saw is a classic example of a first class lever. A second class lever has the load between the fulcrum and the point at which force is applied. A wheelbarrow is an example of a second class lever. A third class lever has the point at which force is applied between fulcrum and the load. The longer the force arm (the distance between the point at which force is applied and fulcrum) the greater the mechanical advantage and the less force needed to move the load. That is why doorknobs are not installed in the center of doors. Force should be applied at a 90 degree angle to the force arm. The same principles hold true when throwing an opponent. For any given throw, we want to understand which type of lever we are dealing with, where the fulcrum is and at which point on the opponent's body we should apply force for the greatest effect.

Let's take as an example a basic hip throw. I have my right arm around the opponent's back and my right hip thrust across in front of the opponent's hips. This throw involves a second class lever with my hips as the fulcrum, the opponent's center as the load to be moved and his upper body acting as the force arm. The further up his back I wrap my arm, the greater my mechanical advantage, and the less force I will have to use to effect the throw. Now let's look at a different example of a second class lever throw. I approach my opponent from behind and my goal is to pull him over backwards onto his back. The load is the opponent's whole body and the fulcrum is his heels. The further up the opponent's body I pull, the longer the force arm and the greater my mechanical advantage. For example, imagine approaching another from behind and grabbing them around the shins, it would be next to impossible to pull them over onto their back by applying pressure so far down the force arm (body). Now imagine approaching another from behind and grabbing with both hands around their forehead. It would take little pressure to pull the opponent over backwards. In this case you have applied force at the furthest point on the force arm from the fulcrum and have afforded yourself the greatest mechanical advantage possible. Once you understand the principle of the lever and which lever is applicable to a specific technique, it becomes possible to design the most efficient method of executing the throw.

PRINCIPLE SEVEN: FOLLOW-UP

Once the opponent is on the ground, the fight is not necessarily over. Although a good throw will very likely prove to be debilitating to the person taking the fall (especially if he is not trained in breakfalls and is being thrown with substantial force onto a hard surface), the thrower must be prepared to continue with the fight or take other appropriate action if the opponent is not rendered completely incapable of further aggression. After executing a throw it is very important that the

thrower not "let his guard down" or assume out of hand that the fight is over. Even if the downed opponent is obviously incapacitated, one must always be aware of subsequent attacks from other aggressors. Not until you are free and clear of the area in which the altercation occurred should the fight be considered "over." This principle deals with several methods of following-up after the opponent has been downed. Please note that following-up does not necessarily involve physically reengaging with the thrown opponent.

Follow-up: Methods

1) End the Throw in a Superior Position:

A superior position in this case refers to one from which you may either escape the area, apply a finishing technique on the downed opponent and which ideally leaves you in a position in which you are aware of and able to respond to the surrounding environment in general. One must practice until throws can be executed smoothly and decisively without loss of balance. The techniques themselves should be set up with the idea of continuous stability in mind. For example, if you set up a throw in such a manner that the opponent's arm(s) are in a good position to grab some part of your body as he falls, you may be in a vulnerable position. Even an untrained assailant will instinctively grab onto anything within reach when falling. During practice, you need to keep this fact in mind and be prepared for the reality of throwing an unwilling opponent in the street. Special care should be given to setting up techniques which leave you in as safe and stable a position as possible during the throw. Having your partner test your position and stability by grabbing hold of and pulling you as he is thrown is a valuable training aid once you have mastered the basics of whichever technique you are practicing. Learn to set up and execute throws so that the opponent cannot break your balance or pull you down with him as he falls.

Taking the above one step further, if your partner is able to break your balance and/or pull you to the ground with him as he falls, practice flowing with the event and reestablishing a superior position as soon as possible. If your opponent breaks your balance as he falls, that is the reality of the situation and to resist will almost invariably make the situation worse for you. For example, you are attempting a basic hip throw. As you begin to pull the opponent over your back, you feel his arm reach around your neck. If you resist the opponent's hold as you throw, chances are you will be pulled down in a headlock or some other disadvantageous position. If, on the other hand, you go with the pull and kick your feet out from under yourself, you will land on top of your opponent with the full weight of your body and odds are you will hurt the opponent sufficiently to end the fight anyway. Again the basic rule applies: do not resist force with force. Train until you can set up your techniques from positions which insure you will be able to keep your balance and superior position as you throw. Have your partner test you by trying to break your balance or pull you down with him as he falls. Finally, if you do lose your balance, practice going with the flow and change to another technique, one which allows you to reestablish dominance as quickly as possible.

2) Continue your Awareness of the Environment:

Just as it is very important to maintain your awareness of the surrounding environment as you engage a single opponent (through positioning and peripheral vision), it is equally important to maintain this awareness after you have completed your technique and the opponent is on the ground. If you decide that your opponent is incapacitated and incapable of further aggression, be sure to "keep your guard up" as you exit the area or deal with others in whichever manner is appropriate. Be aware that fights rarely happen in a vacuum and violent occurrences will sometimes prompt irrational behavior in otherwise sensible people. You may be singled out because of the way you dress, speak or look and once the aggression toward your person is set in motion, others who were originally not involved may join in if they are "sympathetic" to your opponent's "cause."

The best way to prepare for such encounters is to train your intent and awareness realistically as you practice with your work-out partner. Cultivate the habit of expanding your awareness to include your entire immediate environment and maintaining that awareness after you have

completed a technique and on into subsequent techniques. Ideally, from the moment you step onto the mat until the training session is over, you should strive to maintain your mental focus and awareness. Once you have a command of the technical details of the techniques, you should begin training with more than one partner at a time in an approximation of a multiple opponent encounter. Remember, the point is that you want to train to expand your awareness of the environment and be able to monitor your position relative to the other people and objects about you. You fight like you train; the reflexive ability to maintain focus and awareness of your environment may prove as important, if not more important than the number of techniques you know in an actual street fight.

3) Decide on Subsequent Action:

As stated above, the fight is not necessarily over once you have thrown the opponent to the ground. If you have maintained a superior position and are aware of your opponent as well as the surrounding environment, you will be in a good position to immediately asses the situation and decide on the next course of action. In regards to the downed opponent, this course of action usually involves one of two choices: First, you may decide that the opponent is still capable of further aggression and that you have to follow up physically with a strike, lock or submission hold. Otherwise, if you decide the opponent is no longer a threat, you will most likely seek to exit the area and remove yourself from further potential danger.

Here it should be noted that if attacked, under the law you are permitted to respond with only enough force to protect yourself and are required to stop fighting once the opponent is no longer a threat. The decision ultimately lies with you and must be made quickly. If you are balanced, focused and aware after the opponent is downed, you will be able to make the split second decision as to whether the fight with the opponent is over or not. A word of advice: it is dangerous to remain in the area of a violent street confrontation. Once you have stopped the aggressor, staying around to "gloat" over your "victory" or assuming that the situation is no longer dangerous may ultimately lead to your defeat. Killing a single enemy in the midst of battle doesn't mean that the battle is over. Street fights should be viewed in similar fashion. Remember, the "fight" is not over until you are free and clear of the entire area in which it occurred.

PRINCIPLE EIGHT:
THE INTENT FLOWS OUTWARD LIKE WATER (WATER MIND)

The previous seven principles have been presented in a more or less sequential order. Principle Eight is ever present throughout. This particular mental device is an application of calming the mind and expanding the awareness (please see Chapter Two). When your mind is calm and your awareness is expanded, you will be able to direct your intent outward to your environment. It is important to understand the distinction made here between awareness and intent. Awareness refers to a general sense of yourself and environment. You are now focusing on the book you are reading, but your awareness includes at least a vague recognition of the pressure of the chair you are sitting on, background noise, air temperature etc. We want to expand our awareness to the greatest possible degree. Forewarned is forearmed and the earlier we are aware of the direction the flow of events is taking, the quicker we may prepare and react to our advantage. Limiting the range of our awareness to the opponent in front of us precludes the possibility of using the environment to our advantage, as well as leaving us vulnerable to attacks from others. The ability to expand the awareness requires some practice and most people do exactly the opposite in conditions of extreme stress.

Intent refers to the conscious direction of your mind. It is akin to the idea of "will," and is what we commonly associate with being the essence of ourselves. Whenever you use the word "I" you are referring to your conscious intent. Just as you learn to expand your awareness so should you practice focusing your intent. Focusing the intent is what we do when we concentrate on a particular. When we are able to actively maintain a state in which the awareness is expanded and the intent is focused, we may act and react to

the best of our ability and the potential for spontaneity is created.

Water Mind: Methods

1) The Intent is Directed Toward the Opponent (Think In)-:
Your awareness is expanded to include as much of the environment as possible but the focus of your intent flows toward the opponent (or primary opponent if there are more than one). This is best achieved by "thinking in" toward the opponent as if your intent were water shooting out of a powerful hose at the opponent's center. This mental energy likewise projects out of your body and arms thus uniting your mind and body. When facing another at a distance, you should immediately project this flow of mental energy towards them and orient yourself so that you are in a position from which you can initiate offensive or defensive action. Your mind is capable of responding much faster than your body and, if calm and focused, will be able to initiate an appropriate physical response to attack. If your intent is not focused on the opponent or is dispersed, you will inevitably react more slowly and this will greatly reduce your chances of successfully defending against an attack. Where you choose to focus your vision will also have an effect on the focus of your intent. Some schools prefer to look at their opponent's eyes, some at the opponent's chest and others at the opponent's solar plexus. The important point is that the awareness remains "expanded" to take in the opponent's whole body and surrounding environment and one's visual/mental focus should never narrow into "tunnel vision" which excludes the whole while overfocusing on the part.

The way to practice expanding your awareness while focusing your intent is through attention to your peripheral vision. The basic mechanics of such practice involve looking at some point on your opponent's body (his upper chest for example) while paying conscious attention to your peripheral vision. This may prove much more difficult at first than one may imagine, especially when your opponent is moving. It is very important that you do not "look" at your opponent's hands or feet as they move or try to track the motion of punches or kicks. Allow

---

yourself to act and react while looking at a central point on the opponent's torso without being distracted by his peripheral movement. Remember, the hand is quicker than the eye, the torso is not. Narrowing your visual/mental focus to one small area to the exclusion of the whole results in slowed reaction time. Expanding your awareness without focusing your intent is tantamount to "daydreaming." Both extremes should be avoided. You can practice expanding your awareness while focusing your intent at any time, but pay special attention to maintain this balance of awareness during the actual time you spend training martial technique.

2) Connect to the Opponent Mentally Before Physical Contact is Made:

The sooner your mind receives and processes information, the quicker your body is able to make an appropriate physical response. Allowing your intent to flow toward the opponent like water flowing from a hose unites your mind and body as well as giving you a "connection" with the opponent. This connection creates the potential for immediate mental/physical response to any given stimuli. Imagine that you and your opponent are standing at the bottom of a pool of water at a distance of several feet apart. Your opponent begins to move toward you. Long before he reaches you physically, you will be able to feel the pressure of the water he has displaced in your direction. This pressure serves as advanced warning as to the direction and intensity of your opponent's attack. If you are projecting your intent to the opponent as if it were water flowing toward him, you will "feel" his slightest motion through your vision. This gives you the longest possible time in which to react and the greatest potential for appropriate response.

Most trained fighters project their intent in similar fashion to the one described above after they have some experience and confidence in their skills. Much time can be saved in the acquisition of this important ability if you train the focus and "feeling" of your intent consciously from the beginning. After you have developed some proficiency you can step up the training of your intent by practicing connecting with more than one opponent (in motion) and objects in the

environment. A final important point: from the foundation of a calm mind with an expanded awareness, you must "allow" the intent to flow forward without mental coercion. This means as your intent flows out to another your mind should be free of apprehension or any type of "guessing" what the opponent will do. These cause turmoil in the flow of the intent and only result in confusing the self. If the intent flows out without effort, your mind/body will be free to act and react instantaneously.

3) Feel the Opponent as an Extension of Your Center:

Once the opponent is moving toward you, you want to immediately move off the line of attack and seek an advantageous angle. Feeling a mental connection with the opponent will give you advanced warning as to the direction of your opponent's attacking momentum. Previously we discussed blending with an opponent's flow of momentum in order to make a physical connection from which to draw him into our own momentum flow. Once we have made a physical connection we want to continue with our mental connection and feel the opponent's body as part of our own. Our goal is to connect centers and subordinate his center to ours. This is best achieved by a combination of a tactile connection to the surface of his body continuing on with a mental connection through to his center. As stated earlier, our hands are used to make a connection and transfer the momentum of our body into our opponent's body. We need to be able to "stick" to our opponent's center both physically and mentally. In order to do this, our hands must remain relaxed and sensitive and capable of continuous repositioning on the opponent's body. The intent, however, flows outward and through the opponent's center without break.

Although it is not necessary for our hands to remain "stuck" at the point of initial contact with the opponent, our intent should never lose its "contact" with the opponent's center. The ability to "stick" to an opponent is greatly facilitated by utilizing the image of your intent flowing into the opponent like water. When flowing water hits an obstruction, it neither resists nor retreats, it "sticks" to the object in its path and flows around it from every other possible angle. Likewise, allowing your intent to flow into the opponent like water will allow you to stick to the opponent where appropriate while continuously circumventing obstacles as you control his center.

As we lead the opponent into the throw, we need to remain sensitive to his position and motion. Once the opponent is caught in our momentum flow and is subordinate to our center, we want to throw without hesitation. But, it is also important to remember that no technique is foolproof. If you maintain your mental connection with the opponent's center throughout the entire technique, you will have the potential to change or adjust as needed. Water Mind can be summed up as utilizing a calm mind and expanded awareness by allowing the intent to flow forth in a continuous, focused stream toward the opponent in general and through his center in particular. This focus of the intent creates the potential for spontaneous action and reaction and allows you to change and adjust your technique as needed. It unites the physical and mental faculties and focuses them on a common goal, thus bringing all of one's inherent strengths to bear on the task at hand.

CONCLUSION

In this chapter we have discussed types of throws and basic principles. It may be valuable here to summarize briefly the principles presented and their ramifications. Throws are categorized into three general types, namely, Arcs, Circles and Spirals. All throws which may be executed with natural power can be categorized as one or a combination of the above. Understanding the category into which a particular technique fits gives one an immediate reference to relevant principles and key points. In Chapter Three, the throws presented are organized under the above types. It is helpful to remember the descriptions offered in this chapter when practicing the throws presented later on.

The key to mastery and true understanding of any art is through a complete understanding of the basic principles underlying the art. The techniques presented in this work are offered not as isolated methods but rather as physical

illustrations of the principles upon which they are based. It is VERY IMPORTANT that you read and have an understanding of the concepts covered in this chapter before going on to the throws themselves. Constant reference is made in Chapter Three to the ideas, concepts and terminology covered here.

Now let's briefly review the basic principles involved in an effortless throw as they were presented (more or less in sequential order). When confronted by a potentially violent opponent, we attempt to maintain Safe Distance, that is the distance from which our opponent cannot reach us without moving his torso or taking a step. Once the opponent moves toward us, we must reestablish Safe Distance by moving away or connect with the opponent physically. Depending on the type of attack and our relative position to the opponent we may intercept the attack if early or avoid it if late. The most important thing to remember at this juncture is to move off the line of attack. Remember, from the beginning of any encounter until the end we always seek to avoid using force against force. As the opponent moves toward us, we begin to coordinate our movement with his and make a physical connection, joining where there is no relative motion between our respective bodies. We match the speed and rhythm of our motion with the opponent's in order to join centers and become as one body. Once we have joined centers, we want to influence the opponent's body and motion where he cannot resist, making use of his inherent structural weaknesses. We now transfer the momentum of our body through the connection we have with the opponent moving him in the same overall rhythm so that he becomes like an "appendage" of our own bodies. This movement serves to break the opponent's posture by either misaligning his hips and shoulders or his base and sets him up for the throw. We use a combination of coupling, weight dropping, removal of support and levers to cause the opponent to fall. Maintaining a superior position, we asses the situation and environment and immediately decide opon subsequent action. Finally, the entire sequence is controlled and guided by the intent as it flows out into the surrounding environment and into the opponent like rushing water.

THE EIGHT ALLIES

Finally, certain salient points may be extrapolated from the above principles and organized as a group in their own right. These points (The Eight Allies) are inherent in the principles mentioned above but their importance warrants further clarification. When training or designing techniques, reference may be made to the following as a kind of basic checklist of principles to be followed for effortless throws done with Natural Power. The term "allies" refers to things with which one should consciously align. The Eight Allies are as follows:

1) Space/Time
2) Momentum
3) Gravity
4) The Earth (as a support and a weapon)
5) Our Inherent Strengths
6) Opponent's Inherent Weaknesses
7) Leverage
8) Mind/Body Unity

Space/Time refers to our spatial relationships with our environment and our opponent (Safe Distance) and the direct correlation this has on reaction time. Positioning yourself at various distances and angles confers an important time advantage which allows you to obtain a superior position at the outset of an encounter. Being aware of your relative position and its influence on reaction time gives you a great advantage over an opponent who is unaware of these things.

Momentum is the key to delivering tremendous power with minimal effort. Properly applied momentum overcomes strength every time. The correct application of momentum allows the physically smaller and weaker to overcome the larger and stronger. When momentum is favored over brute strength the force which may be transferred is exponentially greater. Imagine trying to chop a piece of wood by placing the axe on the surface of the wood and then pushing down with all your might (brute strength). Even the strongest among us would find it nearly impossible to cut a piece of wood this way. Now raise the axe up over your head and allow it to fall with effortless momentum, you can easily split the wood. By allowing the body to compress-rebound and swing,

we may generate tremendous momentum-power seemingly without effort.

If there is a Master Force in nature with which we should align ourselves it is gravity. The shape and structure of everything on the planet, organic and inorganic, animate and inanimate has been directly influenced by the Earth's gravitational field. From the instant we are born until the very end of our lives, gravity never ceases to be a constant force acting upon us at every moment. To live out of harmony with it invariably results in adverse consequences both to our health and efficiency of motion. Without correctly submitting ourselves to gravity's force, we will never reach our full potential in the martial arts (or athletics in general). Gravity is the force which allows us to generate momentum without effort. It is also the force which is really responsible for "throwing" our opponent to the ground. All we need do is set up the conditions for imbalance in our opponent and allow gravity to do the rest. While practicing solo forms and exercises, our primary consideration is the maintenance of balance and methods of generating power within the gravitational field. And when engaged with another we must never forget that our balance and the balance of our opponent is simply the relationship between our bodies, gravity and the Earth. Just as momentum is the key to generating maximum natural power with minimum effort, gravity is the force which makes this momentum possible. What we must do to take full advantage of the power inherent in gravity is to relax and allow its force to flow through us.

The Earth itself serves as our foundation and the base from which we move. The general definition of "balance" when applied to our physical selves implies the ability to remain in an upright posture on the ground in the gravitational field. The fear of falling is inborn and commonly results in continuous tension as we struggle to hold ourselves "up." Instead of viewing the Earth a something we must hold ourselves off of, we should understand that we are already "on the ground" even as we stand. Once we realize that our "base" really includes the entire surface of the Earth, we may experience a mental release from the fear of falling and relax downward, thereby making a fundamental connection with the source of our stability. If we wish to allow our bodies to compress and rebound as a spring, the Earth is the support against which we compress. Nothing is more massive or more powerful than the Earth itself, and through relaxing into it in harmony with the law of gravity we find our greatest strength. Gravity and the Earth are the two most basic sources of Natural Power.

The Earth may also be viewed as our greatest weapon. Just as a fist or foot are anatomical weapons when striking, the Earth is the weapon when throwing. And unlike the fists or feet, the Earth never gives nor misses. If you throw the opponent to the ground in such a way that he cannot break his fall he will be defeated outright or you will have enough time to follow up and escape.

We want to use our minds and bodies in the most efficient manner, taking full advantage of our inherent strengths. Once we move in this fashion, we may then take advantage of the great natural forces (momentum, gravity and the Earth). Our bodies have inborn mechanisms which allow us to maintain our balance and structure without conscious effort. Imbalance, tension and stress are the results of learned behavior and acquired bad habits. One of the primary goals of practice is to inhibit these inefficient (and often harmful) bad habits, allowing our innate mechanisms to once again reign without interference. This is being true to our nature and aligning ourselves with the way things are. Using something contrary to its design only detracts from the things inherent efficiency and ability to perform its intrinsic function. Our minds and bodies are no different. The key to utilizing inborn strengths to their fullest potential can be summed up in a single word, and that is Relaxation. Relax the mind by remaining as calm and centered as possible while relaxing the body completely. Holding tension anywhere in the body and then attempting to move is like driving a car with the emergency break on; peak performance becomes an impossibility. As stated above, momentum is the key to natural power. And tension in the body only serves to slow down the transfer of momentum through the tissue. What gives the body the correct form for the task at hand is the mind, and not tension. Your mind is the conductor of the many parts which make up the

whole. The brain waves provide the rhythm which the various parts of the body follow, resulting in an overall, harmonious coordination of the parts into a unified flow of movement. This is referred to as "whole body power" and creates the potential for maximum efficiency and maximum power. So calm your mind and relax your body, letting what is already there do what it is designed to do without interference.

When we understand in which state we are the strongest we will naturally understand which states are weak. This is referred to in the martial classics in the statement "know yourself and know others and in one hundred battles you will not be defeated." For example, if we understand that we are strongest when relaxed, we may try to cause our opponent to become tense. Similarly, since we know in which positions we are stable and powerful, we try to break our opponent's posture and cause him to be in a weak position as we attack. Understanding relative strengths and weaknesses also tells us when we should not- attack or issue our power, as the opponent may be in a strong or superior position, one from which he may be able to take advantage of our movement. The important point is to use our strengths against the opponent's weaknesses; following this principle allows the smaller and weaker to overcome the larger and stronger.

Once we are relaxed and balanced and able to take advantage of the great natural forces, we will be able to generate power most efficiently. The question still remains as to how to use this power most efficiently. The answer is to always seek to use properly applied leverage ("leverage" is used here in a broad sense to represent applying power from a position of mechanical advantage). For example, you may have excellent body mechanics and the ability to generate a tremendous amount of force, but if you apply the force at the wrong time or in the wrong place it will have little effect. If momentum is the secret of generating power, leverage is the secret of how to use it. Properly applied leverage will increase the effect of your power many times over and will create the potential for a force your opponent will find unstoppable. Uniting the mind and body is related to using our inherent strengths. However, once we are relaxed our inherent strengths function on an unconscious level, while mind/body unity is the result of a conscious, focused intent. Once the mind is calm, we become more aware and in control of our intent. Mind/body unity comes about when we consciously direct our intent to feel, move or fill our bodies. Water Mind is one example of mind/body unity and is the most relevant to our purposes here (training and fighting). Mind/body unity involves awareness to the state of things as they are and moving the body consciously with the intent. The key to moving the body with the intent lies in using a mental "image" to direct physical perception and motion. For example, if you were walking around the room "daydreaming" and then I asked you to "imagine" that you were walking on very thin and slippery ice, suddenly your tactile sensations, awareness of your balance and attention/intent would all be radically different than they were in the preceding moments. You are in the same place doing the same thing, the only difference is the way you focus your intent. With the image of walking on thin ice, you are able to unify your mind (intent) and body (kinesthetic perception/feeling) in relation to the particular image chosen. Images are the "tools" which allow you to inhibit bad habits until they are no longer there, while helping to ingrain constructive skills and mind/body unity. The concepts and principles presented in this chapter are meant to be used as guidelines for creating and organizing technique and structuring training. Bear in mind that the principles and steps apply to skills relevant to actual fights but the techniques themselves must be trained until they are "second nature." A technique is only useful if it is efficient and can be applied spontaneously. Organize your training around correct principles then practice until the techniques are part of you.

Chapter Two

Body Use

INTRODUCTION

The manner in which we use our bodies is of the utmost importance. Control of our physical selves is the very basis of martial technique (and athletics in general). The techniques in this book are based upon generating Natural Power and applying it in the appropriate manner at the appropriate time. So, logically, before we attempt to learn and practice technique, we must first understand the principles of body use and the methods of generating Natural Power. Natural Power results from uniting the mind and body and making full use of inherent strengths while harmonizing with the the forces of nature. Natural Power involves the force of the entire body which is generated without tension and is expressed through compression/rebound and centripetal/centrifugal forces. This means the body is aligned to maintain total relaxation allowing gravity, other external influences or the shifting of the weight to compress the skeletal structure into the Earth resulting in a "rebound effect" and/or causing the limbs and torso to swing freely about their appropriate joint axis without effort. What this means is that the limbs and torso either compress/rebound like a spring, swing like a pendulum or a combination of both. And all is under the conscious direction of the intent.

There are basically three components to Natural Power: structural alignment, complete relaxation and overall rhythmic momentum. It is possible to generate power with one or two components without the other(s) but the resultant force will be greatly reduced. Good skeletal alignment held with tension may be stable in static poses but will lack mobility, flexibility, sensitivity and any force generated will be seriously inhibited. Relaxation without proper alignment may allow for some degree of sensitivity and the ability to change, but the posture will be weak and little power can be generated (one cannot take full advantage of gravity and the Earth). If the structural alignment is correct and the body is completely relaxed, one will be able to move feeling a natural, whole body rhythm which coordinates all the various parts into one movement flow, resulting in maximum efficiency of motion for the task at hand. The energy produced is often referred to as "Whole-Body Power," with the combined power of the whole being exponentially greater than the potential force which can be generated by any one part. This is the result of correctly coordinated rhythmic movement.

In this chapter the various principles of body use are broken down into eight component parts (for the sake of clarity and for training purposes). In application, the body always moves as a coordinated whole. Below are the principles of body use with appropriate exercises.

PRINCIPLE ONE: ALIGN WITH GRAVITY

A logical place to start is with the very framework around which our body is constructed, the skeleton itself. When the skeletal structure is aligned correctly (and the muscles are relaxed), any incoming force will be translated through the network of bones into the ground; no muscular force of resistance is needed. The bones are aligned in such a manner that force flowing through one flows directly through the next, and so on into the Earth. The absolute minimum effort is used to align the frame, the muscles remain relaxed. Generating power follows the same principle. With correct alignment, the skeletal structure will compress into the ground as a spring, storing a potential rebound force which is capable of generating tremendous power. The power is generated "passively," meaning the only requirements are correct alignment and relaxation, no overt force need be used. This type of energy is directly analogous to a metal spring's; once the spring is compressed, it does not "push" itself back into its original position by force, the rebound power produced occurs "passively." And so it is with our bodies. Gravity, momentum or the outside pressures applied by another provide the force of compression, if we are relaxed and aligned properly, the rebound force which powers our technique occurs without effort.

The most pervasive and influential of the natural forces acting upon us is gravity. From the moment of birth our relationship with gravity begins and for the rest of our lives continues without a second's respite. Tensing in an effort to "fight" the force of gravity is as futile and physically damaging as is collapsing beneath its pull. The logical alternative is to submit to the force of gravity by aligning ourselves with it and using its tremendous power to our advantage. This is the basis of physical health as well as athletic power. Improper skeletal alignment results in a constant and unbeatable "opponent" of force in gravity; alignment with this force results in an inexhaustible ally.

Without correct structural alignment, the full potential of power will never be realized. The following guidelines are meant for dynamic as well as static posturing, and "posture" itself is defined as the "shape" of the body at any given moment (in movement or at rest). Aligning the body correctly with respect to gravity allows one to access and make full use its inherent strengths and the Natural Power which results.

1) The Head Floats Up From the Crown:

The position of the head is vital to the alignment of the rest of the body. Where the head goes, the body follows. When the alignment of the head is incorrect, it becomes impossible to make full use of one's inherent strengths. The importance of the head's position cannot be overemphasized. In order to make full use of the compressive/rebound and rotational energies which power our movements, the body must be held as a relaxed and flexible unit. And the position of the head is of prime importance in the overall alignment of the body as a whole.

The power we seek to generate is elastic and resilient. Imagine for a moment that the body is like a rubber band. If the rubber band is not gently stretched, it remains limp and weak. If the rubber band is stretched too tightly, it is easily broken. If the rubber band is gently stretched from end to end, it is "lined up" correctly and stores great potential power. Similarly, if we either slump (like a limp rubber band) or hold ourselves rigidly (like an overtaut rubber band), we negate the potential of generating elastic Natural Power. Gravity eternally takes care of the "pull" at one end of our bodies with its perpetual downward force. Our job is to consciously allow our head to feel as if it is gently "floating upward," thus creating the necessary gentle "counter-stretch" in our body which allows us to access our inherent strengths and creates the potential for Natural Power. It is

important to note that the correct alignment is effected through mental directives and not brute force. We only need to "imagine" something is occurring and then "feel" the result.

Exercise One: Lengthening the Body

Stand up straight without tensing any muscles. Try to feel as if your hips are directly over your legs (keep your legs straight) and your shoulders are directly over your hips. Feel your head balancing at the top of your torso between your shoulders. Now, touch the tops of your ears with the thumbs of each hand. Extend your index fingers over the top of your head until they touch (reach straight up over your head). The point at which your index fingers touch is the crown, the midpoint on a line drawn from ear to ear over the top of your head. In order to insure proper alignment of the body in general, and to create the gentle "stretch" which is the prerequisite of Natural Power, we need to imagine that our heads are being gently pulled upward from this point (upward meaning away from the torso, not necessarily straight up). A useful image is that there is a helium balloon attached by a string to the crown, which gently and constantly lifts the head away from the torso. The chin may slightly tuck inward (see Illustration 1 on the next page). It is very important not to strain with the muscles of the neck in an attempt to force the head into the alignment. Relax and use your imagination until you begin to feel the head floating upward, aligning and lengthening the body. The new alignment may feel different or unusual at first, but with time it will become the natural state and you will no longer need to focus conscious attention upon it. In fact, this alignment is the natural state, we all maintained this alignment when very young (for proof, look at any small child); improper posture is the result of acquired habits, habits which reduce efficiency and health.

The importance of this basic alignment cannot be overemphasized. Without correct alignment of the head, proper alignment of the rest of the body becomes as impossibility. No special "practice" time is needed, anytime it comes to mind you can engage the image of your head floating away from the torso and reinforce correct alignment. This is especially helpful in that during technique

Illustration 1

practice, it is very difficult to pay attention to too many things at once. Working on your own alignment and body use during solo training (forms and drills without a partner) and during the movements of everyday life (which affords training time every waking hour) will greatly increase the rate at which you improve.

2) The Four Levels and the Centerline:

"Four Levels" is a name borrowed from the Chinese Internal Arts and refers to the relative alignments of the head, eyes, shoulders and hips; each maintains a level or parallel relationship with the other three. Imaginary lines drawn across the top of the head, the pupils of the eyes, the shoulders and the hip joints remain parallel and equidistant in motion or at rest (see Illustration 2). Functionally, this means the head may rotate (about 45 degrees right or left) but should not tilt from side to side or up and down, the eyes should look straight ahead without straining to

look too far up, down or to the sides, the shoulders are not lifted or tilted and the hips should not jut out to either side. Maintaining these spatial relationships insures that the overall alignment of the upper body will be correct and its motion will be unified.

The Centerline is a very important concept and vital to organizing the movements of the body as a coherent unit. It is an imaginary line drawn from the crown of the head straight through the center of the body, which serves as the axis around which rotational movement occurs. The parallel lines (Four Levels) drawn horizontally across the top of the head, through the eyes, and across the shoulders and hips are at a right angles to the centerline (see Illustration 2). Whether standing upright, turning or bending at the waist, the relative distances between the lines of the Four Levels and their 90 degree angle to the Centerline should not change.

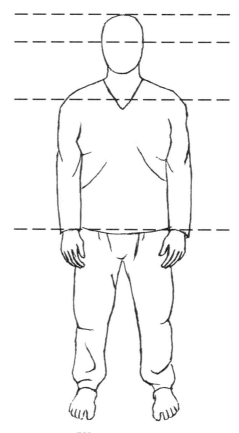

Illustration 2

28

Exercise Two: Level the Shoulders and Hips

Stand up straight with the feet close. Lift one shoulder up toward the ear as far as it will go and hold it there. Have your partner hook both hands over the raised shoulder and pull down. Don't resist the pull, stand as if you are a statue without letting your shoulder drop. You will find that it is very difficult to keep from tipping over toward your partner in the direction of the pull (see Illustration 3). Now stand up straight and drop your shoulders so that they are parallel and relaxed. Let your head float upward as described above. Imagine you have heavy dumbbells in both hands as they hang by your sides. Now have your partner hook both hands over your shoulder again and pull straight down as before. If you keep your shoulders level (with both hands pressing straight down), you will be very stable, so stable in fact that your partner may be able to "hang" from your shoulder (see Illustration 4). This is an example of exaggerating the force of gravity to check the relative strengths of posture. You are much more stable with the body straight and the head, shoulders and hips in parallel alignment. The same type of test may be done by standing up and jutting one hip far out to the side while your partner hangs on the shoulder on the opposite side, this posture is as unstable as the posture with the lifted shoulder.

3) Lift the Chest:

The chest should be held in its naturally open and lifted position without "sticking it out" (which causes tension in the upper back) or letting it collapse (which disrupts stability). The scapula should feel as if they are "falling" down the back. They should not be pulled out to the sides or lifted upward. The tension caused by pushing the chest forward with force "cuts off" the arms from the power of the rest of the body. Collapsing the chest destroys the skeletal alignment so that the natural

Illustration 3

Illustration 4

29

compressive quality of the body is lost. Once the above two guidelines are followed (allowing the head to float up from the crown and keeping the Four Levels), the chest should naturally be in its correct position. But some attention should be paid to not pulling the shoulders back or letting them slump forward.

Exercise Three: Opening the Chest

Stand with the right foot in front the left, about a half step ahead with the back foot turned out to about a 45 degree angle and the front foot pointing straight ahead. Square your torso so that you face straight ahead with your navel pointing in the same direction as the toes of your right foot. Stand up straight with a very slight bend at the knees and let your head float upward from the crown. Relax and be sure not to curl the buttocks under. Have your partner stand a bit to your right side and put his left palm on your chest, thumb down. Your partner pushes in and down toward your rear at

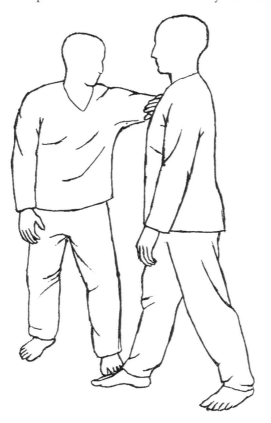

Illustration 5

a 45 degree angle. This posture will be extremely stable as the incoming force flows through your skeletal system directly into the ground. (see Illustration 5). When resisting incoming force from the front or issuing power forward, the chest must be lifted in order to take full advantage of the inherent strengths of the skeletal frame .

4) Maintain the Natural Lumbar Curve:

The area of the waist and hips is very important in the study of martial arts. This region forms the link between the upper and lower halves of the body and is largely responsible for giving direction to the power the body generates. The waist and hips form the foundation of stability. In light of this, the alignment of the hips and its relationship to the rest of the body is extremely important. One simple method of insuring the correct alignment of the hips and pelvis is by maintaining the natural curve in the lower back. Although the lifting of the crown of the head is meant to gently lengthen the entire torso and back, the spine maintains its natural curves and no muscular effort should be exerted in an attempt to "straighten" the spine. Tucking the tailbone under destroys the connection between the upper and lower body and greatly detracts from the ability to use the power of the legs and hips. Conversely, lifting the tailbone too far ("sticking out" the rear) will cause undue tension in the lower back which makes the body stiff. The natural curves of the spine should be maintained throughout all of the postures and motions involved in forms and techniques. Whether turning the waist or bending forward, attention should be given to maintaining correct alignment in the waist and hips.

Exercise Four: Stabilizing the Hips

Stand erect with the feet together. Relax and imagine the head floating upward from the crown. Lock the knees straight by pulling them back gently. Place the back of your right hand on your lower back, in the center of the lumbar curve. Relax and let your rear move back until there is no sensation of tension or stretching in the thighs, but not so far back that you feel tension in the lower back. You should feel no pressure whatsoever in

Illustration 6

your legs or hips. This is the natural alignment of the waist and hip area with the correct amount of curve in the lower back. Keeping the back of your hand on the lower back, turn your left foot out to about a 45 degree angle and step forward a half step with the right foot directly in front of the left (the toes of the right foot point straight ahead). Feel with your right hand to make sure the curve in the lower back does not change. Once you are set, drop both hands by your sides. Square your hips to the front so that your navel points in the same direction as the toes of your right foot. Now have your partner stand directly behind you and put his palms on each side of your lower back, just above the hips, with the four fingers wrapping around each side of your hip bones. Have your partner push straight forward and down at a 45 degree angle. You should be stable to the point of being immovable (see Illustration 6). For contrast, stand in the same position and let your tailbone curve under, rounding the lower back. Have your partner push forward and down at the same 45 degree angle. You will immediately lose your

balance and pitch forward. This exercise is an illustration of the importance of the alignment of the waist and hips in relation to the stability of the body as a whole. Correct alignment allows you to transfer incoming force through the skeletal structure into the immovable ground without exerting muscular effort.

5) The Knees Point in the Direction of the Toes:

Keeping the center of the kneecap pointing in the same direction as the toes insures the correct alignment of the hips, knees, ankles and feet. This rule provides a simple method of maintaining the correct alignment of the lower body. The legs should move as a unit, this means there should be no twisting or torsion in the knees or ankles. The best way to preserve the integrity of these joints, insure the correct transference of momentum through the body and maintain a stable yet mobile base is to adjust the angle and direction the body faces by changing the position of the feet and then shifting the weight from one foot to the other. And the position of the feet is adjusted by rotating the whole leg from the hip. For example, I am facing North in a parallel stance (with both feet facing North) and want to turn 90 degrees to my right to face the East. If I leave my feet in place and turn my waist, my knees will twist out of line with my toes and my legs will torque unnaturally. This stance is as unstable as it is uncomfortable. If, however, keeping my weight on my left leg I first lift my right foot and turn it toe-out from the hip (keeping the knee in line with the toes) until the toes point to the East, and then shift my weight onto my right leg, my torso will naturally turn right 90 degrees in full balance and without strain.

The legs are are the "foundation" of the body and its means of locomotion. It is therefore natural to move and position the body as well as generate momentum by stepping and by shifting the weight from one foot to the other. The rising and falling of the body as well as its rotation and translation through space are all controlled primarily by the legwork. In order to insure creation of momentum without imbalance or residual tension to hold it back, Natural Power is generated "passively." This refers to placing the foot or feet in an appropriate position and then shifting the weight from foot to foot. It is not necessary to "push" the weight of your torso from from one foot to the other, as the tension created in the pushing leg disturbs balance and hinders the transference of momentum. The waist and torso will naturally turn in the direction the toes point if the alignment of the leg is intact (knee aligned with toes). It is not necessary to use effort to create these types of momentum, we only need to align the body and base, letting the mass and gravity do the rest.

Exercise Five: Stepping and Shifting the Weight

This exercise is designed to reinforce the correct alignment of the lower body and the method of moving and turning the torso by shifting the weight. Stand up straight with the feet parallel and about shoulder width apart. Let your head float upward from the Crown and align your body as described in the sections above. Relax your muscles as much as possible and feel as if the bones of your skeleton are "stacked" one on top of the other. Without disturbing the alignment of your body (do not tilt the torso or stick the hip out to the side), shift your weight to your left foot. Bend the knees very slightly and gently lift the right foot, placing it a small step forward with the knee and toes pointing straight ahead (be sure your hips do not move and that your tailbone does not curl under). Now shift your weight to your right leg (don't push off with your left foot), moving with the head level and floating upward (you can imagine you have a glass of water balanced on the crown of your head). The alignments of the upper torso (head floating upward, the Four Levels, the lifted chest and lumbar curve) should remain unchanged, allowing the body to move forward as an integrated unit (see Illustration 7). With the weight over the right foot, and keeping the body and right leg absolutely motionless, bring your left foot up beside the right, suspended slightly above the ground. Now move the left foot forward and shift the weight forward onto it as described above. During the entire time the left foot is moving forward, the body and right leg should not move. This type of stepping exercise trains you to move the body forward in a straight line transferring the momentum created through

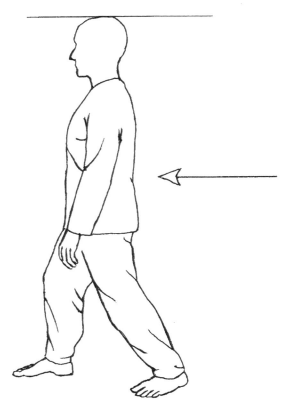

Illustration 7

the entire body (this enables you to engage the entire mass of your body in the task at hand). By turning the legs inward or outward from the hips (toeing in or out with the knees in line with the toes) and then shifting the weight to the angled foot, your torso will naturally turn, creating rotational momentum.

6) Bend the Body at the Hips and Knees:

In order to maintain the correct alignment of the spine and legs, as well as the connection between the upper and lower halves of the body, it is important to compensate for the vertical motion of the torso by bending at the hips, and not the waist. Bending at the hips is involved in two situations; squatting and bending over forward (while one may bend the torso forward without bending the knees, squatting requires a forward bend at the waist in order to maintain relaxed alignment). As much as possible, the knees do not extend past the front of the ankles, especially the knee of the leg which supports the majority of the weight. If the knees move forward into vertical alignment with the toes, the stability of the body is weakened.

For the vast majority of movements, a slight bend at the knees is ideal and provides the maximums of both stability as well as mobility. When the situation requires that the body be lowered, the bend in the knees should ideally not be greater than 45 degrees and should never exceed a 90 degree angle (when the legs approach a 90 degree angle of bend, it is often preferable to drop onto one knee, in which case the angle of bend in both legs remains at 90 degrees allowing the torso to maintain an upright and stable position). In wider stances with the body lowered, the torso should be tilted forward at the hips, with the spine maintaining the same relative position as upright posture (the tailbone should not be

curled under). Widening the stance and lowering the body without compensating with a bend at the hips which angles the body forward (that is, if you keep the torso vertical) destabilizes the body and precludes the use of Natural Power (see Illustrations 8 & 9).

Exercise Six: Bending and Squatting (Part One, bending)

Stand up straight with the feet spread about double shoulder width apart. Lock the legs straight by pulling back gently at the knees. Feel your head floating upward (away from your torso) and your spine lengthening. Now place the backs of the hands on either side of the lower back. Bend forward slowly from the hips, without letting the spine bend (feel with the backs of your hands to see if the lower back begins to round, it should not). Bend forward as far as you can from the hips without changing the relative alignment of the

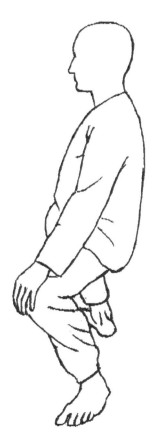

Illustration 8 - Incorrect

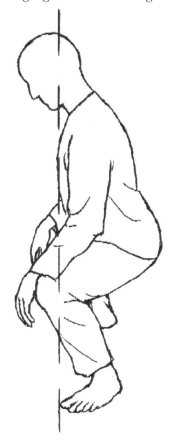

Illustration 9 - Correct

spine and torso (if you are flexible, you may be able to bend the torso forward about 90 degrees). Stop bending forward before the lower back begins to bow into your hands (see Illustration 10). Now slowly straighten to the starting position. Be sure to keep your legs straight and your head lengthening away from your torso throughout the entire exercise. Curving the spine to stretch or as a calisthenic is fine, but for movements which require power, all bending should be done from the hips.

(Part Two, squatting)

Stand up straight with the feet about double shoulder width apart, the feet may be turned out a little. Feel your head floating away from the torso, lengthening the torso. Begin to bend the knees and lower the body into a squatting position, as you do, allow the upper body to tilt forward from the hips in the same manner as Part One of this exercise above (do not let the tailbone curl under). Your knees should be pointing the same direction as your toes and the front of the knees should not pass ahead of a vertical line drawn through the front of the ankles. If you squat low (with the bend at the knees approaching a 90 degree angle), your torso will be tilted forward so that a line drawn

vertically through the tip of your shoulders would touch the front of your kneecaps (see Illustration 11). It may be helpful to imagine you are squatting down with a very heavy backpack on your back. Now slowly return to the starting position. Part One of this exercise is an example of the proper alignment of the torso when bending forward. Part Two illustrates the correct alignment of the upper and lower bodies when squatting.

7) Maintain the Alignment of the Hips and Shoulders:

The torso must be moved as a unit or the integrity of the body's alignment will be lost. A basic rule is to maintain the alignment of the hips and shoulders. This means lines drawn straight down the sides of the body from the shoulders will pass through the center of the hips (see Illustration 12). This alignment should be maintained whether bending forward, tilting backward, or twisting from side to side. Just as the torso bends from the hips, it should rotate from the hips also (and not from the shoulders). When twisting the upper body, stop the rotation of the shoulders

Illustration 10

Illustration 11

34

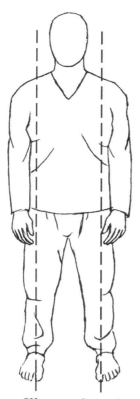

Illustration 12

at the same time the rotation of the hips ceases. In the chapter on Principles we discussed how misaligning the opponent's hips and shoulders breaks his posture and sets him up for a throw. In relation to ourselves, we must never allow our hips and shoulders to be pulled or twisted out of alignment with the other, as misalignment here not only greatly reduces our potential power but also leaves us vulnerable to our opponent's technique.

Exercise Seven: Rotating the Torso

Stand up straight with the feet a narrow shoulder's width apart. Let your head float upward and relax the whole body. Unlock your knees a little and bend them very slightly (be sure not to curl your tailbone under). Keeping the knees aligned with the toes, begin to turn the hips left and right about 45 degrees each way. Pay attention to rotating around your centerline (see Number 2 above). Let your head move as part of your torso (keep your nose pointing the same direction as your navel

as you turn). Your arms are limp and heavy and swing from side to side as you turn. Only turn the hips as far as is comfortable without allowing the knees to twist (the knees may move forward and backward a little) or the shoulders to rotate out of vertical alignment with the hips. This exercise reinforces the feeling of the proper shoulder/hip alignment and the method of generating rotational momentum with the legs and hips.

8) Let the Weight Fall Through the Center of the Feet:

Since the feet are our actual point of connection with the Earth during stand-up fighting, their relative placement and position is very important. In general, the feet should be placed flat on the ground (especially the foot which bears the majority of the weight) with the weight of the body evenly distributed along the entire surface of the foot. The center of gravity usually falls just ahead of the center of the foot. Allowing the weight to rest too far toward either the ball or heel (except when stepping or rotating the leg) may result in instability. Paying attention to the equal distribution of weight on the soles of the feet aids in maintaining the correct alignment of the knees and hips as well; when the body weight rests too far toward the edges of the feet, the knees tend to buckle either inward or outward. This, in turn, misaligns the lower body, resulting in overall instability.

Stepping is usually done heel to toe, like normal walking, although there are exceptions. The important point is to continually allow gravity to transfer directly through the body and legs, through the feet and into the ground, with the minimum amount of energy necessary to maintain the alignment of the skeletal structure. This is essential in manifesting Natural Power and realizing the goal of generating power without effort. Incoming forces which threaten the balance may be dealt with one of three ways; you may compensate for an unbalancing pressure by moving the feet (stepping), by remaining stationary and adjusting the body in place or by a combination of both. But maintenance of the correct transference of weight through the feet is essential in all cases. Incorrect foot positioning corrupts the alignment at its very base and precludes free and frictionless movement.

Exercise Eight: Balancing on One Foot

Stand up straight with the feet together. Allow the head to float upward and relax the body. Unlock the knees by bending them very slightly (be sure not to tuck the tailbone under). Without leaning to the side, shift all of the weight to your left foot. Check to see that the weight is evenly distributed along the entire bottom surface of your left foot (try to feel gravity transferring straight down into the Earth). Now slide your right foot straight ahead as far as it will go without disturbing the posture or moving your hips (see Illustration 13). Continue by moving the right foot out to the right and circle it all the way to the rear until the leg is extended straight behind you (see Illustration 14). Keep the right leg straight (but not rigid) throughout the movement, and do not let the ball of the foot leave the ground. The left leg will have to bend and straighten slightly to compensate for the movement of the right leg. During the movement, it may be helpful to imagine that you have a full glass of water balanced on the crown of your head. Now slide the right foot straight forward past the left until it is extended straight ahead of you and repeat the circle to the rear. After circling the leg in this manner for a number of repetitions, repeat, circling the leg in the opposite direction (extend the leg to the rear and circle it around to the front). Then switch legs and repeat. This exercise trains the ability to maintain balance on one leg while adjusting the posture to compensate for motion, as the body is aligned with gravity over a single point of balance.

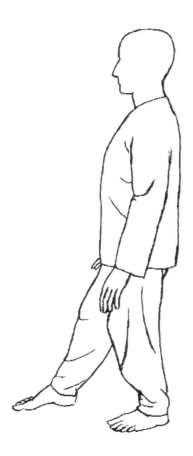

Illustration 13

Illustration 14

36

PRINCIPLE TWO:
RELAX COMPLETELY AND LET THE BODY WEIGHT SINK

Besides correct anatomical alignment, complete relaxation of the body is perhaps the most important prerequisite to making full use of the body's inherent strengths. Relaxation allows one to align with the great natural forces and generate Natural Power. Tension in the muscles hinders movement, causes imbalance, slows momentum and makes one more vulnerable to the opponent's technique. It is hard for that which is stiff to adapt efficiently to external force and respond flexibly to circumstances. Tension interferes with the natural elastic nature of the soft tissue and reduces its ability to compress when under pressure and rebound with force. Rigid structures are often most easily toppled or broken. When generating momentum (the key to power), tension serves as a kind of "brake" which inhibits the smooth transference of momentum through the body, stifling power. If you pinch a hose, the flow of water is obstructed. Much the same thing happens when you tense the muscles, the flow of momentum is obstructed and tension anywhere in the body detracts from one's ability to generate force.

As stated in Chapter One, gravity is an all pervasive and inescapable force of nature. To fight against it is illogical and ultimately futile. Once we submit to gravity's pull and ally ourselves with it, we may avail ourselves of its power. First we have to align our skeletal structure so that the downward pull of gravity transfers through our bones and into the Earth without having to tense or strain our muscles in an effort to "hold ourselves up." The next step is to relax completely and allow our soft tissue to "sink" under gravity's force. If one relaxes completely, things will naturally "fall into place" and align, one on top of another, in the proper sequence. Besides obstructing the smooth flow of momentum through the body, inappropriate tension also results in weak links in the chain of alignment. The key to generating power without tension or strain is to maintain relaxation in stillness and in motion in order to make full use of the body's inherent strengths in cooperation with the great natural forces of gravity,

momentum and the Earth. Following are several exercises which will help in establishing proper alignment with complete relaxation.

Exercise Nine: Relaxation and Sinking

It is not enough just to align the skeleton with gravity, this alignment must be held without undue tension in the muscles. When aligned correctly and completely relaxed, although the postural muscles will be working to hold you erect, you should not feel the slightest bit of tension anywhere in the body. Stand erect with the legs straight and the feet about shoulder width apart; align yourself as described under Principle One: Align with Gravity (head floating up from the Crown, shoulders and hips level, chest lifted...). Now, relax completely and imagine that you are a skeleton with no muscles to hold it up. Your only means of maintaining upright posture is by balancing your bones one on top of the other. Allow all of your muscles to hang limply from your frame. Close your eyes and scan your body with your intent to make sure that there is no residual tension anywhere in the muscles. Be very careful not to lose the alignment of the frame (don't slump over or let your chest collapse). Now continue to relax all the muscles until you get a real sensation of them "sinking" or feeling heavy. For example, you may become aware of the weight of your arms as they hang from your shoulders. You may feel as if the pressure increases at the bottoms of your feet or that you feel "heavier" than before. Be sure to relax the muscles on both sides of the body (pay as much attention to relaxing the muscles at the back of the body as you do to the muscles at the front). Continue standing for a few minutes, feeling the weight of your relaxed muscles as they hang from your frame. Breathe naturally with your belly relaxed and you will automatically take full breaths (as the muscles of the abdomen and waist relax, the diaphragm will relax in turn, allowing the lungs to fill completely).

Exercise Ten: Expansion

With complete relaxation comes an expansion of the soft tissue. As muscles relax, they expand and allow the body to align itself with gravity. Besides the expansion of the soft tissue, there is also a feeling of the whole body expanding vertically as the force of gravity "rebounds" from from the Earth up through the frame. Standing balanced and completely relaxed will result in a feeling of expansion and lightness, even as you feel your body submitting to the downward pull of gravity. Once you have completed Exercise Nine and have cultivated the feeling of balancing the frame without muscular exertion, begin to feel your muscles and body as a whole becoming light and expanding. Feel that there is "space" between the joints and the torso is lengthening upward and expanding outward simultaneously. Be sure not to use the slightest bit of force or muscular exertion (but if your body spontaneously moves to relax further or makes adjustments in alignment, it is important not to interfere). You should feel as if you are occupying the greatest amount of space possible (which is impossible if you "contract" your body or muscles). Stand for a few minutes, feeling both light and stable at the same time.

Exercise Eleven: Relaxation in Motion

Now that we have the ability to stand with correct alignment and complete relaxation, it is helpful to make simple motions while maintaining this alignment in the relaxed state. Continuing from the above exercises, gently raise and lower the arms lightly through space. Take care not to tense the muscles or move to such extreme angles or extend the limbs so far that tension or misalignment results. It may be helpful to imagine someone else is lifting your arm from the wrist and moving it in various patterns through space as you remain completely relaxed. Move the arms from the wrist or fingers without lifting the shoulders (for example, if your arm is extended straight out in front of you at shoulder level, it should feel as if the arm is hanging limply, suspended by a string from the ceiling that is tied around the wrist, the arm and especially the elbow should feel as if it is "hanging.") Next, turn the torso from the hips keeping the shoulders and hips in line (imagine someone is standing behind you holding the outside of your hips and is turning your torso for you). Finally, keeping the head, shoulders and hips level, shift the weight from leg to leg by moving the hips right and left (try not to "push" your torso with the legs). Practicing martial drills, forms and sets in this manner will

further reinforce the feelings of correct alignment, relaxation and balance.

In summary, it is absolutely essential to relax completely, letting the parts of the body "fall" into place naturally as the soft tissue sinks and expands. Without proper relaxation we can never make full use of the tremendous power inherent in gravity, momentum and the Earth. Relaxation with correct alignment also makes available the tremendous power inherent in the body itself, allowing it to compress/rebound and swing with centripetal and centrifugal forces.

PRINCIPLE THREE: CALM THE MIND AND EXPAND THE AWARENESS

In discussing the use of the body, including posture, movement and various states of being, it is important not to lose sight of the fact that the ultimate control lies in the mind. The intent leads and the body follows. When the mind and body are unified (working together under conscious control), all of the one's power is directed and focused into a single flow. Efficient action is born of clear and informed conscious decision. If the threat of physical attack results in panic and erratic thinking, subsequent action and reaction will most likely be far less than optimally effective. When calm, the mind is free to think clearly without the emotions interfering and confusing the brain. If the mind is allowed to become clouded by fear or panic it will be difficult to apply appropriate techniques of self defense.

Everyone knows that it is best to keep a "cool head" when dealing with potentially dangerous situations. The question is how to prepare mentally for such situations before they occur. Just as physical ability is improved during training, mental ability should be refined through training as well. The first step is to calm the mind by removing conscious conflict. By "conscious conflict" I am referring to the conflict that occurs when the mind is divided against itself. When practicing movements and techniques, conscious conflict often arises when we want the situation to be other than it is, and then try to "force" the desired mental reality onto the external reality that is actually occurring.

The important point is that in order to change a situation without creating conflict or struggling, we need to first accept what is actually going on at the time and work from there. And this is entirely a mental process at the outset.

In order to work with what is actually happening, we need to be calm and clear-headed enough to see it, and then accept and work with it. Failure to do so results in "denial." For example, if you are confronted by an angry individual, refusing to face the fact that he may try to punch you may very likely cause you to hesitate, resulting in your being struck. No matter how much you may dislike the situation or want to avoid a fight, you need to see the situation and its potential danger as it is and make decisions accordingly. Resolution to the facts often produces a kind of calmness (as it eliminates conscious conflict) which, in turn, promotes clear thinking and efficient action. Calm thinking resulting in accepting things as they are coupled with physical ability acquired through training go a long way towards improving your chances of successful action should the need to defend yourself ever arise.

In addition to remaining calm and focused, it is important to train the ability to "expand" the awareness so that it includes not only your whole body, but also the surrounding environment. In order to unite the mind and body we need to expand our awareness to fill our entire bodies, to become aware of our kinesthetic sense and feel our whole selves as one entity. The relaxation practices described above (Exercises 9, 10 & 11) are good methods of training the awareness to include the whole body, in fact, the expansive feeling which results from complete relaxation automatically brings about an expansion of the awareness (as the mind and body are essentially united, the state of one has a direct effect on the state of the other). When working with another, practice expanding your awareness until you can take in the surrounding environment without overfocusing on any one element (it may be helpful to focus the awareness on the peripheral vision). Overfocusing on one thing causes the reaction time to other stimuli to increase. Here again, it is important to pay attention to the practice of expanding the awareness during the time you spend practicing techniques. Conscientious practice results in

"internalizing" reactions so that they become automatic. Only techniques which have become a "part" of you are really useful in an actual martial encounter. Going through the motions of a technique by rote without complete conscious awareness results in a good part of the training time being wasted. Be patient and conscientious in training; resist the temptation to "cheat" by using inappropriate force in an attempt to cover errors and placate the ego. Relax completely and fill your body and the surrounding environment with your mind.

PRINCIPLE FOUR: GENERATE POWER THROUGH STRETCH/REBOUND AND ROTATION

There are basically two ways to generate power without using tension or effort: the first is to allow an external, compressive pressure stretch the muscle and connective tissue, storing energy which will cause the tissue to rebound or "snap back," creating a pulse of force; the second is to allow the limbs and torso to rotate or swing like pendulums, generating centripetal/centrifugal forces. Once again, it is of the utmost importance to maintain correct structural alignment and complete relaxation. Aligned and relaxed, the limbs and torso are free to compress-stretch/rebound under pressure and to swing freely around their proper axes.

There is always some amount of compression-stretch/rebound occurring, especially in the lower body (with the exceptions of jumping in the air and groundfighting, at least one foot is always in contact with the ground). When shifting the weight or stepping, the entire weight of the body sinks and causes a stretch throughout the muscle and connective tissue of one leg or the other. The rebound or "snap back" generated by this stretching of the muscle and connective tissue generates the power for all types of techniques. One leg may compress-stretch/rebound while the other swings (a step or kick). The arms may compress-stretch and rebound as part of the body as a whole and produce a kind of short, pulse energy to push or strike. The arms may also swing, generating energy in a whip-like fashion. Lets look at these two basic methods of generating power in turn.

Stretch/Rebound:

When the body is properly aligned with gravity (and relaxed) there is constant interplay of compression-stretch/rebound occurring. Imagine a skeleton with rubber bands connecting the bones together. In addition, imagine that all the bones of the entire skeleton are coated on the outside by a layer of soft and elastic rubber "skin". If we stand the skeleton up in balanced alignment and then press downward on its shoulders, the compressive force will cause the rubber bands between the bones and the rubber skin to stretch, thereby storing a potential rebound force throughout the entire frame. When the compressive pressure is released, the elastic nature of the rubber bands and rubber skin will cause them to 'snap back' into their original, neutral state, thus producing a pulse of force which transferes from the ground up through the bones. This is what actually happens when the relaxed and correctly aligned body is subjected to external, compressive pressures. The connective tissue between the bones and the muscles and skin have much the same elastic properties as the rubber bands and rubber skin in the example above. It should be noted that the elastic tissue both stretches and snaps back without conscious effort. In fact, any extraneous contraction of the muscles will only serve to inhibit the stretch/rebound that naturally occurs with the application and release of compressive pressure.

Stretch/rebound power may manifest throughout the entire body as a single unit which includes the arms (as in a push or short, shocking strike). It may also be used in combination with rotational momentum (with one limb stretching/rebounding as the other limb swings, as in a step or kick, or with the lower extremities stretching with the resultant rebound momentum being transformed into rotational momentum by the hips and expressed as a swinging motion in the upper extremities, as in a hook punch). Channelling this flow of energy into motion is one of the keys to generating force without effort. Proper alignment

of the frame is essential to take full advantage of compressive force.

The first step in training the utilization of stretch/rebound power is to pay attention to aligning the body with gravity at all times. Again, the goal is to translate all incoming pressure into a vertically descending force which flows into the ground; paying attention to alignment with gravity automatically lines the frame up correctly. Just as we can generate much more force by taking advantage of momentum over muscle force alone, we can generate much more rebound force by utilizing the elastic nature of our soft tissue than we could with muscle power alone. We can support much more weight with our frames than we can lift with our muscles. For example, most of us would find it impossible to lift a 250 pound barbell and place it across our shoulders (this would require great muscular strength), but most of us could support the weight if we were standing erect and the barbell was lowered onto our shoulders from above (our aligned frames could easily support the weight). In fact, mentally exaggerating the pressure of gravity is a good tool when training the alignment.

Exercise Twelve: Alignment and Compression

Stand erect with the feet about shoulder width apart. Let the head float up from the crown and align the body as described under Principle One above. Try to relax completely and balance yourself as if you were a skeleton without muscle to hold yourself up. Stand for a few minutes until you feel relaxed and centered. Now begin to consciously pay attention to the downward pull of gravity. You may feel the pressure at the bottoms of your feet increase, and the weight of your arms as they hang down from your shoulders. Now consciously intensify this feeling of pressure by imagining that the downward pull of gravity is increasing. Try to imagine a much greater than normal downward pull through your entire body (another useful image is that you are standing underneath a powerful waterfall and must resist the downward force of the water). You will find that you will spontaneously adjust your alignment and the lifting of your intent to the crown of your head in order to compensate for the perceived increase in downward pressure. Although the feeling of pressure may be intense, be sure not to tense any muscles as you do this exercise. If you wish, you can lift and move your arms, take steps, bend your body or practice any martial arts form or pattern while keeping the image of intensified gravitational pressure. This exercise is very helpful in training the overall alignment of the body in the gravitational field and may be utilized on occasion to reinforce correct postural alignment.

It should be evident that this compression-stretch/rebound effect will be greatly hindered if the soft tissue (muscle) is not completely relaxed. Even if the skeleton is properly aligned, tension anywhere in the body will impede the flow of momentum generated through stretch/rebound. The muscles and skin are also elastic in nature and will "snap back" into their original shape once external pressure is removed. Appropriate muscle tone is brought about by aligning the body correctly, relaxing completely and maintaining an "expansive" feeling throughout the whole body. Correct muscle tone is neither limp nor rigid. A coiled noodle will not snap back (it is limp), neither will a coiled pretzel (it is rigid). So, alignment and relaxation go hand in hand creating the conditions necessary for this stretch/rebound "elastic" power. Remember, once you are aligned correctly and relaxed, you don't have to "do" anything to produce power other than allow yourself to be compressed, the momentum will rebound out of your body unhindered and without effort.

Rotation:

Rotation basically involves "swinging" the limbs and torso around their appropriate axes (joints). For example, the arms rotate or swing around the shoulder joints, the legs swing around the hip joints and the torso swings from the hips as well. Rotation also involves "twisting" the limbs as well as swinging them. We have already discussed the advantages of using momentum over muscle power alone. Swinging the limbs and torso is the primary method of generating such momentum. Swinging movements are by far the most powerful that a human can generate. As stated above, as long as we are standing on at least one foot, some compression will occur, but the momentum generated through compression-stretch/rebound from the base (legs)

is often translated into a swinging momentum in the torso and upper extremities. It is swinging that allows us to generate maximum power (that's why we "throw" rather than "push" a punch).

Walking is a good example of an interplay and exchange between the momentums of stretch/rebound and swinging. As we walk, we allow gravity to compress our weight into one leg (resulting in the stretching and subsequent rebound of the muscles and connective tissue) as our hips move forward and translate the momentum into a swinging motion of the forward stepping leg and foot. Once the forward foot steps down, we shift our weight over it and again allow gravity to compress us into the forward foot, which takes over as our base and source of stretch/rebound power. Normal walking is an alternation of compression-stretch/rebound momentum translating into rotational momentum which powers the "swing" of the forward stepping foot, which in turn compresses and the exchange is repeated. As we walk, our arms also naturally rotate around the shoulders and swing freely forward and back. This is a most basic example of the momentum of compression-stretch/rebound in the lower body translating into rotational momentum in the upper extremities, which results in naturally effortless power expressed through the arms. In fact, this shifting of the weight and the stretch/rebound and rotational momentums which naturally result are the basis of our martial power (true to the Martial Classics which assert "boxing is like taking a walk." Literally!). If you maintain correct alignment and relaxation, you are, in effect, practicing the correct methods of generating martial power every time you take a step.

Once again, the free flow of rotational momentum is not possible without complete relaxation. Tension in the limbs acts as a "brake" to free swinging, rotational movement. Translating the momentum of stretch/rebound generated in the lower body into rotational momentum in the arms, torso or legs is not possible if the muscles are tense, as momentum cannot flow through (you cannot crack a frozen whip). Another benefit to swinging the arms and legs freely (besides generating maximum power) is that if the swinging limb is stopped unexpectedly or misses the target, the balance of the body as a whole will remain undisturbed. For example, if I throw a hook punch by generating momentum with my legs and waist and allow this momentum to flow through my relaxed arm, and my arm misses the target, I will not "throw" myself off balance because my arm was completely relaxed. By leaving my arm relaxed there is no tension which serves to "connect" my arm with my torso. A missed or stopped blow will not influence my center of gravity, leaving me able to immediately respond to the new situation. The same holds true for a throwing technique; I use my hold on the opponent to transfer momentum through my relaxed arms into him while counter-force applied by my opponent to me will not transfer through my relaxed arms back into myself. Whether the momentum be primarily compressional or rotational, total relaxation is vital. And this relaxed state allows the momentum produced in the lower body (legs and hips) to translate through the arms, causing them to swing freely and powerfully without tension or effort.

Correct alignment (especially of the base and torso) is also necessary. In order to transfer momentum through the body and out through the limbs in the most efficient manner, the torso must maintain its correct alignment. For example, if you are swinging your arm in a roundhouse type of motion (punching for instance) and just before the hand connected with the target you collapsed your chest, the entire rhythm, momentum and focus would be interrupted, destroying the power of the motion. It is very important to maintain the alignments described above under "Principle One: Align With Gravity" at all times.

Both expressions of Natural Power (stretch/rebound and rotational) may best be described as a "wave of force" (see Appendix section On the Mechanics of Force for a discussion of "jing"). We seek to generate a wave of momentum which flows through our bodies unhindered, with each part contributing to the power of the whole, in the correct sequence and direction. It may be helpful to compare this method of power with a wave in the ocean. The ocean water does not in itself create the momentum of a wave. Rather, a flow of energy passes through the water and causes it to move. The moving water is the externally observable manifestation of the invisible energy passing through it. This energy needs a "relaxed"

medium to move through. Relaxed here is used in the sense of neither tense nor slack. There are no waves on a frozen pond (ice is too "tense") or in a fog (the mist is too "slack"). The energy which produces ocean waves requires water in its naturally "relaxed" and passive state. So it is for waves of force through our bodies. If we tense our muscles, we are frozen as ice and waves of momentum cannot pass through us. If we are misaligned with its resultant slack muscle tone, momentum again will not flow. Only when we are relaxed and aligned can we generate and make full use of waves of force.

PRINCIPLE FIVE: MOVE AT THE SPEED OF GRAVITY

We have discussed gravity as one of the natural forces with which we seek to ally. Our structure and functions have all been and presently are directly influenced by gravity's pull. Besides aligning with gravity (statically and dynamically), we need to allow our movements to conform to the speed of gravity's downward pull. If our movements resist the speed of gravity, true relaxation and rhythm will be destroyed. Obviously, moving at the speed of gravity does not mean all parts of the body move at the same speed. The speed of motion of various parts of the body is always in relationship to every other part. For example, a slow rotation at the center of the body will result in a very rapid rotation at the outer perimeter of the body. The important point is to coordinate all motion into a united rhythm in harmony with the gravitational pull. What this amounts to in practical terms is correct timing.

The first step in correct timing is maintaining relaxation. As explained in the section above, tense or slack muscles ruin momentum flow and make proper timing impossible. In fact, completely relaxing the muscles allows their weight to "sink" continuously with gravity's pull. In effect, relaxed muscles constantly "fall" at the speed of gravity into their natural positions, with the pull of gravity providing proper tonus. In this state, muscles come into play as they are needed and allow momentum to transfer through uninhibited. This helps to lay the foundation for the proper rhythm of the whole body in motion (see Principle Six below).

Moving a part of the body with the speed of gravity in harmony all other parts is under the direction of the intent. The intent coordinates all motion between relative parts while maintaining relaxation in respect to gravity's pull. For example, you generate momentum with the body and allow it to transfer out of your hand, as in a punch. If you attempt to speed up the blow by "pushing" your arm out too early the action creates tension and actually results in a loss of power. If you hold the arm back, again power inhibiting tension is created. If you allow your body to compress-stretch and rebound and the limbs to swing freely at the speed of gravity, you will be able to maintain the balance (alignment) and complete relaxation necessary for Natural Power to occur, without strain of undue effort. This type of movement feels comfortable and easy.

Exercise Thirteen: Rotational Movement and the Speed of Gravity

This exercise involves the stretch/rebound force translating into rotational motion in the shoulders as the arms swing. It also trains the feeling of moving the arms with the speed of gravity. Stand erect with the feet about shoulder width apart. Align the body with gravity and relax completely. Unlock the knees and hips and swing both arms up over the head, until the fingers point straight upward (see Illustration 15). Now allow the arms to drop, swinging around the shoulder joints in a downward curve (do not let the elbows bend and the arms to fall down with a jerking motion). Imagine energy flowing out through the arms as they swing down and toward the rear (see Illustration 16). Make no effort to accelerate the hands and do not hold them back. The knees will bend a slight amount (as the frame compresses under the momentum of the downward swing) when the arms swing down and through toward the rear. Continuing the exercise, as the arms naturally swing from the rear to the front, allow the frame to "bounce" slightly (in the knees and hips), rebounding and adding momentum to the arms which powers another upward swing. You may continue the upward and downward swing of the arms, feeling the frame compress

and the speed of gravity as the arms ascend and descend. Your hands will naturally accelerate on the downswing, reaching top speed as they reach their lowest point (when the fingers point straight down). The hands again accelerate as they swing forward, slowing gradually to a stop as the hands reach their highest point (when the fingers point straight up). This natural acceleration and deceleration of the hands is analogous to tossing a ball straight up into the air; the ball will gradually slow its ascent as its momentum is dissipated under gravity's downward pull, will seem to pause for a second at the point of transition from ascent to descent, and will gradually accelerate as it falls once again toward the center of the earth.

As stated above, although we seek to organize movement in harmony with the speed of gravity's pull, this does not mean we move each part of

Illustration 15

43

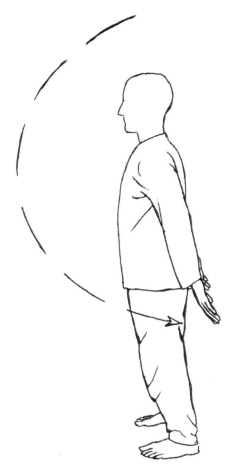

Illustration 16

in the air, the gymnast is not able to push off anything to increase his momentum or force (this is now completely subordinate to the speed of gravity), but he is able to control the speed of his maneuver by changing the angle and direction of his body. Like the gymnast, we seek to control the speed and direction of our movement in harmony with the speed of gravity while remaining on the ground.

PRINCIPLE SIX:
MOVE RHYTHMICALLY

All things in the natural world possess an inherent rhythm. Things move in cycles and alternate between opposite ends of an underlying continuum. This continuum is that which is unchanging beneath the rhythms which are recognized as continuous change. Our bodies also have cycles and move in certain rhythms. For our purposes (generating Natural Power for martial technique), we need to organize the movements of our bodies in accordance with a rhythm which is in harmony with its structure and the forces of the environment which influence it. This rhythm of movement is really a continuation of moving at the speed of gravity, which we discussed above. Correctly timed rhythmic movement (rhythm is the very basis of "timing") is the key to whole body power and generating power without effort. Rhythm is power.

When the movements of individual parts of the body are not in a harmonious rhythm with all other parts, movement is awkward and "uncoordinated." The coordination of the various movements of the body into a harmonious rhythm results in an overall movement which is graceful, powerful and comfortable. In most cases, uncoordinated movement is the result of too much effort and focusing on the movement of one part of the body without consideration of the body as a whole. One of the keys to coordinated, rhythmic movement is to relax and move with as little effort as possible. In Exercise Thirteen above, we can observe the rhythm that naturally occurs when we relax and move at the speed of gravity. As our arms swing up and down, there is a natural rhythm which alternates between acceleration, slowing gradually

our body at the same speed, nor does it mean we always move any one part of our body at the same speed. The actual speed at which any given part of the body moves is controlled by the angle and direction of the body as a whole (always in relation to the speed of gravity). For example, imagine a gymnast who has vaulted himself into the air. He now has no connection whatsoever with the ground and his body as a whole is literally falling at the speed of gravity. But he can still vary the speed at which various parts of his body move by changing the angle and direction of his torso and limbs. Perhaps he is rotating in space (as in a forward or back flip). If he extends his limbs and body, he will slow the speed of rotation. If, on the other hand, he pulls in his limbs and rounds his body, his speed of rotation will increase. Once to a moment of stillness and then acceleration again, repeating exactly the same sequence. Any attempt to change this natural rhythm results in stiff and stilted movement and a subsequent loss of power.

The above outlined principles (alignment with gravity, complete relaxation, a calm mind, coiling and swinging, moving at the speed of gravity...) are the prerequisites for rhythmic movement. When these principles are not followed, rhythm is lost and power is lessened. For example, when throwing a punch, untrained individuals will often lift their shoulders, or tense their arm at the moment of impact, or will raise their elbow as they punch. Any of these actions will detract from the rhythm of the movement and reduce power. Most athletes have had the experience of a peak performance which felt "effortless." In fact, one of the hallmarks of superior athletes is that their actions normally appear to be smooth, relaxed and without effort. A case in point is the expert swimmer whose body motions appear to be relaxed and unhurried but who glides through the water at a rapid pace. Contrast this with the novice swimmer who thrashes about in the water expending great effort while barely moving at all. The former understands whole body rhythm while the latter does not.

How does one tell when the body is moving with correct rhythm? This is not an easy question to answer as the one who moves must rely on subjective feelings as opposed to a cut and dried formula. There are, however, guidelines with which the practitioner may compare his or her subjective experiences. The first rule is that movement with correct rhythm should feel practically effortless. There should be no straining or use of tense force. A general rule of thumb is that you should not be able to tell from where (which specific part of the body) your power comes. For example, if you push someone and you can feel it was the power of your arms which did the pushing, you were not moving with correct rhythm or using whole body power (as you were primarily using the strength of your arms). When you apply force to another and achieve the desired result without feeling any part of the body in particular was using force, you are most likely moving with appropriate whole body rhythm. Compare your martial movements with walking. While walking, there is a natural whole body rhythm and no one part of the body is using excessive force. It is this sort of naturalness we are looking for in the movements of our martial art.

Another helpful guideline is to keep the range of all motions within the bounds of mechanical advantage. If the limbs are extended past a certain point or to extreme angles, they lose the support of the rest of the body and are "cut off" from their power source. Trying to apply force in such positions necessitates the use of brute force in the misaligned limb and prohibits correct rhythm and whole body power. It is a natural response to use our limbs within their ranges of maximum efficiency, as movement here is comfortable and efficient. For example, you would not attempt to hammer a nail into a piece of wood at arms length in front of you, nor would you try to drive a nail behind your back. Martial arts movements should follow similar principles of natural ranges of motion and positions of power.

Following are several guidelines which help define the range of motion within which we are able to make full use of Natural Power: The arms should not be extended so far forward that the upper back "hunches over" or the shoulders are raised. The elbows should not be pulled back so far that they stick out behind the back. When the arms are extended straight out to the sides, the hands should not reach back beyond the point at which they are passing the sides of the body. The arms should remain more or less "in front of" the torso so that the muscles remain relaxed (see Illustration 17). Training extreme ranges of motion and unnatural angles of movement are like fitting a square peg into a round hole, they go against the body's innate reflexes and are inherently less powerful than relaxed movements in comfortable ranges of motion. The same applies to the positioning of the stance and the steps. Extremely low and extended stances are weaker and less stable than those within the ranges of natural comfort and they greatly hinder rhythmic movement. Pay attention to maintaining a comfortable and relaxed alignment which allows correct whole body rhythm to spontaneously arise.

Illustration 17

PRINCIPLE SEVEN:
EXHALE SMOOTHLY WHEN APPLYING FORCE

The breath has a profound influence on both the state of the mind and the condition of the body. In fact, breathing practice is often used as a method of training mind/body unity, as breathing is a function that is automatic (an unconscious function of the body) and which can also be consciously controlled (a conscious function of the mind). The ability to breathe smoothly and fill the lungs completely is important not only to health but also to the ability to generate power. Besides this, the rhythm of the breath has a direct influence on the brain waves and the rhythm of body motion. Erratic breathing results in erratic movement. Standing in correct anatomical alignment and relaxing completely will automatically encourage correct, full breathing. But the rhythm of the breath requires conscious direction until it becomes automatically timed to the motions at hand.

In general, it is helpful to exhale when applying force to another. Anyone who has ever lifted a fairly heavy weight knows that it is much easier to generate force when breathing out as opposed to inhaling or holding the breath (which is particularly detrimental as holding the breath during exertion causes the blood pressure to rise and may result in dizziness or even unconsciousness). During exhalation, one feels as if the weight "sinks" and the body becomes more stable. Exhalation releases tension and promotes mental calmness, leaving the mind clear and aiding one's control of the body. As our goal is relaxed, rhythmic movement, and the rhythm of the breath directly influences the rhythm of body motion, smooth and even exhalation becomes vital to smooth, rhythmic body motion. "Choppy" breathing results in choppy movement which destroys the overall flow of momentum-power through the body as a whole. The key to correct, rhythmic breathing is a smooth, quick inhalation followed by a smooth, slow exhalation. The relatively quick inhalation minimizes the time one is vulnerable to attack and maximizes the time one may apply force (during exhalation).

When applying a technique, the goal is to exhale smoothly from beginning to end, avoiding rapid alternations of inhalation and exhalation between individual movements. Take for example a technique which involves a continuous series of blows. In a technique of this type there are two distinct breathing patterns which may be employed. The first pattern involves a shallow inhalation before each blow followed by a short, forceful exhalation as the blow is delivered; this is followed by another short inhalation before the next blow and a short exhalation as the blow is delivered and so on. This breathing pattern allows one to exhale as force is delivered, but because each subsequent blow is preceded by a short inhalation, the net effect is a cycle of breathing akin to "panting". Rapid cycles of inhalation and exhalation are associated with "panic breathing" and tend to overstimulate and confuse the brain while promoting erratic movement. In contrast, if you inhale smoothly, completely and rapidly and then apply your punching combination while exhaling smoothly throughout, your mind will remain calmer and more focused, and your movement will be smoother and more rhythmical, thereby increasing the amount of power delivered without breaks between the individual movements. The same holds true for techniques which involve throws. Exhaling smoothly throughout the technique will facilitate and reinforce the ability to connect with the opponent, lead him into your momentum flow and transfer the momentum of your body into him without a break. It is very important to apply techniques in a smooth unbroken flow as any break in the motion may allow the opponent to regain his balance and escape or counter your technique. Smooth exhalation also aids the intent in flowing outward like water, before, during and after the throw is completed.

Power Breathing:

You may practice this exercise standing or sitting (be sure you are aligned correctly and maintain relaxation throughout). The purpose is to promote mind/body unity and to train the correct rhythm of breathing as applied to martial technique. Relax the belly and breathe in through the nose smoothly and fairly rapidly (try to fill the lungs completely within a five second span). Feel as if the entire abdomen is filling with air from "the bottom up" as water fills a glass. This promotes a full breath and focuses the intent on the center region (one's physical center of gravity) as well as enhancing stability. Now exhale smoothly and slowly through the nose or mouth. Make a faint but audible sound and pay attention that it is not choppy or intermittent (the sound of your exhalation should be one long, even and continuous "note"). Try to make the sound of your breath a deeper tone to facilitate the sinking of the breath and the relaxation of the belly. Feel the air coming from deep within the abdomen instead of from the mouth. It may help to imagine your breath sinking into the lower abdomen as you exhale, which helps to cultivate a centered stability. Maintain the smooth and even exhalation for about fifteen seconds or longer, but not so long that you are left short of breath. Remain relaxed throughout the entire cycle of inhalation and exhalation. Repeat the cycle for as long as you wish, aiming for a smooth rhythm. It is advisable to practice Power Breathing while remaining stationary (either sitting or standing in place) before attempting to match the breath with martial forms and techniques.

Practicing Power Breathing with relaxation and good posture will help to center the body and mind which results in deeper levels of relaxation. Although the exercise is primarily aimed at developing the condition of mind/body unity, increasing potential power and the ability to coordinate the breath with smooth, rhythmic body motion, its practice is also conducive to releasing stress and building health. Practice the exercise separately and then combine it with martial forms and techniques. A final word of advice: never force either the inhalation or exhalation until there is any discomfort, strain or shortness of breath. The durations of the breathing cycle given above are only suggestions. The most important point is to establish a smooth rhythm of breath while remaining centered, comfortable and relaxed.

PRINCIPLE EIGHT:
MOVE THE BODY AS A COHERENT UNIT CENTERED IN THE HIPS

Principle Eight more of less ties together the previous principles into an overall rule of body use. Correct alignment, relaxation, a calm mind, rhythmic movement at the speed of gravity and Power Breathing are all coordinated so that conscious intention, physical movement and the cycles of breath are united in a coherent flow. Once the above Principles are understood and internalized, the whole process of movement may be organized around one's center. The center referred to is the actual physical center of the body, which is the hip and pelvic region. Most of the prominent Asian martial arts place a great importance on this area of the body as not only the physical but also energetic center of one's being.

The hips and pelvis form the physical center of the body, and the point of connection between the body's upper and lower halves. Momentum generated by the lower body is given direction by the center region. The bend at the hips is also the area which is mainly responsible for neutralizing and dissipating incoming forces from outside the body. When the body is erect, the physical center of gravity is located mid-point between the hips, inside the torso. It is important to realize that this point will shift and change location in relation to the body's posture and movement. For this reason it becomes difficult to organize and guide all movement from one static point in the body (as the body's actual "center" of gravity is constantly changing as motion occurs). However, keeping a more diffused, "peripheral" awareness of the entire hip and pelvic region when moving is often a helpful method of uniting the mind and body and training centralization of power and balance. Feel the entire torso as a single, flexible unit (like a ball filled with air) that is heavier at the bottom (in the hip and pelvic region) than at the top. It is essential that the basic structural alignments be maintained in order to create the conditions necessary for this state. Maintaining the lumbar curve and bending the body from the hip joints as opposed to the lower back will "connect" the torso with the lower body. Leaving

the shoulders and arms completely relaxed and in positions of mechanical advantage will also serve to "connect" the arms with the torso. With these alignments intact the body will become a flexible unit with the hips and pelvis serving as the base and center of motion.

One of the keys to maintaining correct anatomical alignment, connection throughout the body and true balance (in motion and at rest) is to keep the center of gravity directly over the base, with the base being defined as the area between the two feet. No matter where the feet are placed, if you draw a straight line from the toes and heel of one foot directly to the toes and heel of the other foot, the area between these lines is the area of one's base (see Illustration 18). If you are standing on one leg, the area of your base is only as large as the supporting foot. Imagine a straight line passing at a right angle to the floor toward the center of the Earth (the line of gravity). If this line passes through your center of gravity and falls within the area of your base, your posture (static or dynamic) is stable (see Illustration 19). Once the line of gravity which passes through your center of gravity falls outside your base, you must immediately readjust either the position of your torso, feet or both to reestablish the vertical alignment of the center of gravity with the area of the base or you will fall to the ground (we sometimes move our center of gravity outside our base on purpose when we wish to roll or fall to the ground, as when we execute a sacrafice throw). Remember, although the physical center of your body is the region of the hips and pelvis (and this area with its direct connection to your legs and torso serves as the center of your mass and power), the center of gravity is not limited to one fixed location in the body; it moves as the posture changes.

Once you understand and have internalized the above principles of body use through conscientious practice of the exercises, the mental and physical orientation contained in the following exercise may serve to tie together Exercise One through Thirteen into one "master exercise." It is helpful to go through the Body Use Exercises individually to get a feeling for the specific principle I am attempting to illustrate so that we have a "common ground" from which to communicate. Once the particular skills and methods of body

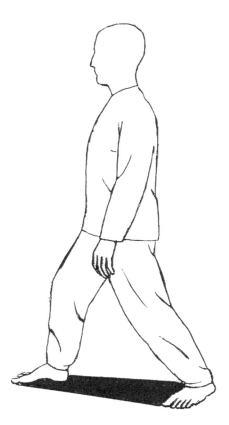

Illustration 18

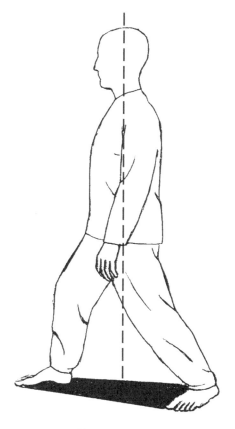

Illustration 19

use presented above are internalized and again become the natural state, the particular use of the intent outlined in the exercise below may serve as a simplified and all-encompassing state of mind/body unity from which all movement originates. Although the preceding exercises are helpful for reinforcing various aspects of correct body use and Natural Power, and may be useful to return to when attempting to master new movement patterns or eliminate specific problems, the state of being presented in Exercise Fourteen is the fundamental method of aligning the mind and body with the principles of Natural Power, the power borne of non-effort and non-interference with one's inherent nature. I have referred to this state of being elsewhere as "true balance."

Exercise Fourteen: True Balance; Using the Body as a Coherent Unit

The following "exercise" is really more a method of uniting the mind and body and training the intent to "feel" the body as a whole and unified entity, with the resultant ability to maintain this overall mental and physical unity in motion and at rest. In this state, the intent "fills" the body as a whole and all of the above mentioned principles of body use are automatically adhered to. Although complete mastery of this state of being is more of an ongoing process of refinement rather than something that can be obtained absolutely, still it can be said that to master this is to master body use.

First, stand up and become aware of gravity. Allow your body to align itself so that it takes the absolute minimum amount of effort to keep yourself from falling. Every muscle in your body should feel as if it is completely relaxed and expanding, that you are taking up as much space as possible with all parts of your body. Your center of gravity is balanced directly above your base. You are now aligned correctly and completely relaxed. You are in a unified and balanced state. Your mind and body are unified, your physical self is in the state of balance which offers no resistance to your innate functions and you as a physical entity are in balance with the external forces of the natural environment.

The key to maintaining this state of unity and balance, and one which insures the generation and utilization of Natural Power in motion is only this: in all movements and postures, allow the intent to move the body so that you are never consciously aware of any muscle contracting or tensing or using force. Of course muscles will contract, but they do so without your being consciously aware of them. Moving about in this manner feels effortless and demands that you adjust the angle and placement of your body as a whole so that gravity continuously transferres through you and into the ground without the effort involved when you are misaligned or tense. Whenever you feel muscles straining adjust yourself so that this pressure is released. Allow the body to compress and swing and avoid using clumsy or stiff force. To move without overt effort guarantees your center of gravity will be directly over your base, thus insuring maximum stability. The maintenance of relaxed muscles allows the frame to compress and rebound without hindrance. Extreme angles and ranges of motion or unnatural postures will automatically be avoided as they cause tension and discomfort. You will be free to move easily in any direction from this state of comfortable, centralized balanced. In fact, the optimal utilization of all our innate strengths, alignment with natural forces and the opportunity to take maximum advantage of momentum automatically avails itself when we maintain this state of true balance in motion and at rest. With practice and experimentation you will discover that it is possible to maintain this state of relaxed unification and balance when sitting, jumping and even when rolling on the ground.

CONCLUSION

It should be noted that all of the principles of body use included in this chapter are mutually reinforcing and are, in reality, different methods of arriving at the same goal. This goal is free and easy motion without effort or strain, a state of mind/body unity and true balance. This state of being allows us to make full use of our inherent strengths, generate Natural Power, remain stable in stillness and in motion, and provides us with the attributes necessary for effective action in martial encounters.

All of the principles and techniques of throwing presented in this book have as their foundation the principles of body use found in this chapter. Spending time practicing and experimenting with the ideas and principles presented here will hopefully serve as an aid in furthering self awareness. In the following chapter little reference will be made to the principles of body use, but they are implied in every technique. It is very difficult to control others until we are able to control ourselves. Through conscientious practice and awareness of how we use our minds and bodies we may not only come to a greater understanding of our own strengths and weaknesses, but because of the common bond of our humanity we also become more aware of the strengths and weaknesses of others. This is perhaps the foundation of effective action and is reminiscent of the famous quote from The Art of War-: "know yourself and know others, and in one hundred battles you will taste victory one hundred times."

Part Two
Chapter Three

Analysis and Applications

Introduction

Before we begin with the techniques themselves and their practical applications, it is important that you have read, studied and are familiar with the concepts and terminology presented in the preceding chapters. In the descriptions of the throws and the analysis sections which follow, constant reference will be made to the material previously covered in Chapters One and Two. Once you have a good understanding of how the throws work (the principles) and how to generate momentum and apply power (body use), technical proficiency will come steadily with practice. Although the principles of entering, connecting and throwing can only be made manifest and actually applied by practicing the techniques themselves, you should already have internalized the correct methods of body use before you attempt the throws. If you have not, you may find it extremely difficult to pay sufficient attention both to yourself (your balance, motion, posture...), and how you are interacting with an opponent. Once you understand how to use your body correctly and have practiced the exercises offered in Chapter Two until they are second nature, you can turn your attention fully to the task at hand (the methods of setting up and throwing your partner/opponent).

Following are some guidelines which will help you structure your practice for maximum benefit. Included are suggestions for a sequence of training as well as things you should be aware of and pay special attention to as you train.

GUIDELINES FOR PRACTICE:
1) If there are specific drills for the throw, then practice them first until you are familiar with them. Building good habits and the correct feeling for the movements before you attempt to throw your partner will help you to internalize the correct movement patterns and responses.
2) Practice cooperatively in the early stages of learning a new technique. This is most important. The partner being thrown should allow the thrower to set up and apply the

technique without resistance at first. Remember, you are learning new skills and not competing. Cooperative practice is probably the most important variable in training which determines how proficient students will eventually become. Those who struggle and compete during the learning stages rarely achieve a very high level of technical ability (which the ability to apply "techniques" in a real combat situation is based on). When I say "cooperatively" I mean that the partner receiving the technique neither struggles to resist nor "falls for" the partner applying the technique. Obviously, anyone can counter a technique if he or she knows what's coming beforehand. During the acquisition stage of practice, allow your partner to apply the technique without resistance yet do not fall if the technique is incorrectly applied.
3) Pay special attention to the set up and entry (setting the opponent up involves creating or taking advantage of an opportunity to make a physical connection. Once we have a connection we maneuver ourselves and the opponent so we may "enter," obtaining an advantageous position and connecting our center with our partner's center. In the text which follows, "set up" and "entry" are used together and the term "set up" is often used to denote the whole process). Taking the time to correctly set up a throw is what makes the technique possible in the first place. The best technique in the world is useless if you do not have the opportunity to apply it. Taking the time to set up a throw is analogous to taking the time to aim a gun. The odds of hitting a target are very high when the gun is correctly aimed. Likewise, the odds of successfully completing a throwing technique are much higher if the throw is properly set up. An excellent method of training is to practice setting up and entering the throw very slowly and smoothly until extraneous motion is eliminated. Once you can enter the technique correctly in slow motion, simply adding momentum (not tension) will make the technique viable in a real fighting situation.

4) Practice the techniques from a static entry first. This means the partner taking the fall should stand still and allow the thrower to enter the technique without providing any momentum. There are several advantages to practicing techniques in this manner, especially in the early phases of training. First, the throw is easier to set up as the partner to be thrown is stationary. The variables which require attention are limited (the partner practicing the throw does not have to worry about getting hit, evading, matching momentum...). On the other hand, the throw must be exact because the partner being thrown is standing in a stable and balanced posture providing no momentum which could potentially be used against him. Starting throws from a static posture allows you to move through the technique in a step by step and precise manner without the pressure of being hit.

5) After you become proficient at setting up and executing the throws on a stationary partner, begin to practice applying the techniques against realistic attacks. It is important, however, to control the speed of practice, especially in the beginning. Have your partner attack you in "slow motion" and respond accordingly (in slow motion) until your reactions and movements are smooth and efficient. Once the proper motions are internalized at slow speed, begin to pick up the pace and practice the techniques with a partner moving at normal speed (always within the bounds of safety, never practice so fast that the partner taking the fall is in any danger of injury).

6) Always remember to be aware of your own kinesthetic sense. It is important that you do not get so caught up in throwing your partner down that you forget the basic principles of body use. If you discover that during the application of a technique you are tense, off balance or are vulnerable to counter attack, go back and practice the technique until you have corrected whatever is causing the problem. This is important even if you are successfully throwing your partner. For example, you may find you are having to use a little brute force in order to throw your partner, but the throw is working none the less. Continuing to practice in this manner will build bad habits of body use and will ultimately retard your progress. If you run into an opponent who is larger and heavier or more skillful than the practice partner

you could throw with brute force, you may find your technique ineffective. Correct and precise training will instil the constructive reactions, sensitivity and correct movement patterns that will allow you to perform at your best in an actual fight. Avoid the temptation to "cheat" during training just to complete the throw.

7) The best indicator of a technique properly executed is that it should feel effortless. The throw applied correctly to another should not require any more effort that the movements of the throw executed in the air. Although you will feel the opponent's mass and the pressure of his weight, you should not feel the need to exert brute force or strain when executing the technique. If you are straining, you are doing something wrong. Also bear in mind that any technique is "conditional" to the situation at hand. This means the appropriate technique must be applied at the appropriate time. You cannot arbitrarily choose a particular throw and apply it whenever you want. Practicing the throws cooperatively will aid in internalizing which throws are appropriate to which situations. Maintaining balance and relaxation will allow you to change from technique to technique as the situation demands.

8) Another vital key to progress is exchanging feedback with your training partner. Since your partner is the one being thrown, he or she is best qualified to give you constructive feedback on the feeling and result of the technique applied. For example, after executing a technique ask your partner if they felt as though they could have either resisted or countered the throw, or if they felt you were using inappropriate force. Work with each other in the spirit of cooperation and with an honest desire to help the other improve.

9) Finally, be sure you are proficient at breakfalls before attempting any of the techniques in the book. Most styles of combat martial art include systematic training in breakfall practice, and there are many competent teachers with whom you can learn the methods of landing safely after being thrown. Although the correct methods of breaking one's fall can be gleaned from the pictures of the throws following, it is important to be trained specifically in breakfalls before actually being thrown. And, of course, always practice on a soft and padded surface (wrestling or judo mats are ideal).

The Throws
Part One

ARCS

(1) THE SHOULDER STROKE

General Description

This is a simple throw which catches the opponent in a surge of momentum, uprooting him and sending him crashing to the ground as if he were caught up in a breaking wave. This throw is specifically a side arc as it causes the opponent's head to travel sideways from the upright position to the right or left while the fulcrum of the rotation, his outside foot, remains stationary. It is a fairly unique throw in that the great majority of arcing throws involve rear arcs, and less frequently front arcs, with side arcs by far the least common. Because this technique is relatively easy to set up and execute, and because it clearly illustrates most of the major principles of throwing discussed in Chapter One, it is a good throw to begin with. In addition to its simplicity and ease of entry, opportunities to apply the Shoulder Stroke often occur in real life combat situations. The angle of entry and the fact that the throw makes use of one's entire body mass in motion makes it especially well suited for use by smaller and lighter individuals against the larger and stronger. The resultant fall is potentially devastating if applied to an unsuspecting opponent on a hard surface because of the sudden transference of momentum and the awkward angle at which the opponent hits the ground. When set up and executed correctly, the Shoulder Stroke may be applied with minimum effort against opponent's more than double your own body weight.

Since the speed at which momentum is transferred from thrower to thrown may be controlled, it is advisable to begin very slowly, allowing the partner taking the fall to land gently on his side. Once both partners are familiar with the mechanics and feeling of the throw, momentum may be added (but always within the bounds of safety). Practice entering and executing the throw on a stable and stationary partner in a precise and relaxed manner until you are able to go through the whole process smoothly, decisively and without effort. Once proficient against a stationary opponent, begin to set up the technique from a variety of "realistic" situations. The variations offered in the Combat Application section are only examples of possible applications and are by no means exhaustive. As with all subsequent techniques, practice until the mechanics of the throw are internalized and may be applied with no gap between intention and action.

Method of Application

(1) You and your partner face each other at minimum safe distance (hereafter, we will refer to your partner as "B"). B stands with his right foot forward and his right arm extended to the front at about shoulder height. B's outstretched arm is representative of any type of punch, push or grab. Stand up straight, balanced, and completely relaxed with your feet about shoulder width apart. Feel the body lengthen and expand as you relax. Your intent pours outward toward the opponent like water (see Figure 1).

(2) Shift your weight to your right leg and then cross step forward and slightly to your left with your left foot as you brush B's right forearm toward your right with your left hand (cross stepping involves stepping forward, placing the foot down toed out as the heel of your rear foot comes off the ground, with the rear knee held close behind

54

the knee of the forward leg). This moves the attacking limb (B's right arm) away from you as you simultaneously shift your weight to your forward left foot (which moves your body slightly to the left off the line of attack). Be sure to toe your left foot outward. Although your body will move left as you shift your weight to your left foot, avoid leaning to your left. Lower your body slightly as you move forward (see Figure 2).

(3) Continue your forward motion swinging your right arm up from under your left making contact behind B's right elbow. Rotate your hand palm outward and continue moving B's arm to your right as you grab his upper arm behind the elbow (be sure to grip gently with the intent). Continue your forward momentum and begin to bring the right leg forward (see Figure 3).

(4) With your right arm extending out in front of you and remaining unbendable, step up with your right foot past the front of B's legs with a deep step (your right leg should pass just in front of B's legs). Your extended right arm will push B's right arm around toward his rear, causing his torso to turn to his left (aim as though you are trying to push B's right elbow into his left shoulder, the resultant rotation of his torso will misalign his shoulders and hips). Continuing the forward momentum, shift your weight to your right leg, pressing your right shoulder into B's right side, thereby joining centers (see Figure 4). Be sure to keep your head tucked close behind B's right shoulder.

(5) Continue shifting your entire weight to your right leg, pushing with your rear left leg and moving your torso (shoulder) straight into B's right side at an upward 45 degree angle (push directly toward B's left side in order to shift his weight entirely over his left foot). You are transferring the momentum of your body through your right shoulder into B's center. B's right leg will now be weightless and will begin to come up off the ground. Reach around the back of B's right leg with your left arm so that your hand hooks around the inside of his right knee (be sure not to attempt to grab and "lift" B's leg too soon, wrap it only after his weight has been pushed completely over his left leg, leaving his right leg "weightless"). As you

wrap B's right leg, let go of B's right upper arm and drop your right arm down so it wraps around the front of his waist (your right hand holds his left hip) (see Figure 5).

(6) Continuing your forward momentum, bring your left leg up behind your right and lift B's right leg upward (toward your armpit) as you lean a little to your right and slightly down into B's side. Your body moves in an arc and the transference of momentum to B causes him to be uprooted (brings his center of gravity up) and then drops his center of gravity outside his base (outside his left foot). The result is that B will fall in an arc toward his left side. Be sure that your right knee does not extend past your right ankle as you shift the weight to your right foot (see Figure 6).

Analysis of Entry

In order to successfully set up and enter this throw, it is important to move into B transferring your momentum directly through his center in a straight line from one side to the other. To execute the throw from the safest angle, thereby minimizing the opponent's chances of counterattack or escape, it is very important to push B's lead arm around toward his rear shoulder. Not only does this check his lead hand (pushing from behind his upper arm prevents him from striking back with his elbow or attempting to wrap your neck in a front headlock), the motion also serves to break his posture by misaligning his hips and shoulders. Keeping your head tucked behind B's shoulder as you move into him is also intended as a safety measure should he free his right arm before he is taken off balance. Pressing your head at the back of his shoulder prevents him from building up any momentum should he attempt a rear elbow strike with his lead hand. Additionally, setting up the entry in this manner allows you a safe avenue of escape toward the opponent's rear should you need to abort the throw. By cross stepping slightly to the left with your left foot while simultaneously slapping the opponent's lead arm in the opposite direction, you effectively move yourself off the line of attack and create the momentum to enter the throw in one smooth flow.

Figure 1

Figure 2

Figure 3

Figure 4

Figure 5

Figure 6

The Shoulder Stroke - Method of Application

Most importantly, your intent flows out from you and into the opponent like water from a powerful hose. During the basic stages of training, treat your partner's extended right arm as an obstacle which will literally be swept aside as you flow inward like the current of a strong stream. Your body follows the forward flow of intent and continues moving into the opponent until his whole body is caught up in your momentum flow and is swept away. Practice connecting with your partner mentally while still at Safe Distance, before any physical contact is made.

Analysis of the Throw

As stated above, the Shoulder Stroke is side arc. The opponent's head travels in an arc from the upright position to the ground to either the right or left side. The throw involves a second class lever with the outside edge of the opponent's rear foot serving as the fulcrum, his torso (the center of his body) as the load to be moved and the point at which your shoulder presses against his side as the point of application of force. The length of his body from the point of application of force down to the fulcrum (the outside of his rear foot) acts as the force arm. Since it is mechanically most efficient to apply force at a 90 degree angle to the force arm, as you shift your weight into the opponent you should transfer the momentum of your mass into the opponent at an upward angle of about 45 degrees to the ground.

The opponent's posture is broken when you push the elbow of his lead arm around toward his rear shoulder. This causes his shoulders and hips to be misaligned vertically. Once the opponent's posture is broken you continue to step past him and press your shoulder into his lead side, it is at this point that you join centers. The point of contact between your shoulder and the opponent's torso is the place through which you transfer the momentum of your body into his. Be sure not to lean forward in an attempt to strike the opponent with your shoulder, the pressing of your shoulder into the opponent should be gentle and continue in a smooth acceleration and should not be a percussive bump. Pressing your shoulder into B at a smooth rate of acceleration is the key to blending the motions of your respective torsos. If you knock

B away by smashing into him you will be unable to match the rhythm of your motion with his. By connecting with B gently and then accelerating your mass into him in a smooth flow, you will not alarm him and cause a reflexive recoil reaction, and his center will be subordinate to yours. As you continue moving into the opponent, the resistance of his mass will soon take the slack out of your connection as his ribs compress inward, resulting in a direct connection between your respective centers.

It is important to drive straight into the opponent from the side in a direct line toward his rear foot, moving forward and upward at a 45 degree angle. The upward angle allows you not only to take full mechanical advantage of applying force at a right angle to the force arm, it also prevents the opponent from squatting in an attempt to lower his center of gravity and increase his stability. Once the opponent's center of gravity is pushed over his rear foot, the area of his base becomes only as big as the sole of one foot. You now have control of the momentum of his body and can lead the opponent into the throw. Wrapping and lifting his forward leg helps to change the angle of the forward momentum into a downward angle (toward the ground) as well as safeguarding against any attempt by the opponent to turn and run. Continuing your forward momentum moves the opponent's center of gravity outside the area of his base, removing his support and causing him to fall.

It is important to keep the flow of momentum constant and continuous throughout the throw. This necessitates projecting the intent forward and then downward in an arcing flow. It almost feels as if you and the opponent are caught up in a breaking wave which surges upward and then crashes downward in a powerful arcing motion. After the opponent hits the ground, be sure to maintain the outward flow of the intent and be aware of both the downed opponent and your surrounding environment. As the opponent is projected away from you, stop your forward flow of momentum and allow your rear foot to step up behind your front foot. Stand stably and centered so that you are again in the neutral "ready posture" and are able and to move in any direction.

Analysis of Body Use

Pay attention to your posture as you face your partner before actually moving in to connect with him. Be sure you are standing in a centered and balanced manner and that your entire body is relaxed, with the crown of your head floating upward. Your vision should be directed toward B's upper chest with awareness on the peripheral vision.

During the initial movements, your hands and feet move together (the left hand cross checks B's right forearm just before your left foot cross steps forward; your right arm swings up from beneath B's right arm and catches behind B's elbow as you step forward with your right foot). This insures unitary motion and whole body power which continues right through to the completion of the technique. After you have made the initial contact with B, extend your right arm pushing B's right upper arm around toward his left. Following, as you step up with your right foot and shift your weight from the left cross stepping foot to the advancing right foot, be sure that your right arm does not collapse or bend at the elbow. The right arm remains extended with energy so that the forward momentum generated by the legs and torso is transferred directly through your right arm, which pushes B's right elbow toward his left shoulder. In short, do not use your right arm to push the B's right arm, use your whole body to push and turn him. This is a very important point. If you step past B with your right leg allowing your right arm to collapse and then attempt to push B's right arm toward his left shoulder, you must rely entirely upon the strength of you right arm alone.

As you shift your weight to your right leg and begin to uproot B by pushing upward at a 45 degree angle, lead the rising motion by allowing your head to float upward (do not "brace" yourself by pulling downward as you move in to uproot). Once you have pushed B's weight over his left foot, leaving his right foot unweighted, drop your left arm heavily and wrap up his right leg. As you continue the throw, imagine lifting his right leg by raising your left elbow rather than by pulling up from the hand. Your hand only adheres to the inside of his right knee lightly. Allow your

left arm to bend at the elbow as you lift B's right leg so that your shoulder does not raise. Keep the arm as relaxed as possible. At the same time your right arm will be wrapping B's waist. Do not try to hug his hip too tightly. Try to wrap around his hip making contact with the entire inside surface of your right arm.

Do not lean forward too much when pressing your right shoulder into B's right side. Keep your posture upright and your center of gravity well within your base of support. When lowering your body as you enter the throw (as you move in to press your right shoulder into B), be sure to bend at the hips keeping your back aligned (do not bend in the middle of your back). During the stepping and shifting of the weight, pay attention to the Four Levels (see Chapter Two). The technique should be completed in one smooth motion from beginning to end; this necessitates generating momentum in one smooth wave of force. Therefore, it is important to practice until you can coordinate the movements of your hands and feet, the shifting of your weight and your breathing (try to exhale smoothly throughout the throw) into a smooth rhythm.

Combat Applications

Following are various "real life" situations in which the Shoulder Stroke may be appropriately applied. It is important to realize that there are conditions to every technique. Understanding a throw and practicing until the mechanics of the technique are internalized are necessary prerequisites to being able to apply any technique for real. The next step is to practice until it is possible to set up techniques more and more efficiently and then to cultivate the ability to flow from one technique to another. But the basics must be mastered before going beyond to more advanced forms of training. Before you attempt the techniques in less structured situations, it is vital that you have spent enough time drilling them with a cooperative partner. When applying the throw in various situations, variations in set up and execution are often necessary. It is important to understand that all variations are based on the "prototype" or original throw and ultimately have the same feel when applied, regardless of the route taken to enter the technique.

Once you feel you have a concrete grasp of the throw and can apply it smoothly and successfully against a stationary partner, begin to set up and execute the throw in various combat situations. As always, train slowly and cooperatively with safety in mind. The suggestions given below represent only a few of the many situations in which the Shoulder Stroke may be successfully applied.

Straight Head Punch/Jab Defense

Stand at Safe Distance, the opponent has his right foot forward and his hands raised in an "on guard" position. Aim your gaze toward his upper chest making sure you do not try to focus on or follow the movements of his hands (see Figure 7).

The opponent lunges forward and extends his right arm in a straight strike toward your face. Step out to your left with your left foot a half step and shift your weight to the left, moving your body off the line of attack. As you step, swing your left hand up and toward your right, as if you are slapping your own right shoulder (be sure the arc of the left hand's movement moves as high as your face). This motion is a cover that protects your face and slaps the opponent's incoming fist away from you; it is not a block, be sure not to look at the punch, rather, maintain the focus of your vision on the opponent's upper torso/head area (see Figure 8).

Almost simultaneously, your right hand swings up from under your left and connects behind the opponent's right elbow. Immediately rotate your right arm outward and begin to push the opponent's right arm toward your right. Continuing the motion, grab behind his elbow and extend your arm as you shift your weight to your left foot completely in preparation for the right foot's forward advance step. Lower your body a little and press your right shoulder into the opponent's right side (see Figure 9).

Keeping the forward extension of your right arm, step forward with your right foot past the front of the opponent's legs and push his right elbow toward his left shoulder. As you push, raise

your body upward at a 45 degree angle, your right sholder pushing into the opponent's right side. As the opponent is uprooted and his weight shifts to his left foot, wrap your left arm around the back of his unweighted right leg, grabbing inside his knee (see Figure 10).

Continue your forward momentum, as you drive upward and lift the opponent's right leg, throwing him in a side arc onto his left side. Be sure to enter and complete the throw in one smooth flow of momentum, paying attention to the salient points described above (see Figure 11).

As the opponent falls away from you, release him and let your left foot come up a half step behind your right. Watch the opponent and maintain your awareness of the surrounding environment (see Figure 12).

Front Choke Defense

The opponent reaches up and grabs your throat with one or both hands. Immediately bend your arms at the elbows and grab the opponent's wrists from underneath. Do not make a big movement with your hands, but rather "sneak" them up under the opponent's wrists and grab. Try not to grab his wrists too tightly, simply hold them firmly where they are in space. As you grab his wrist, step back a half step with your right foot and shift your body back, taking your throat out of the opponent's grasp (the feeling should be one of holding his wrists stationary and backing your throat out of the grasp; see Figure 13).

As soon as your neck clears the opponent's hands, immediately spring out of your right foot and step forward with the left foot a half step, toed out. At the same time as the forward step, swing your right arm up under the opponent's right and rotate your arm outward grabbing behind his elbow. Extend your right arm and shift your weight to your left foot (see Figure 14).

Continue with the throw as above, lowering your body a little and pressing your right shoulder into the opponent's right side. Step up with your right foot and uproot the opponent at a 45 degree upward angle, wrapping his right leg with your left and throwing him in a side arc (see Figure 15).

Figure 7

Figure 8

Figure 9

Figure 10

Figure 11

Figure 12

The Shoulder Stroke - Straight Head Punch/Jab Defense

Figure 13

Figure 14

Figure 15

The Shoulder Stroke - Front Choke Defense

(2) REAR HEAD TILT

General Description

This throw involves tilting the opponent's head back, taking the slack out of his spine until the pressure applied at his head transfers directly into the opponent's hips. Continuing to tilt the opponent back results in his upper body (and his center of gravity) moving outside the area of his base, causing the opponent to topple over backward in a rear arc (the opponent's head travels in an arc from the upright position to the ground toward the opponent's rear while his feet remain stationary). Once properly set up and set into motion, it is virtually impossible to escape from this throw. And a very small expenditure of energy will land even very large and heavy individuals flat on their backs.

It is a true axiom of body mechanics that where the head goes the body follows. If we view the entire length of the body as a force arm with the fulcrum at the heels, applying force to the opponent's head (near the end of the force arm) maximizes mechanical efficiency. This particular technique takes advantage of this principle in applying force to the head in order to lead the other's body. Because the throw is set up from the opponent's rear and is entered in such a manner that he can't see it coming, it is relatively difficult to counter the entry.

One may use this throw to set up subsequent techniques such as holds and chokes. It is also a useful technique to use when breaking up a fight or when you wish to immediately subdue and control another. Although there is little chance of injury during the set up phase of the technique, extra caution should be used when actually taking the partner (or opponent) to the ground. There is a very real chance the person taking the fall will land on the back of their head, which may result in serious injury. During training, be sure to walk through the technique slowly and "cradle" your partner's head to avoid injury. Likewise, discretion must be used in actual application.

Method of Application

(1) Approach B from behind. B should stand upright and balanced (see Figure 16).

(2) Step forward with your right foot to the center point between B's legs and reach up with both hands, palms up, extending them just over the tops of B's shoulders, close to the sides of his neck (see Figure 17).

(3) Simultaneously lightly drop your forearms on the tops of B's trapezius muscles as your palms press up under each side of B's jaw (it feels as if you are cupping B's jaws and supporting his head from below). The point of contact with the tops of B's shoulders should be about the middle of your forearms (about half way between your wrist and elbow on the ulna or little finger side of your arm; see figure 18).

(4) Break the opponent's posture by dropping your elbows heavily and pushing slightly forward with your forearms as you push B's chin first forward then upward with your fingers. B should be made to lean forward slightly and then his head is pushed a little more forward before being tilted up and over to the rear. Move B's head forward and up in a smooth circle. Do not attempt to pull his chin directly backward as he will be able to resist (see Figure 19).

(5) Once B's head is tilted backward (he is made to look upward), continue dropping your elbows heavily. (the point of contact of your forearms and B's trapezius muscles is the fulcrum around which your rotate your arms. The position and action of your arms constitutes a first class lever with his head as the load to be moved and the dropping of your elbows and body weight as the point of application of force). This action will cause B to arch back and will lock his head directly to his hips. Holding B in this locked position slide your left foot back a half step and shift your weight back to it, carrying B's head back with you (be sure not to move away from B, your arms do not straighten as you shift your weight back but rather you move with and carry B back as one unit). B will now be overbalanced toward his rear and

Figure 16

Figure 18

Figure 19

Figure 20

Figure 21

Rear Head Tilt - Method of Application

will be leaning against you, reliant on you for his support (see Figure 20).

(6) Continuing your rearward momentum, take a long step back with your right foot and allow B to fall in an arc onto his back. Be sure to slide your hands around to the back of his head as he falls and cradle his head so that it does not hit the ground. Once B loses his balance and begins to fall, stop applying downward force and allow B to tuck his chin in preparation for a breakfall (see Figure 21).

The entire throw, from the second you make contact with his top of the opponent's shoulders and chin until he falls backwards, is done in one smooth circular flow of force.

Analysis of Entry

Obviously, when practicing this throw as a drill there is no consideration of Safe Distance as you approach from the rear. You need to approach directly behind B's centerline (applying the technique from one side or the other changes the opponent's falling momentum into a spiral, which in turn calls for a different method of causing him to fall). When moving the two hands into position, try not to telegraph the action by making contact with B's shoulder area or neck before the hands are in the proper position. Setting up the throw roughly or with force will alert the opponent as to your intentions and will increase the odds of resistance or counter. Your forearms are moving upward at a slight angle as they extend over the tops of B's shoulders, and once you drop your arms onto the tops of B's trapezius your palms continue pushing his chin toward his front in the same forward flow of energy. B should feel as if at the instant of contact his entire center moves forward over his toes and slightly upward.

When setting up this throw in a combat situation, it is helpful if you can first cause the opponent to lean back, at least slightly. If you maneuver around behind your opponent and he bends forward, it will be very difficult if not impossible to set up the throw. Pushing or striking the opponent from the front, or pulling him from the rear and then moving immediately into the technique is

usually the best way to enter successfully. Once you catch the opponent's jaw, however, it is extremely difficult to escape from or counter this throw.

As far as your intent is concerned, you should feel its flow as if you are a wave which surges up directly beneath your partner and breaks toward his rear, sucking him over backward in its crest. For this reason (the flow of force surges straight up from beneath B), it is important that you move in close behind B so that your centers are joined even as you make initial contact with your hands and arms. Try not to reach out forward for his head, rather stand very close behind him and feel as if the energy surging up from your feet flows directly upward through B's body, catching him under his chin.

Analysis of the Throw

This technique principally makes use of a second class lever. If we view the opponent's entire body as a force arm from his heels to the top of his head, we have the longest potential force arm possible. As we know, force applied at a right angle to the force arm at the point furthest from the fulcrum maximizes one's use of force. Applying force to B's head (the furthest point from the fulcrum located at his heels) allows us to break his posture and take him down with the least amount of effort (the load to be moved in this case is B's center, which we want to put on the ground. Remember that your hands are only the connections through which you transfer your momentum, they should remain soft and relaxed throughout the technique.

Although applying force at a 90 degree angle to the force arm is most efficient, we have to take into consideration that the person we wish to move is flexible and capable of resistance and change. In order to take the slack out of B's head/torso, we need to first move his head forward and then upward in a circular manner. This insures his chest will arch, which in turn will lock his head and spine into his center (hips). Once B is set up with the slack taken out of his head-torso-hip connections, we may continue the motion by taking him over backward to the ground. Attempting to pull directly back on an opponent's chin often results in him ducking his head and bending forward at the waist, which makes it much more difficult to effect the throw. As pointed out in the section above, your arms work as a first class lever in a see-saw manner when tilting B's head back (with his chin as the load to be moved, the point at which your middle forearms contact his shoulders as the fulcrum and your elbows as the point of application of force).

You need to stand very close behind B in order to join centers. After you have tilted his head back and broken his posture (the torque on his head and subsequent backward arch it causes breaks B's vertical shoulder/hip alignment), it is important to move B back as if he were a part of your body rather than first stepping back and then pulling his head (the correct feeling of the throw is as if you were holding B in a rear bear hug and pulling him back as you step backward). Once B's body is arched back and his hips are locked, a very small rearward pressure will cause his center of gravity to move outside the rear parameter of his base. B will now be leaning back dependent upon you for his support. All you need do at this point is step back and let him fall (removal of support). Remember that your hold on B's chin is only a connection through which you transfer your momentum.

Once his head is tilted backward and his hips are locked, "feel" through your hold on his head down through his entire body and move his mass through his head. This is very different than jerking someone's head backward and attempting to pull them to the ground with brute force. Although the latter method may work, it leaves much more opportunity for your opponent to counter or escape. If at any time you need to abandon the throw, or if your hold on B's jaw slips, you have a safe avenue of escape as you are already behind him. In addition, during an actual encounter, you can intensify the destructive potential of the technique by kneeing the opponent in the back after you enter the throw, before throwing him down. You can also strike the opponent on the face or throat as he falls.

As stated above, the overall rhythm of this throw is in a wave-like flow which surges upward from directly beneath B and breaks toward his rear, carrying him over backward in a rear arc. As you begin to push B's chin forward and tilt

his head back, be sure you connect softly and complete the throw with a smooth acceleration of force. Any jerky movement will tend to break your connection with B's center and afford him an opportunity to escape.If you are in a combat situation and need to amplify the force of the throw, as you step back and let the opponent fall, allow your hands to roll up from under his chin to above his face. Dropping your weight and pushing down suddenly and heavily with both hands (as if his head were a basketball that you are going to bounce hard against the ground) will amplify many times over the force with which the opponent's head lands on the ground and could result in serious injury (needless to say, this variation of the throw should only be used when there is a serious threat to your person; never practice pushing your partner's head down with force during practice). During practice, once your partner begins to fall, stop pulling his head so that he has time to tuck his chin and breakfall. If you feel that his downward momentum is too great for him to break his fall in time, quickly slide your hands around to the rear of his head to prevent the back of his head striking the ground. When applying the throw in a street situation, be sure to step back with your lead leg far enough so that the opponent has enough room to fall without landing on your leg. You may even swing your retreating front foot around behind you and turn out of the opponent's way as he falls. Be sure to end the throw in a balanced posture.

Analysis of Body Use

The entire technique requires that you maintain an upright posture throughout. As you enter behind your partner and scoop up his jaw from below, consciously feel the upward pull on the crown of your head. This will help you create the upward surge of energy necessary to catch B's center and uproot him. Feel your intent flowing upward toward B's head before your hands actually connect beneath his jaw. Keep your arms relaxed and heavy and allow the weight of your elbows dropping to create the lever action which tilts B's head back. Once B is arched back and the slack is taken out of his body (you have a direct connection through his head and torso with his hips), feel as if you and he are fused into one body. Keep your arms bent and your chest close to B's back as you step back and move him as part of you. As you step back, do not lean back and attempt to pull B over with the power of your arms alone, rather, keep your back straight and move B with the momentum of your whole body, centering the movement in your hips.

Moving your rear (left) foot back a half step before your front foot steps back aids in creating momentum without disconnecting your respective centers. After your left foot takes a half step back, continue shifting your weight over it but be careful not to lean back. As soon as your weight is over your left foot, continue the momentum stepping back with your right foot as you pull B over backward. The rearward stepping should be in one continuous flow of momentum. As you move backward, allow your hands to pull B and drop at the speed of gravity. This means your arms move in concert with your body and then fall heavily as B goes down. Resist the urge to jerk B's head back with your hands (as this will break your overall body rhythm and ruin the timing of the technique). As always, when shifting your weight be sure that your body is aligned so that your center of gravity remains directly over your base. Exhale smoothly for the duration of the technique, allowing your body weight to sink as you step back and pull B down in a rear arc.

Combat Applications

To execute this throw, you need to be behind your opponent. If you are attacking someone directly who is unaware of your presence (for example, if you are breaking up a fight), you may approach from the rear, setting up and finishing the technique as practiced in the Method of Application section. When attacked from the front or during a "hands up" fight, you will need to set up the throw indirectly and create a condition in which you have an opportunity to move to your opponent's rear. The easiest method of entry to an opponent's rear involves moving directly outside his forward foot, while controlling his forward arm. Oftentimes when ducking a punch you will again find yourself behind the opponent, and in position to apply this throw. The throw is easiest to apply when the opponent is arched backward slightly. If you are combining the throw with striking techniques, once behind the opponent a blow to his kidney (which causes him to arch his back) will provide the necessary set up.

Jab/Straight Punch Defense

As stated above, the easiest method of entry to the opponent's rear when initially face to face is around the side of his lead hand and leg. A straight punch toward your face gives you the opportunity to enter directly to the opponent's rear.

You are facing the opponent at Safe Distance. Stand erect and relaxed with your vision aimed toward the opponent's upper chest. You may have your hands up in a defensive posture. Focus the flow of your intent on the opponent, while remaining aware of your peripheral vision (see Figure 22).

The opponent steps forward with his right foot and throws a right straight punch at your face. As he crosses Safe Distance, step forward and out toward your left at a 45 degree angle with your left foot toed in (it is very important to toe in your left foot on the step, that is, point your left toes toward the opponent, otherwise your flow of momentum will be aimed away from him). As you step, swing both hands up and push outward from behind the opponent's punching arm in order to "bounce" his punch away from you. Keep your arms relaxed and "springy" and don't attempt to "block" his arm at any specific place. Use the movement of the arms to close off the entire right side of your head rather than attempting to block the incoming punch specifically. Allow your right foot to slide up and slightly toward your left rear as you step and shift your weight to the left foot. Your intent flows outward toward the opponent's centerline. (see Figure 23).

Continuing, immediately lift your left foot, allowing yourself to spring forward out of your right foot (don't lean back and shift your weight to your right foot first, only lift your left foot and "fall" forward). Step around behind the opponent with your left foot so that you are more or less directly behind him. As you step, move your left hand around the back of the opponent's neck and insert it over his left shoulder; your right hand slides up over the top of his right arm and palm strikes the opponent straight into the right side of his jaw, causing his head to turn so he looks directly forward (as you move and strike, keep your right elbow down to guard against the opponent trying to strike back at you with his right elbow; see Figure 24).

Moving in very close to the opponent's back, bring your right foot up behind the opponent and push up under his jaws with both hands as you drop your forearms onto the tops of the opponent's trapezius muscles. Continuing the motion, drop your elbows heavily and push the opponent's head forward and then tilt it back in a circular motion (see Figure 25).

Continuing the momentum, step back with your left foot a half step and bring the opponent with you, breaking his posture by causing him to arch backward. Follow with a long step back with your right foot, allowing the opponent to fall in a rear arc. Be sure to end the throw in a balanced position and maintain your awareness of the opponent and your surrounding environment (see Figure 26).

Front Kick Defense

The Rear Head Tilt is also a good technique to use if you enter to an opponent's rear after he attempts a front kick.

Face the opponent at Safe Distance. Look toward his upper chest and pay attention to your peripheral vision (see Figure 27).

The opponent steps in and raises his knee in preparation for a front thrust kick to your stomach. As he steps and lunges forward extending his foot, step forward and outward at a 45 degree angle with your left foot, toed in. Simultaneously swing your right arm down and to your right rear to knock the opponent's kick away from you (do not attempt to "block" the kick with your right arm. Depending on the timing and angle of your step, you may not even contact his leg at all. Only swing your right arm down close by your side as a cover in case your step is slow or the opponent kicks at an outward angle; see Figure 28).

After the step and cover, your weight will be on your left foot and your hips will be turned toward the right. Continuing, step up with your right foot toward the opponent's back and extend both hands up over the opponent's shoulders (you may strike either side of his neck if necessary) turning the palms up under either side of his jaw (see Figure 29).

Continuing the motion, push the opponent's head forward and then dropping your elbows heavily cause him to look upward. Step back with your left foot a half step and continue with your right, pulling the opponent back in a rear arc (see Figure 30).

Figure 22

Figure 23

Figure 24

Figure 25

Figure 26

Rear Head Tilt - Straight Jab/Straight Punch Defense

Figure 27

Figure 28

Figure 29

Figure 30

Rear Head Tilt - Front Kick Defense

(3) HIP DISPLACEMENT

General Description

The Hip Displacement is a unique throw in that it causes the opponent to fall in a rear arc, however, the opponent's feet move laterally during the fall. When caught in the momentum flow of this technique, it feels as if you are caught up in a wave which pitches you backward and sideways simultaneously. During the throw, you literally displace the space occupied by the opponent's hips with your own hips. The result is that the opponent is projected sideways; you simultaneously apply pressure downward and to the rear across the front of the opponent's throat, causing him to fall in a rear arc. The Hip Displacement can be used to great effect when very close to the opponent face to face, in many standing grappling situations and as a counter to attempted throws. When correctly set up and applied, its momentum is virtually impossible to escape.

Method of Application

(1) Stand facing B from the front. B stands with his right foot forward. Reach out and take hold of B's right wrist with your left hand (be sure to keep your left hand and arm relaxed, use soft grip to hold his wrist; see Figure 31).

(2) Step forward and to the left at a 45 degree angle with your left foot, stepping outside and just past B's right foot, placing the foot down toed in. As you step, simultaneously swing B's right arm back and out toward his right rear (be sure to leave your left arm relaxed and naturally heavy so that the weight of your arm takes the slack out of B's right arm as you swing). As you step up and swing B's arm up to his right rear, simultaneously move your right hand up the front of B's chest, then extend your right arm over B's left shoulder, pointing toward his rear (see Figure 32).

(3) Keeping energy flowing out of both your arms (do not allow them to collapse as you move forward), shift your weight to your left leg and continue pushing B's right arm toward his right rear with your left hand as your right arm begins

to put pressure across the front of his throat (see Figure 33).

(4) Continuing your forward momentum, bring your right leg up and step behind B toward his left rear, toeing your right foot in as you step. The outside of your right hip will make contact with the rear of B's right hip as your leg moves behind him. Continue extending both your arms (it is very important not to let your arms collapse as you move forward) and turn your right hand thumb down behind B's left shoulder (as if you are pouring a glass of water onto the ground) as your right foot touches down to B's right rear. B will be thrown toward his left rear corner in a rear arc, and will land flat on his back (see Figure 34).

Analysis of Entry

Although this throw can be applied without controlling B's right arm, it is much easier and ultimately more effective to enter the throw stretching B's right arm out to his right rear corner. Once the slack is taken out of B's arm and his posture is broken to his rear, you have created an avenue of entry into the technique. As you step up with your left foot and swing B's right arm toward his right rear, extend your right hand and move it up the front of B's chest, close to his body. It is important not to raise your right arm horizontally and then attempt to swing it around B's throat from a distance. This type of "clothesline" motion telegraphs your intentions and will alarm B, giving him a chance to intercept your right arm with his left arm. Moving your right hand up the front of B's chest very close to his body allows you to move the arm into position from an angle that B cannot see (you cannot see your chest with your peripheral vision when looking straight ahead). Your right hand should "slide" up the front of B's chest (close to it, but without actually making contact) and over his left trapezius, extending toward his rear palm down until the crook of your right elbow is against B's throat. Now your right arm connects with B where there is no relative motion. In actual application, if the opponent grabs your wrist, the throw may be entered directly as in the standard technique above (often with the addition of a striking technique) or may be set up off punches

Figure 31

Figure 32

Figure 33

Figure 34

Hip Displacement - Method of Application

(usually by intercepting early). Normally, you will not want to step past an opponent's side and to his rear until you have broken his posture as described above.

It is very important when stepping up with your left foot to toe it in and point your toes in the general direction of B's center. As soon as you step, shift your weight to your left foot (be sure to keep your hips level). Once you swing B's right hand up to his rear and step forward with your left foot, your flow of intent should be aimed through B's centerline. The correct focus of intent will be difficult to achieve if you do not toe in your left foot so that your torso is turned toward B's center.

In addition, toeing in the left foot provides stability and turns your entire flow of momentum in the correct direction (aimed toward B's left rear).

Analysis of Throw

As explained above, this throw is a rear arc which involves projecting B sideways as he falls. Swinging B's right arm back and up toward his right rear takes the slack out of his arm and connects your hold (at the wrist) directly with B's center. It is very important not to relax the pulling pressure on his arm at any time during the throw. As you swing B's arm out, you simultaneously step up

71

with your left foot toed in. As explained in the section above, it is vital to toe in the left foot to insure stability and correct focus of momentum. As you shift your weight to your left foot and bring up your right in preparation for the actual hip displacement, you continue to push B's right arm toward his right rear corner (keeping your intent moving forward and into B and your posture upright). This will break his posture by misaligning his shoulders and hips along their vertical axis. Your right arm (which is wrapped around the front of B's throat) also continues its forward pressure as you shift your weight to your left foot. This causes B to lean backward slightly. At this point, B is set up for the throw.

Continuing with the above momentum, keep your posture straight and step with your right foot behind B toward his left rear corner. As the right front side of your hip presses into the rear of B's right hip, turn your right toe inward (remember to turn the leg as a unit from the hip) as you step down behind B. The toeing in action causes your right hip to rotate and aids in uprooting B and displacing his hips. It is at this point (as your hips touch) that you physically join centers. In order for the throw to work without effort there must be even pressure at two points, B's right hip and his throat. If you maintain correct, upright posture and move in at the correct angle, your right arm and hip will push in with equal force. The result is that B will find his entire torso being displaced in space as a unit. Moving B as a unit prevents him from adjusting either above or below in an attempt to escape the throw. It may be helpful to imagine transferring momentum into B evenly with the hip and the right arm simultaneously. Throughout the entire throw, from the initial entry until B is projected to the ground, you should feel as if there is a strong force pulling your hands away from your body toward the front. At no point in the technique should you relax this forward flow of intent. It is also important not to crash into B or attempt to bump him of his feet. Extend your arms and move into B at a smooth rate of acceleration. Accelerating into B without impact makes it possible for you to sweep him up into your momentum flow, match the rhythms of your movement and make B's movement subordinate to yours.

The Hip Displacement causes B to fall primarily through removal of support. You literally displace his base and cut his legs out from under him. Turning your right arm over and dropping it heavily as you step into B's hip is also a form of weight dropping which puts pressure near the top of B's body, the weight of which causes his head and torso to fall over his base in a rear arc. There is also a slight coupling effect as B's hips are displaced slightly forward (caused by the toeing in of your right foot which creates a spiral energy at the hip) and his upper torso is pushed to the rear by the weight of your right arm as it turns thumb down. As B projects away from you, be sure to place your right foot down and allow your left foot to slide up a half step behind it in order to maintain an upright and balanced posture. Continue looking in the direction of B's fall and mentally project your intent outward in that direction. Remain aware of both B (as he lands) and the surrounding environment. In actual application, if the opponent manages to resist the throw, your superior position makes it possible for you to change into any number of follow up techniques instantaneously.

Analysis of Body Use

From the beginning of the throw to the end your body maintains an upright posture. There is no need to squat or lean at any time during the technique. It is especially important to shift your weight carefully, moving your body as a coherent unit to insure a smooth flow and transference of force. It is helpful to consciously focus attention on allowing the crown of your head to float upward throughout the technique. This aids in keeping your torso aligned and consequently the ability to apply even pressure to B's torso (at the hip and throat). It is also helpful in the early stages of training to move through the throw in a step by step manner, paying attention to the relative alignment of the Four Levels as described in Chapter One. Step forward and swing your arms with the speed of gravity, keeping them relaxed. In addition to maintaining the upward pull of intent at the crown of the head, center the movement of your body in your hips.

72

As you swing your arms forward (the left swinging B's arm to his rear and the right swinging up and across the front of B's throat) and step with the left foot, feel the impetus for the arm movements coming from the forward momentum of the body. In other words, do not step first and then attempt to "shove" B's arm up behind him. It is most important to keep a constant forward intent flowing out of the arms (as if your arms are hoses with a strong current of water spraying from your fingertips). Although your intent maintains its strong forward flow, it is important to shift your weight from your rear right foot to the front left foot without your torso leaning forward.

Maintain a continuous forward flow of whole body momentum as you shift your weight to your left foot and then step across behind B, shifting your weight to your right foot. Do not squat over the left leg and attempt to spring off it as you press your right hip into B's right hip. As you shift your weight over your left foot, do not allow the knee to move forward of the ankle. Let your weight compress the left leg, stretching the soft tissue and utilize the momentum of the rebound out of the ground to propel you toward B's rear. Only maintain your upright posture and step behind B as if he was not there. As B begins to lose his balance and fall to his left rear, turn your right hand thumb down behind his left shoulder and allow the weight of your arm to overbalance him to his rear. Try to avoid pushing down with strength as this tends to cause you to lose your balance and may give B something to hold onto as he falls. Finally, once you have a good grasp of the mechanics and flow of the throw, practice entering and executing the entire technique during one smooth exhalation.

Combat Applications

This throw is useful in various grappling situations and as a counter to another's attempts to throw you. The Hip Displacement can also be used as a follow up technique when other sweeps and throws prove unsuccessful. The throw blends well with striking techniques, especially strikes to an opponent's face or throat which cause him to lean back.

Wrist Grab/Cross Defense

The opponent grabs your left wrist with his right hand standing with his right foot forward (see Figure 35).

The opponent begins to pull you in with his right hand and raises his left hand in preparation for a punch to your face. Since he is already within the parameters of Safe Distance, you must act immediately. In this instance it is advisable to intercept the attack early. Move with the force of his pull (resisting the opponent's pull will result in the use of force against force will most likely result in you losing your balance) stepping forward and to the left a little with the left foot toed in. Simultaneously swing your left arm down and toward the opponent's right rear as you strike straight up with your right palm directly into the opponent's nose or chin. Moving and striking in this manner not only moves you off the line of attack, your strike also acts as a barrier between your head and the opponent's left punch (see Figure 36).

The force of your strike will cause the opponent to lean back and will intercept his forward flow of force (if the opponent leans back to escape the blow it makes no difference, he is still set up for the throw). Continuing, shift your weight to your left foot and extend your right arm past the front of the opponent's throat (be sure not to retract your right hand after the strike). Your right hand is now extended over his left shoulder (be sure to keep the forward flow of intent in both your arms, your left arm continues moving the opponent's right arm toward his right rear; see Figure 37).

Step with your right foot toward the opponent's left rear, turning your right foot toe in and pressing your right hip into the rear of the opponent's right hip. As the opponent loses his balance, turn your right hand thumb down and drop the arm heavily across his throat. The opponent falls in a rear arc to his right rear (see Figure 38).

Backsweep Defense

In this variation the Hip Displacement is used to counter an attempted backsweep (for example, such techniques as judo's o-soto-gari or a chest push and backsweep). Although the set up and timing of entry are somewhat different than the above technique, the throw itself is the same. The trick is to catch the opponent and displace his hips as he lifts his sweeping leg in preparation to throw. Although in this variation of the technique the opponent will not have his posture broken to the rear, the fact that he is standing on one foot as we apply the counter is sufficient to allow us to uproot and project him.

The opponent grabs you by the lapels from the front (see Figure 39). He begins to twist your shoulders, causing you to lean to your right. Once the opponent has secured a hold on you and begins to unbalance you with the twist, it is important not to resist his force (as this will result in your being held in a disadvantaged position). As you are twisted toward your right, relax and sink your weight into your right foot. Try to maintain the relative alignment of your hips and shoulders, but don't tense your upper body (see Figure 40).

As the opponent lifts his right leg to the rear in preparation for a backsweep (to complete the technique he will swing his right leg back into the back of your right leg and throw you to the ground

Figure 35

Figure 36

Figure 37

Figure 38

Hip Displacement - Wrist Grab/Cross Defense

Figure 39

Figure 40

Figure 41

Figure 42

Hip Displacement - Backsweep Defense

onto your back), shift your weight to your left foot and lift your right leg a little. Push off your left foot, stepping sideways with the right foot toed in behind the opponent's legs (see Figure 41).

Move sideways into the opponent pressing the outside of your right hip into the right rear side of his hip. Move your torso across evenly (try not to thrust your pelvis out to the side or lean your upper body sideways) so that your right hip and right side press into the opponent's right hip and side of torso respectively. As you move sideways, extend your right arm past the opponent's right shoulder (bring your posture back to the upright position as the opponent loses his balance). Move into the opponent with even pressure above and below. The opponent is thrown to his left rear in a rear arc (see Figure 42).

Roundhouse Punch Defense

In this example the Hip Displacement is set up and entered by pushing the opponent's right arm straight back to his rear at shoulder level (as opposed to swinging his arm arm to his rear from below, as in the standard technique). Here, the Hip Displacement is set up off a roundhouse punch, but the same principles of breaking the opponent's posture are applied.

You are facing the opponent at Safe Distance. Be sure to relax and connect with him mentally (your intent flows toward his centerline) before he actually begins moving. The opponent cocks his right arm and begins to move toward you in preparation for a roundhouse punch (see Figure 43).

Relax and step forward and to the left with your left foot at a 45 degree angle, stepping down with the foot toed in. As you step, simultaneously swing your left arm up and push it forward with your body (try not to swing your arm out and away from your body, rather, the arm and body move forward as a single unit. This greatly increases the stability of the arm and prevents you from opening your centerline if the opponent "fakes" the punch). Be sure to maintain the direction of your gaze toward the opponent's upper chest/head area (do not look at his punching hand). This entry is a classic example of "intercepting early," as we seek to stop the forward momentum of the opponent's swing as early as possible, effectively stifling his power. As you step in and swing your left arm up to cover, simultaneously swing your right palm straight up into the opponent's nose or chin in order to disturb his offensive momentum (see Figure 44).

Continuing, grab the opponent's right upper arm at the triceps and pull it to your left, moving it away from his body as you simultaneously push it toward his right rear (this will result in the opponent's shoulders and hips losing their vertical alignment). As you move the opponent's right arm out and to his rear, shift your weight completely to your left foot and extend your right hand past his throat over his left shoulder (see Figure 45).

Continuing your forward momentum, step your right foot behind the opponent toward his left rear corner and displace his hips as in the techniques above. Be sure to follow up by bringing your left foot up a half step behind your right and finish the technique in a stable and relaxed posture, with your awareness expanded to include your surrounding environment (see Figure 46).

Because the Hip Displacement projects the opponent away from you, you will not have the opportunity to maintain control of him as he lands on the ground. Therefore, it becomes especially important to maintain your focus of intent and awareness of the environment after the completion of the throw. Although this technique results in a fairly hard fall, the opponent may or may not be incapacitated. Be alert as to his condition and prepared to decide on subsequent action (escape or follow up techniques).

Figure 43

Figure 44

Figure 45

Figure 46

Hip Displacement - Roundhouse Punch Defense

(4) FRONT HIP PUSH

General Description

This is a very simple throw which is easy to set up and apply. It involves applying leverage to the front of the opponent's hip at an outward angle which causes him to fall in a rear arc. The technique is suitable to many situations and may be entered smoothly from both punching and grappling attacks. One advantage of the throw is that the connection with the opponent, joining of centers, breaking of the opponent's posture and actual takedown are really only different stages of the same forward movement. Consequently, this technique requires very little time to execute. Because the technique attacks the opponent's base directly, the Front Hip Push is well suited for application against a taller and heavier opponent. Once the basic method and angle of the application of force are understood, you may modify the basic technique by using different parts of your body to effect the throw (for example, you could throw the opponent by applying pressure with your palm, forearm, foot or knee). This potential variability in the methods of application of force gives the thrower a much broader spectrum of situations in which this technique can be successfully applied. When caught in the throw, it feels as if someone grabs your belt from the rear and yanks you to the ground.

Method of Application

(1) Stand facing B from the front at Safe Distance. B stands with his right foot forward. Your intent flows toward B, focusing on the front of his waist (see Figure 47).

(2) Take a small step forward with your left foot toed out, putting the foot down a few inches in front of B's right foot. Shift your weight to your left foot and then continue moving forward, stepping up between B's legs with your right foot, toed in a little. The inside front of your right thigh should make contact with the inside of B's right leg. As you step in with your right foot, lower your body and put your right forearm across the front of B's right hip (at the crease where his upper thigh joins

the torso). Your left hand hangs straight down (see Figure 48).

(3) Shift your weight to your right foot, simultaneously pushing forward and slightly outward (towards your left) on the front of B's hip, bending forward at the hips (aim the push toward his right rear). B's leg will buckle outward and his posture will be broken (see Figure 49).

(4) Continuing with the above push, reach down with your left hand and grab around the back of B's right ankle with your left hand. Continue pushing B's hip back and downward at a 45 degree angle with your right forearm, bending forward at the hips until B falls backward in a rear arc (see Figure 50).

(5) As B falls, bring your left foot a half step up behind your right and return to the upright ready position. You may either let go of B's right ankle as he falls or continue holding it in preparation for a follow up technique (see Figure 51).

Analysis of Entry

Since this throw is entered from the front, Safe Distance needs to be taken into account. Although you will not have much of an "angle" on B when you enter, the speed at which B's posture is broken and his balance disturbed makes it difficult for him to counter. Care must be taken, however, to set up and enter the throw smoothly and quickly to avoid counter attack, since you are in range of both of B's hands. When entering the standard technique, the key is to step up between B's legs and shift your weight to the forward foot in a continuous motion, the momentum of which literally sweeps B's center backward off its base. The central point is that the entire technique from entry to finish should be completed in one weight shift from your left foot to your right foot.

Your intent is aimed through B's right hip toward his rear right. When you step in with your right foot be sure to toe it in a little so that as your weight shifts over your right foot, your hips will naturally turn to the left a little, thereby aiming your push toward B's right rear. When you connect with B's hip, do not strike him with your

Figure 47

Figure 48

Figure 49

Figure 50

Figure 51

Front Hip Push - Method of Application

right elbow or forearm (which tends to knock him back a step, precluding direct entry into the throw). Press your forearm gently into the front of B's hip, accelerating smoothly at a constant rate throughout the technique. In practical application, this throw is most often set up after you strike at your opponent's face and cause him to lean back, which divides his attention and gives you time to enter the throw.

Analysis of the Throw

As discussed above, this throw is entered and completed in one movement. Therefore, as you step up with your right foot between B's legs and press your right upper forearm against the inside front of his hip, you have already joined centers. Pressing with the forearm closer to your elbow will allow you to line up your humerus bone (the bone in your upper arm) with your torso, thereby creating an unbendable wedge between your mass and B's hip. As you shift your weight to your right leg, the slack between your forearm and B's hip will immediately be taken out and you will break his posture. It is vital to push from the inside of his hip at an outward angle as this pushes B's right upper femur out and away from its connection at his hip. This causes B's right leg to be pushed away from his center and the resultant misalignment breaks his posture (through misaligning his base). Continuing the outward and downward pressure at B's hip causes him to fall to his rear.

The structure of our legs is such that we are least able to resist pressure applied from the inside of the leg toward the outside. If B is standing in a stable stance with his right foot a step ahead of his left, with the weight on his right foot (the standard Forward Stance of Karate or Bow Stance of Kung Fu), pushing at the front of his hip straight toward his rear transfers your force directly into his back leg and actually adds to his stability. The stability of the stance is less resistant to pressures applied to the outside of the leg inward or from the rear forward, but the stance is least resistant to pressure applied from the inside of the leg (pressure applied anywhere from the hip down to the ankle) toward the outside. We take full advantage of this inherent structural weakness

and aim our push outward and at a 45 degree angle downward toward B's right rear.

Your momentum is transferred completely through the connection you have at B's hip. Grabbing around B's heel with the left hand serves two purposes. First, it causes you to focus your intent at a the downward angle necessary to make B fall (because you have to "bend over" in order to reach around his ankle). Secondly, holding B's ankle gives you an added measure of control as he falls, and sets up potential follow up techniques as well as protecting you from B's foot should it fly up toward you as he falls. Holding around his ankle (the end of the force arm), gives you the greatest leverage advantage when controlling his leg.

Once B's posture is broken, the forward lean of your torso actually causes him to fall. This is not so much the result of pushing B down forcefully as dropping the weight of your upper body into his hip (once B's posture is broken, you do not want to "push" his hip down and out as much as allow the weight of your body to "fall" into it at the speed of gravity. This results in a smoother and more powerful transference of force into B). It is weight dropping which actually causes B to fall. Allowing your weight to compress into your right (front) leg at the speed of gravity allows you to create a powerful surge of momentum through B's hip. Once your weight has transferred into your right leg, the forward momentum will naturally stop and you immediately allow the upward intent at the crown of your head to return you to the upright posture, bringing your left foot up a half step behind the right.

Once you have returned to the upright ready posture, you may choose to let go of B's ankle or control the leg as you follow up (B is especially vulnerable to leg locks or a right kick to the groin). Maintain awareness of the surrounding environment and continue to focus your intent in the direction of B's fall.

Analysis of Body Use

The entire technique from start to finish involves one long step and the shifting of the weight from the rear to the front foot, with a simultaneous forward lean of the torso. The feeling of the thrower is of taking a long step forward and then bending down to pick something up off the ground. It is important to transfer your weight forward with a smooth acceleration into B's hip as you shift your weight from the left rear foot to your front right foot. Avoid stepping between the opponent's legs with your right foot, stopping your forward momentum, and then bending forward to push his right hip. This would necessitate using the force of your right arm alone rather than the transference of the momentum of your entire body. As you shift your weight to your right foot and begin to bend forward, be sure to bend at the hips and not in the middle of the back. As you bend forward at the hips and begin to press the front of B's right hip, be careful not to round your shoulders or "hunch" your back. Keep your shoulders relaxed and your chest lifted, maintaining the Four Levels as you bend. Also be careful not to raise your bottom up as your head lowers. Sink into your right foot as you bend forward at the hips. Keeping your rear down and letting your weight compress into the front foot causes your torso to "fall" into B's hip at the speed of gravity, which is the ideal speed at which to transfer momentum into him.

Step in deep enough with your right foot so that after you have transferred all of your weight to it, your right shin will still be perpendicular to the ground. Too small a step with the right foot may result in your right knee extending past your right ankle at the completion of the forward weight shift, causing your torso to lean too far over your right leg at the completion of the throw. Remember, take a deep step with your right foot so that you can compress fully into it and maintain stability throughout the technique. Your hips should continue to lower as your torso bends forward. Once B is actually falling, you may begin to raise your body upward by lifting at the crown of your head, thereby returning to the upright ready position.

In the standard version of the throw illustrated above, you use the upper part of the forearm just below the elbow to press into B's hip. Pushing with this area of the arm allows you to use the bone in the upper arm as a wedge between your own center of mass and B's center of mass. Your right arm may remain completely relaxed as you transfer momentum through it. If you want to connect with B's center sooner, you can extend

your right arm until it is almost straight (so that the bones of your upper and lower arm are in straight alignment), and press the front of B's right hip with your right palm instead of the forearm. In this case, you can begin transferring the momentum of your mass into B from a greater distance. The basic principle of pushing from the inside of the hip toward the outside rear and downward remains the same.

The general flow of your intent is in a straight line through B's right hip toward the floor, aiming the focus of the intent at a point a couple feet behind and to the right of B's right hip. Feel as if you generate a wave of force which surges up from your feet and catches B at his hips, breaking toward his rear. Exhale smoothly as you drive B's hip toward the ground. Once B has fallen, you must immediately decide whether or not to follow up. Even if you maintain your hold on B's right ankle, his left foot is free and potentially capable of kicking you. Kicking or stomping B's groin is a possible follow up which is both quick and debilitating. Alternately, you can lock B's right ankle or roll him over and pin him from behind (the descriptions of which are beyond the scope of this book). If you choose to disengage and leave without a follow up, move back to your left rear, away from B's free left foot.

Combat Applications

The Front Hip Push is a simple and direct throw which is entered and completed in one movement. Since the throw is applied directly from the front, it is important to set it up correctly, thereby minimizing the opponent's chances of counter. This technique is especially useful when you are unable to move to an opponent's outside angle or rear (which is most often your best strategy in a fight). Although the fall appears to be fairly mild in comparison to others which involve lifts (techniques which cause the opponent's feet to leave the ground), the impact upon landing can be quite forceful. When correctly applied with full momentum, the pressure applied at the opponent's hip locks his knee, preventing him from sitting out of the throw by bending his legs. Falling stiff legged often results in the opponent having the "wind" knocked out of him as he bumps the back of his head on the ground. Caution should be exercised when training with your partner.

Straight Punch Defense

Face the opponent at Safe Distance. Aim your vision at his upper chest area and be aware of your peripheral vision (see Figure 52).

The opponent steps forward with his right foot and throws a right straight punch toward your face. Step back and slightly to the left with the left foot, following by sliding the right foot back a half step until your feet are about shoulder width apart. Keep the focus of your intent aimed in at the opponent. As you step back, simultaneously slap across the front of your face with your left hand toward your right shoulder to deflect the incoming punch. This is not a block, stepping back and slightly toward your left rear with your left foot moves you off the line of attack and out of the way of the punch. Turn your hips slightly toward the right as you step, so that the center of your chest is aimed toward the opponent. The left hand slaps toward the right to close off the entire plane through which the opponent's punch passes. You are covering the right side of your face and possibly deflecting the punch, not blocking. Be sure not to take your eyes off the opponent's centerline; keep your head floating up from the crown and your vision aimed toward the opponent's head as you move (see Figure 53).

Lift your right foot and step forward between the opponent's legs, placing your foot down toed in. Your right shin should be touching the inside of the opponent's right lower leg (see Figure 54).

Shift your weight to your right foot as you begin to squat a little and bend forward at the hips, placing your right forearm on the front of the opponent's right hip. As you shift your weight to your right leg, your right knee will move forward into the inside of the opponent's inner leg, contacting just below his knee. This will push his right knee outward, breaking his posture by misaligning his base (see Figure 55).

Continuing, bend forward from the hips and press your right upper forearm into the the opponent's right hip. As you complete the weight shift to your front leg allow the momentum of your center to transfer through your right forearm into

the opponent's right hip, aiming the push toward the opponent's right rear. Reach down with your left hand and catch behind the opponent's right heel as he falls. Because you have toed in your right foot, the angle of the push will be toward the opponent's right rear corner. Be sure to bend forward at the hips, dropping the weight of your torso into the opponent's hip at a downward angle. The opponent falls onto his back in a rear arc (see Figures 56 & 57).

In this variation of the Front Hip Push, you use your right shin to break the opponent's posture (misaligning his base) before your forearm begins its push. If the opponent lunges past you with his punch, you will not be able to apply this technique, but you will be able to enter any technique that is applied from the rear.

Defense from Standing Grappling

You and the opponent are locked in standing grappling (with your right hands holding behind each other's neck and your left hands holding each other's upper arm). Both of you have the right foot forward. Be sure to leave your arms relaxed and heavy. Tension in the upper body will make it easier for the opponent to push or pull you off balance. If the opponent moves in any direction follow his motion keeping "square" with him (don't let him get an angle on you). Relaxing and following the opponent in this manner makes it difficult for him to strike or throw you and results in a more or less neutral position (see Figure 58).

Slide your left palm around the outside of the opponent's right arm until it is underneath the outside point of his elbow. This will be easier if you swing your left foot back toward your right rear a half step (see Figure 59).

Suddenly push the opponent's right elbow up and out to the side at about a 45 degree angle, so that his arm is lifted parallel to the ground (see Figure 60).

Continuing, let go of the back of the opponent's neck with your right hand and bend forward at the hips, pressing your right upper forearm into the front of his right hip. The lifting of his right elbow, forward bend at the hips and the placing of your right forearm on his right hip should follow one another without pause (see Figure 61).

Figure 52

Figure 53

Figure 54

Figure 55

Figure 56

Figure 57

Front Hip Push - Straight Punch Defense

Figure 58

Figure 59

Figure 60

Figure 61

Figure 62

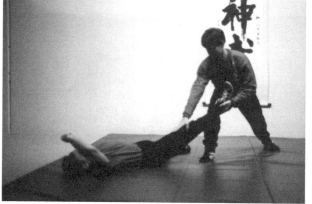

Figure 63

Front Hip Push - Defense From Standing Grappling

Step forward a half step with your right foot between the opponent's legs and shift your weight forward. As you shift your weight forward, continue bending forward at the hips, transferring the momentum of your mass through your right forearm into the opponent's right hip (pushing downward at an angle toward the opponent's right rear). As you push the opponent's hip back toward his right rear, drop your left hand down and grab behind his right ankle (see Figure 62).

The opponent falls onto his back in a rear arc (see Figure 63).

This technique must be set up, entered and completed in one smooth movement. Be sure to keep your intent focused on the opponent and be ready to follow up if necessary.

Front Headlock Defense

The opponent reaches around the right side of your neck with his right arm attempting to pull your head down into a front headlock (see Figure 64).

At this point, it is dangerous to resist the opponent's downward pull as the use of force against force will most likely result in you losing your balance. Bend forward with the opponent's pull and step in deeply between his legs with your right foot. As you step in and bend forward, press your right forearm into the front of the opponent's right hip, breaking his posture at the base (see Figure 65).

Continuing with the forward momentum, push the opponent's right hip downward and to his right rear as your left hand drops down to hold behind his right ankle. The opponent falls onto his back (see Figure 66).

This technique is useful once the opponent has managed to wrap his arm behind your head and begins to pull you down. At this point, go with the pull and stepping in deeply with your right foot, allow your body to drop forward more rapidly than the speed at which the opponent is attempting to pull you down. As you step in and drop your weight, the transference of momentum at the front of the opponent's right hip will push his center backward and away from you, misaligning his base and preventing him from tightening his hold around your neck. Further forward pressure causes him to fall onto his back.

Figure 64

Figure 65

Figure 66

Front Hip Push - Front Headlock Defense

Part Two

CIRCLE

(5) OUTSIDE HIP THROW

General Description

This is a variation of the standard hip throw found in many schools of martial art. The Outside Hip Throw is inherently safer to enter than the standard version (which enters between the opponent's arms) in that the outside position from which one enters makes it much more difficult for the opponent to counter. This hip throw variant also results in a harder fall than usual because you control the arm the opponent would normally use to break his fall. In addition, if the opponent manages to resist the throw, entering from the outside leaves open more options for follow up techniques, as well as a safe angle of escape.

As discussed in Chapter One, circular throws cause the opponent to rotate around his center (hip) area with his feet making a 360 degree revolution in the air. The Outside Hip Throw is an example of a forward circle. The basic feel of the throw is as if you are caught in a wave which pitches you head over heels as it breaks. This technique is especially easy to set up and apply on taller opponents. We will also make full use of the stretch/rebound capabilities of our lower limbs in order to "bounce" the opponent up and over our hips and onto the ground.

Method of Application

(1) Face B from the front. Step up with your left foot and grab B's left wrist with your left hand. Keep your head up and your eyes level (see Figure 67).

(2) Swing your left arm up and out toward your left, pulling B's left arm straight out at shoulder height directly in front of him. Be sure to pull his arm forward and out until the slack in his arm

is taken up. As you swing B's arm up, turn your torso to the left a little and step up with your left foot toed out, in front of B's left foot. As you step, simultaneously swing your right arm up behind B's middle back, "hugging" him close to your right side (see Figure 68).

(3) Lean into B a little (being careful to stay over your base, do not rely on B for your stability) as you begin to swing your right foot forward, taking a step in front of B's legs toward his right. As your right foot lands (you should put your foot down about a foot in front of B's right foot), toe the foot in and turn your torso to the left, simultaneously thrusting your hips across the front of B's hips. Your rear should extend past B's right side. Be sure to maintain the slight forward lean into the back of B's left shoulder; you have now pushed the majority of B's body weight over his right foot. As your right foot steps down and you turn your body toward the left, slide your left foot in a half step toward your right foot and allow the momentum to compress you into your feet, bending your knees and hips slightly. Your weight should be evenly distributed over both feet (see Figure 69).

(4) As the compressive force of your weight causes a pulse of energy to rebound out of your feet (when your compressed lower body stretches back into its neutral position), allow your legs to straighten with the upward surge of force and bend forward at the hips, pulling down on B's left arm (pull his left arm toward your left hip) as you continue to hug his back firmly with your right arm. B will be thrown over your hips in a forward circle onto his back. It is important not to thrust your hips into place and then attempt to lift B over your hips; the impetus for the throw comes from the rebound of force out of your feet which literally "bounces" B over your hips and onto the ground. At no time

Figure 67

Figure 68

Figure 69

Figure 70

Figure 71

Figure 72

Outside Hip Throw - Method of Application

should you feel as if you are lifting B over yourself with your arms, nor should you feel as if you must support his weight at any point during the throw. B should "roll" over your hips without you having to bear his weight (see Figure 70).

(5) If you wish to pin B after the throw, maintain your grip on his left wrist, and stepping back away from B's side with your left foot, press behind his left elbow with your right forearm as you pull his arm toward your left hip. Twist your right forearm clockwise to apply pressure to B's elbow joint. The combination of your momentum and the leverage behind B's left elbow will cause him to roll over onto his face (see Figure 71).

(6) If you want to immobilize B, drop your right knee onto the back of his left shoulder close his triceps. Drop your body weight straight down through your right knee. Lift B's left arm and place his wrist on top of your right collar bone, close to the right side of your neck. Lift your head and chest and lean forward a little toward B's head as you pull inward on the back of his elbow. The forward lean of your body will cause pressure at B's shoulder while the inward pull behind his elbow locks the joint, causing pain and potential hyperextension if the pressure is great enough. (see Figure 72).

Analysis of Entry

In order to set up and enter this throw you need to be outside B's arms (in contrast to the more common variation of the hip throw which would be set up by reaching underneath B's left arm with your right arm, thus leaving his left arm free to grab around your head or neck as you attempt to throw). Therefore, in order to enter the Outside Hip Throw you need to position yourself at an angle from one of your partner's front corners (in this example you are facing him from his front left). It is very important to control B's left arm (preferably by holding somewhere below his elbow) and to swing it up and forward, taking the slack out of his arm in order to make a direct connection with his center. With B's arm pulled straight out to his front at shoulder height, you now have room to enter by stepping forward with your right foot across the front of B's body.

Your intent flows into B from his front side and then changes its direction of focus as you join centers so that both you and B are facing the same direction. You move into B, catching him in your momentum flow which pushes him sideways and then surges up under him, flipping him over in space. Your intent leads the motion and must change direction in a smooth curve from its aim at B's side to the ground in front of him. If at any point during the throw B resists or moves to catch his balance, you have the option of moving to his rear or simply pushing him away.

Analysis of the Throw

Once you have stretched B's left arm out in front of him, you have created the opening needed to enter the throw. As you step in front of B with your right foot and hug around his middle back with your right arm, you want to press into B's body and make contact with as much surface area as possible. This enables you to connect with his center more completely and allows you to transfer the momentum of your mass into him over a greater length of his body. Now the wave of energy surging up from your base will apply pressure along the entire side of B's upper body. The entire inside length of your right arm, and the right side of your torso should be in contact with B as you enter the throw. It is important that you do not "crash" into B's left side as you step in with your right foot and wrap your arm around his back. Moving into B with force will tend to knock him away from you, preventing you from wrapping up and controlling his body. Move into B and wrap him up gently, continuing with a smooth acceleration of momentum as you turn to throw. Moving in from B's side in this manner allows you to join centers and subordinate his center to yours as you cause his weight to shift to his right foot. Leaning into the back of B's left shoulder breaks his posture by misaligning his shoulders and hips. As your right foot touches down at B's front right, his motion is subordinate to yours and he is positioned to be thrown.

This throw involves a second class lever. We are using B's torso as a force arm with the fulcrum just below his hips (the point at which our right hip contacts his lower hip area) and are taking the mass of his torso (center) as the load to be moved. It is, therefore, more mechanically efficient to wrap our right arm around B's mid-back or higher to maximize our leverage (the further up B's back we apply pressure, the longer our force arm). It is also vital to place our hips at a point below B's hips so that the load (his center) is at a point between the fulcrum (our hips) and the point at which we apply force (where our right arm wraps around his back). If your hips are above B's hips, you have not created the opportunity to apply leverage and will be forced to attempt to lift B over your hips with brute strength alone. This is why it is easier for the shorter partner to enter and throw the taller. When the taller partner enters the throw, he or she must squat low enough to place their hips below the hips of the shorter partner taking the fall. In actual application, if the opponent is considerably shorter than yourself, you may want to opt for a different technique. On the other hand, if your opponent is about the same height or taller, this throw can be entered comfortably and will most likely result in the opponent taking a hard fall (and, as always, body weight also makes a difference in the amount of shock received when taking a fall. The amount of force received by the body increases proportionately as body weight increases. It's true that the bigger they are, the harder they fall).

Causing B to shift all of his weight to his outside foot creates for him a very unstable condition in that his entire base of support becomes only as large as the bottom of one foot. Once in this position, B has very little power in his base from which to resist the subsequent lift of the throw. Therefore, in setting up and entering the throw, not only do we seek to break his posture by misaligning his shoulders and hips, we also want to reduce the area of his base to its minimum before we lift and throw. While it is possible to complete the throw by only breaking B's posture and allowing him to remain with his weight distributed over both feet (in a wider base), it is much more efficient for us to exploit the inherent structural weaknesses of the instability of a smaller base of support. Therefore, as you lean into the back of B's left shoulder to break his posture, be sure to step far enough across the front of his body with your right foot so that the pressure of your mass pushes his mass over his right foot.

After you have stepped across in front of B with your right foot, toe in the foot as it touches down. Shifting your weight to your right, toed in foot naturally causes your hips to turn toward the left. Continuing the motion, thrust your hips back in front of B's right hip as you turn your torso to the left. The forward step of your right foot, the left turn of your torso and the rear thrust of your hips follow one another in smooth succession. At this point, relax downward, allowing gravity and momentum to compress your mass into your feet, stretching the tissue of your lower extremities. As the stretched tissues "snap" back into their neutral position, a pulse of energy travels through your body from the ground up. Allow this pulse of energy to straighten your legs so that your hips "bump" B's hips suddenly upward. This creates the upward surge of force which lifts B up and over your hips. Immediately following, bend forward at the hips and holding B's torso firmly against yours, allow the weight of your upper body to "fall" forward and pull B over your hips and onto the ground in front of you. Be careful not to collapse your upper body as you bend forward. Lead the motion by allowing the crown of your head to lengthen your torso away from your hips as you bend. In addition, the action of your forward bending torso should be one of weight dropping and not of forcefully pulling B over. Once you are in position with your hips thrust past B's right side and your right arm wrapped around B's back, you have physically joined centers where your hips contact his. As you bend forward with the flow of momentum rebounding upward from the earth, feel as if B's body is a part of yours, subordinate to your own center. Throwing B over your hips should be as easy as bending over by yourself.

During practice with your partner, remember that you are controlling his left arm, the arm he would normally slap the ground with to break his fall. To insure a safe landing, either release B's left arm as he rotates over your hips so that he may break his fall or hold him up a little with your right arm to slow the momentum of his descent. In contrast, if you apply this throw during an actual fight, you may hold onto the opponent's wrist and prevent him from breaking his fall. Holding onto the opponent's wrist also allows you to roll him over into a hold or pin as described in the Application section. Be sure to keep your weight evenly distributed between both feet as B rotates over your hips and lands. If B ends up projecting outward and away from you, hanging onto his wrist may jeopardize your stability. In this case it is advisable to release his wrist as he falls. Regardless of whether you maintain your grip on B's wrist or release it as he falls, you should end the throw bent forward at the hips with the weight distributed evenly over both feet and your torso in correct alignment. Stand up straight before moving on to the follow up technique, with your intent still focused on B while remaining aware of your surrounding environment.

Analysis of Body Use

The mechanics of this throw primarily involve pressing the weight of your upper body into B in order to break his posture and cause him to shift his weight over one foot. The pressure of your weight then changes from a sideways push to a push from B's rear, the momentum of which is provided by dropping the weight of your torso forward. The actual lift at B's hips is generated by allowing your lower limbs to compress/stretch then rebound with a pulse of upward energy which is transferred up into B's hips. It is very important, therefore, to first shift your weight as a single plane of force which presses into B's side, followed by compression/stretch and rebound out of your base and finally the forward bend of your torso which provides the weight dropping induced momentum that ultimately causes B to rotate over your hips.

As you step in front of B with your right foot, it is very important not to allow your own body to move forward without simultaneously pushing B toward his right foot. For example, you step in front of B with your right foot while wrapping your right arm around his back. You continue to shift your weight toward your right foot but allow B to remain in the same relative position. You will find that your right arm will now be behind you, with the arm stretched back to a weak angle. If at this point B resists the throw by leaning to his left, you will find that you will be unable to complete the throw (see Figure 87). As you shift your weight to your right foot, be sure to lean into the back of

his B's shoulder and break his upper body posture so that you can push his weight over his right foot, all the while maintaining the correct angle between your right arm and torso (your right elbow should not pass behind the plane of your left shoulder. You should maintain the alignment you would have if you were hugging a large barrel. See Figure 88). Move your body into B as a single unit , creating one plane of vertical force.

Once you have broken B's posture and have stepped across in front of him with your right foot, relax and sink a little, bending your knees and hips slightly. At this point, it is very important not to allow your posture to "collapse" underneath B. Keep the feeling of your torso lengthening and the image of your legs and hips as powerful springs which will rebound strongly as a result of the applied pressure. As you pull B forward over your hips with your right arm and begin to feel the pressure of his weight, immediately allow your compressed lower body to spring upward. The upward thrust of energy should occur without effort as it is the result of your lower extremities rebounding naturally to their neutral position. Continuing, bend your torso forward at the hips, letting its weight fall forward as you pull B over your hips in a forward circle. Be careful not bend at the waist as this tends to result in you having to pull B over your hips with the power of your arms alone. Bending your body at the hips and dropping the weight of your torso forward insures an acceleration of momentum at the speed of gravity. The smooth acceleration this creates is optimal for throwing B over your hips without effort. Be sure to keep the feeling of your torso lengthening as you bend, insuring the alignments of the Four Levels remain intact. Dropping the weight of your torso forward at the speed of gravity is only possible if you bend forward at the hips. As you bend forward, keep your body weight centered over the centers of your feet, to insure your center of gravity falls well within the area of your base.

As B rotates over you, your right arm releases its hugging pressure and you allow him to fall. Keep the focus of your awareness on B after he lands. If you wish to pin, place your right forearm below B's left elbow as described in the Method of Application section and step back with your left foot, allowing your momentum to pull B over onto his face. Exhale smoothly for the duration of the throw.

Combat Applications

To enter the Outside Hip Throw you must be outside the opponent's arms and have a hold on one of his wrists. The most expeditious method of entry would be directly to the opponent's outside angle in defensive reaction to a punching or pushing attack. This throw may also be set up from grappling situations, especially those which allow you to control one of the opponent's arms.

Right Cross Defense

Stand facing the opponent at Safe Distance. The opponent is on guard and ready to punch. Stand up straight and relaxed and aim your gaze toward the opponent's upper chest while remaining conscious of your peripheral vision.

The opponent lunges forward, stepping toward you with his left foot as he throws a right punch toward your face (see Figure 73).

As his torso crosses Safe Distance, step forward and out to the left at a 45 degree angle with your left foot toed in. As you step, swing both hands upward and outward loosely, connecting behind the opponent's elbow and wrist areas, deflecting his arm toward your right side (this is not a "block" in the sense that you are attempting to stop the opponent's blow. You are stepping off the line of attack and avoiding his force, your arms form a physical barrier as an added measure of safety while you reach out to connect with him physically). Keep your intent aimed in toward the opponent's center (be careful not to let the direction of your gaze wander off the opponent's centerline). Your arms are relaxed and heavy and maintain a "springiness" which presses in gently toward the opponent's center (see Figure 74).

Immediately after connecting with the opponent, grasp his right wrist with your right hand and pull his right arm away from his body and slightly downward in the original direction of his punch. As you do, strike the opponent in the face or nose with your left palm, sliding it close over the top of his right upper arm/shoulder area. Leave

your arm relaxed and heavy as you strike (this is a short, shocking type of blow intended only to stun the opponent, thereby delaying his reaction time while we enter the throw. Do not pull your left arm back or otherwise "cock" it in preparation for the strike; see Figure 75).

The blow will stun the opponent momentarily and will disturb the focus of his attention. You now take advantage of his confusion and wrap your left arm around his upper back, taking a half step toward B's left side with your left foot, placing the foot down toed in. Now turn your torso to the right slightly while leaning into the back of B's right shoulder to break his posture (see Figure 76).

Continuing the momentum, shift your weight to your left foot, as you push B's weight over his left foot. Turn your torso to the right, sliding your right foot a half step in toward your left foot as you thrust your hips past the opponent's left side (see Figure 77).

Squat a little, compressing into your base then spring your hips upward, lifting the opponent upward at the hips. Continuing, bend forward at the waist throwing the opponent over your hips in a forward circle (see Figure 78).

Double Wrist Grab Defense

The opponent steps up with his right foot and grabs both your wrists with straight grabs (see Figure 79).

Relax your arms completely (any tension in your arms will "freeze" your body and gives the opponent a direct connection to your center). Leaving your arms and body completely relaxed, step up and to the right with your right foot at a 45 degree angle, placing the right foot down toed in. As you step, bend your right elbow and point the outside tip of the elbow at the opponent's center. Your right hand rotates palm down as you step and bend the arm (you are moving your body in and bending your arm at the elbow while leaving your right hand more or less in the same relative position in space. Do not attempt to pull it out of the opponent's grasp; see Figure 80).

Continuing the forward motion, as your right hand nears your left hip, grab the opponent's left wrist with your left hand as you continue rotating

Figure 73

Figure 74

Figure 75

Figure 76

Figure 77

Figure 78

Outside Hip Throw - Right Cross Defense

Figure 79

Figure 80

Figure 81

Figure 82

Figure 83

Figure 84

Outside Hip Throw - Double Wrist Grab Defense

your right hand out of his grip, turning your torso to your left a little as you do (see Figure 81).

Continuing the motion, pull the opponent's left arm straight out in front of him as you back chop his left lower rib area with your right hand (see Figure 82). Note: The forward step, bending of the right arm, grasping of the opponent's left wrist and right back chop occur in one fluid motion without pause.

Taking advantage of the opponent's reaction to your strike, slide your left foot up a half step as you swing your right arm around the opponent's upper back. Continuing, lean into the back of the opponent's left shoulder in order to break his posture (see Figure 83).

Step in front of the opponent with your right foot, putting your foot down about a foot in front of his right foot, toed in. Be sure to push the opponent's weight over his right foot (see Figure 84).

Slide your left foot a half step in toward your right foot. Squat a little and compress into your base as you turn your torso to your left and thrust your hips past the opponent's right side (see Figure 85).

Now spring upward under the opponent's hips and bending forward, drop the weight of your torso. The opponent is thrown in a forward circle (see Figure 86).

Figure 85

Figure 86

Outside Hip Throw - Double Wrist Grab Defense (Con't)

(6) HEADLOCK HIP THROW

General Description

The mechanics of this throw are very similar to those of the previous technique, the Outside Hip Throw. In this variation however, we control the opponent's head by wrapping his neck tightly before we throw. Because the body follows where the head leads, wrapping the opponent's neck affords us a great measure of control over the opponent's entire body. An added benefit to wrapping the opponent's neck is that the pressure we exert on the sides of his neck restricts blood flow to his brain, and immediately weakens his ability to resist our momentum. In effect, we are strangling the opponent as we throw him to the ground. We may further capitalize on the hold we have on the opponent's neck after the throw by continuing the pressure on his neck, which will quickly result in unconsciousness. If, for some reason we are unable to complete the Headlock Hip Throw as planned, the control we have on the opponent's neck leaves open a number of potential follow up techniques.

This throw is a forward circle; the opponent's feet will travel in a 360 spin around his hips as he falls. The flow of momentum during the throw is very similar to the Outside Hip Throw, although in this variation your hips will be thrust a bit further past the outside of the opponent's hip before he rotates over them. The opponent spins in a tighter circle than the Outside Hip Throw, and he feels as if his head is being pulled through his legs toward his rear. The Headlock Hip Throw is especially useful in face to face standing grappling situations or when you have no opportunity to move off the line of attack at a safe angle. Finally, the wrapping of the opponent's head also presents additional opportunities to strike him as you enter and execute the throw.

Method of Application

(1) Stand facing B about one step's distance from him, holding his right wrist with your left hand. Stand up straight and relaxed, with your intent flowing straight into B's center. Look toward his upper chest area. Be sure to hold his wrist with soft grip and not brute force (see Figure 87).

(2) Swing your left hand up and to your left side, keeping the arm relaxed. You will pull B's right arm straight out toward his front at about shoulder height. As you swing your arm outward, toe out your left foot. (see Figure 88).

(3) As you shift your weight to your left leg, extend your right arm, shooting it over B's left shoulder and around the back of B's neck from his left side, making contact at the left rear side of his neck with the radial (thumb side) of your right wrist. After you make contact with B's neck, wrap your arm around his neck while "filing" with the top of your forearm against B's neck (slide your arm with friction against B's neck so that his neck is twisted tightly as you wrap your arm around it). Wrap your right arm as far around B's neck as possible, so that your right elbow crook is behind the back of his neck. As you complete the wrapping of B's neck, step up with your right foot toed in and put the foot down about a foot in front of B's right foot. Hold B's head firmly, squeeze the sides of his neck between your biceps and forearm, and keep your arm relaxed and your right shoulder down. B's head will be twisted so that he looks up towards his left and you will have shifted his weight onto his right foot. (see Figure 89).

(4) Swing your left foot back to your right rear as you turn your torso to the left. Your left foot stops when it is parallel to your right foot. You should now have your left side toward B's chest. As you step back and turn, pull B's right arm around your torso toward your left hip, wrapping his arm firmly around your right side as you continue to pull his head forward. Thrust your hips back until they extend past B's right hip and lower your body slightly. The overall feeling is as if you a "wrapping" B around your hips (see Figure 90).

(5) Continuing the momentum, pull B's head down toward your left knee as you suddenly extend your legs and "bounce" your hips upward, throwing B over your hips in a forward circle onto his back. During practice, release B's neck as he lands so that he may safely break his fall (see Figure 91).

Figure 87

Figure 88

Figure 89

Figure 90

Figure 91

Headlock Hip Throw - Method of Application

97

Analysis of Entry

The Headlock Hip Throw is entered from the front and is extremely useful when you find yourself caught in between an opponent's arms (whether he is striking or attempting to grapple). In order to enter and set up the throw, you need to grasp and control one of B's arms, holding it either at the wrist (as in the standard technique above) or around the upper arm. Once you have control of B's wrist, it is important to swing his arm outward, leading the arm away from his torso in order to take the slack out of his limb. Toeing out your left foot and shifting your weight to the left leg also helps to pull B's weight over his right leg and weaken his base as you step in for the throw. The important point to remember is that it is unsafe to attempt to wrap B's neck and turn your back to him before you have control of one of his arms, and have extended that arm out and away from him. In addition, swinging B's arm out to his front and shifting your weight to your left foot also serves to move you toward a safe angle, away from B's centerline.

Once B's arm is set up, the throw should be entered smoothly and completed in one uninterrupted flow of momentum. Very often, this technique sets up well when you are able to move into an advancing opponent and intercept his power early, controlling one of his arms and possibly striking him to set up the throw. The focus of your intent should be through B's center aimed toward his right rear, with the feeling of catching B from the left side of his center and sweeping him up and over in a forward circle. It is also worth noting that this throw may be set up and executed virtually in one spot and requires very little space in which to maneuver.

Analysis of the Throw

Once you have extended and taken the slack out of B's right arm, you are ready to wrap his neck. As you shift your weight to your left foot, be sure to keep pulling B's right arm outward and away from his torso, and begin to pull it toward your left hip. Extend your right arm at a 45 degree angle over the top of B's left shoulder toward his right rear. Make contact with the left rear side of

his neck and extend your arm forcefully as you wrap the arm around to his right side. It is very important to "file" into his neck in order to take the slack out of his neck muscles, thereby twisting his head until it locks his spine down to his waist (twisting his neck rotates his spine, locking his vertebrae in turn from his neck all the way down the length of his spine to his hips, just as twisting the link at the top of a chain eventually takes the slack out of the entire length of the chain, causing the the link at the bottom end of the chain to be directly controlled by the pressure applied at the top). It is at this point that you gain control of B's center (you control B's center when you have locked B'a spine from his neck all the way to his hips). Filing and twisting B's neck in this manner also results in direct pressure against his carotid arteries, effecting a strangulation as B is thrown (be very careful not to squeeze your partner's neck too tightly during practice; if he is rendered unconscious during the throw, he will be helpless to break his fall).

The initial pull on B's right arm and the subsequent wrapping of his neck follow one another in smooth succession. The net effect is that B's posture is broken as the momentum and pressure serves to misalign his shoulders and hips. As your right arm wraps tightly around B's neck, the arm should make contact with as much of the surface of B's neck as possible. Your right arm should remain completely relaxed and heavy and its combined momentum and weight will cause B to tilt forward toward his toes as his weight is simultaneously shifted to his right foot.

Causing B's center of gravity to shift over his right foot greatly facilitates the execution of the throw itself. The pull on B's right arm, coupled with the shift of your mass toward your forward stepping right foot and the force of your right arm wrapping his neck combine to break B's posture and shift his weight over his right foot. He now stands with his shoulders and hips misaligned and the entire area of his base only as large as the bottom of one foot. This situation allows us to take full advantage of the inherent structural weakness of his small base of support. Continuing, as you swing your left foot back beside your right and extend your hips back past B's right hip, your left outside hip should make contact with his frontal hip area. You have now completed the joining of your centers. It is vital that you continue to pull B's head forward as you swing your left foot back into position, continually "wrapping" him around your body, otherwise, you will be forced to twist your body at the waist in order to thrust your hips into position and will jeopardize your alignment. From the instant your right arm contacts the back of B's neck until the throw is complete, there is constant forward pressure which pulls him forward and ultimately over your hips.

As your right arm wraps around the back of B's neck, you begin the transference of momentum from your mass through his. Your right arm also transfers momentum by its pulling action on B's right arm. Be sure to maintain a constant downward pulling pressure on B's arm throughout the throw. The pull on B's arm coupled with the push at the back of his neck causes B to fall forward over his toes. As he falls, the barrier of your hips stops the forward motion of B's hips, translating his forward fall into a forward rotation. Just as in the Outside Hip Throw, the forward bend at your hips which pulls B over you should be an effortless "falling" forward of your torso. Once B is set up correctly and your own hips are in place, you only need to allow your upper body to fall forward at the speed of gravity, which is the ideal speed at which to cause B to rotate over your hips and onto his back. Remember, the overall feeling of the throw is as if you are wrapping B around your hips.

As with all correctly applied hip throws, the Headlock Hip Throw involves a second class lever, with the fulcrum at your hips, the length of B's back serving as the force arm and the back of his neck as the point of application of power. Therefore, it is vital to lower your hips until they are below B's hips. You will note that applying force at the back of B's neck allows us to take advantage of a longer force arm, as the force is applied close to B's head (the top of B's head is the extreme end of the force arm, so the closer to it we apply our force, the greater our mechanical advantage).

Once B rotates over your hips and begins his descent, release your hold on his neck and allow him to slap out on the mat. You can help to insure he lands safely by pulling upward a little on his right arm so that he rotates completely and lands

more toward his left side (allowing him to slap out with his left arm, rather than landing on his head). If you lose your balance during the throw or wish to take the fight to the ground, you may hold onto B's neck and right arm and kick your own feet out to your left, landing with the entire weight of your body on his ribs (be very careful with this in practice). You will end up in the "scarf hold" position and may apply a finishing choke or joint technique. If you choose to remain on your feet after the throw and want to be in an advantageous position to apply follow up techniques, lower your body by bending at the knees and hips, keeping your weight squarely over your base as B lands. Release his head as he falls but maintain your control of his right arm. As B lands, pull his arm upward and drop your right knee onto his right rib area, keeping your left foot flat on the ground. You are now in a dominant position from which you may strike B with your right hand, or apply a joint locking technique. If you choose to release an opponent altogether as he falls (you may wish to escape the area immediately or deal with another opponent), you can release just as he rotates over your hips at the apex of the throw. Releasing at this time will often result in the opponent taking the brunt of the fall flat on his back as he accelerates into the ground (the results of which can be to incapacitate the opponent; don't release your partner too early in practice unless he expects it, has mastered breakfalls and you are on a heavily padded surface). Releasing early will allow you to return immediately to the upright ready posture, free and clear of the opponent you have just thrown, and ready for subsequent action.

Analysis of Body Use

The alignments and mechanics of the Headlock Hip Throw are very similar to those of the Outside Hip Throw. As you swing B's right hand upward and forward with your left, be sure to grip it lightly with your intent and swing it smoothly (it is counterproductive to squeeze B's wrist tightly and then attempt to jerk it upward, as brute force results in automatic resistance). As you swing B's arm outward, toe out your left foot and begin shifting your weight over your left leg. This creates the initial momentum you will use to move in and wrap up B's neck, and will ultimately translate into the downward momentum which causes him to flip over your hips. The shifting of your weight to your left foot also supplies the impetus for the right arm as it extends up and files around the back of B's neck. The impetus which swings B's right arm outward and extends your right arm around the back of his neck both come from the shifting of your weight to your left foot. As you shift your weight, be sure to keep the crown of your head floating upward and move your body forward in a unit, stopping the shift when your center of gravity is directly over your left foot. Center the weight shift by moving from the hips. As your right arm extends around the back of B's neck, you will naturally begin to turn your torso toward the left. Be sure that your right arm remains relaxed and heavy as it files around the back of B's neck.

Once you have stepped up with and toed in your right foot, shifting your weight to the right leg will naturally cause you to continue turning toward your left (because the foot is toed in; be sure to keep your right knee pointed in the same direction as your right toes). During the shifting of the weight, it is most important to continue the forward pull on B's right arm (toward your left hip) and the wrapping push on the back of his neck. If you discontinue pulling B around your hips as you step up with your right foot, your own posture will be jeopardized. As you complete the shifting of your weight over your right foot, continue the left turn of your body and swing your left foot back into position beside your right in the same flow of momentum, without pause. As you step back with your left foot, continue the pull on B's upper body and bend at the hips and knees as you thrust your hips back past his right hip. Avoid bending over at the waist as this misaligns your posture and destroys the relative alignment of the Four Levels. Once B is wrapped around your hips, allow the energy you stored by bending at the hips and knees to rebound up out of your feet, bouncing B's hips upward. This upward thrust should be an effortless rebound of momentum (a result of the inherent stretch/rebound of your lower limbs) and not a forceful lifting of B's weight.

Continuing with the momentum of your hip's upward thrust, bend forward at the hips (not the waist) and allow your torso to fall forward, pulling B over you and onto the ground. Here again the momentum is provided by gravity and not by a forceful pulling from your arms and back. Although you will feel B's lower torso and hip area roll over your hips, at no time should you feel as if you are lifting or supporting his weight. As B rotates over you, you may either release him in mid-air, immediately returning your posture to the upright ready position, or you may choose to release his head and maintain control of his arm. If you choose the latter, be sure to bend your knees and hips and lower your body into a stable squat position as B lands, to prevent the momentum of his fall from pulling you forward and off balance. Exhale smoothly for the duration of the technique.

Combat Applications

Although the mechanics of the Headlock Hip Throw are similar to those of the Outside Hip Throw, the situations most conducive to entry are opposite. Whereas the Outside Hip Throw is most easily entered when outside of an opponent's arms, the Headlock Hip Throw is most easily entered when caught between an opponent's arms. The Headlock Hip Throw is often a good option in standing grappling situations, when the opponent is grabbing or holding the back of your neck or shoulders. Other appropriate situations for the throw are when an opponent attacks with a roundhouse or "haymaker" punch, affording you a direct entry to his inside line.

Roundhouse Punch Defense

From outside Safe Distance, the opponent steps in with his right foot and cocks his arm for a roundhouse punch (see Figure 92).

Seizing the opportunity to intercept early, step straight in with your left foot and simultaneously swing your left hand up to check the incoming blow while your right hand pushes straight forward with a palm heel strike to the opponent's chin (strike at a slightly upward angle). Be sure to keep your arms relaxed and heavy, feeling as if your elbows are hanging heavily toward the ground and your hands are springing forward. The net

Figure 92

Figure 93

Figure 94

Figure 95

Figure 96

Figure 97

Headlock Hip Throw - Roundhouse Punch Defense

effect of your forward momentum and strike will catch the opponent before he has a chance to shift his weight to his right leg and will result in his upper body being forced back toward his rear, effectively "uprooting" his center of gravity, and stopping his forward momentum. Be sure to keep your posture balanced over your base and allow the forward momentum to provide the impetus for your cover and strike, effecting an upward surge of momentum originating in your feet and rushing up through your body and out your hands in one continuous flow. Your momentum enters the opponent's upper body at an upward slanting angle at his chin which breaks his incoming horizontal force vertically. Avoid stepping in first and then attempting to strike (see Figure 93).

Now that the opponent's momentum and posture are broken (your strike will cause him to lean back, misaligning his shoulders and hips), drop your left arm heavily and catch above the opponent's right elbow or around his wrist holding with soft grip. As you grab with your left, toe your right foot in and turn your waist to the left, using the momentum to extend your right arm, filing around the back of the opponent's neck (see Figure 94).

Continuing the turning and wrapping momentum, swing your left foot back beside your right, thrusting your hips out past the opponent's right hip, as you bend your knees and hips a little. Be sure to maintain the pulling/wrapping pressure which wraps the opponent around your hips (see Figure 95).

Now allow the stored energy to rebound out of your feet, causing you to thrust upward under B's hips. Continuing the momentum, let your torso bend forward at the hips and fall forward, pulling the opponent over your hips and onto the ground (see Figure 96).

You may lower your body into a stable squat and maintain control of B's right arm, dropping your right knee onto his right ribs, ready to apply a follow up technique (see Figure 97).

Front Choke Defense

The opponent reaches up with both hands and grabs around your neck, attempting to choke you from the front as he pushes you backward (see Figure 98).

Relax and bend at the hips a little, then sinking your weight slide your left foot a half step to your left rear (it is important to react immediately and sink your weight as you pull the front of your hips inward, as if you were about to sit in a chair, so that the opponent cannot force you to arch backward. Once you are arched over, it is very easy for the opponent to attack your groin with his knee and/or push you backward onto the ground). As you squat and step back, simultaneously extend both arms upward with the palms close together (in the "prayer" position) between the opponent's arms (see Illustration 99).

Turn your waist to the left a little as you extend your right arm up and over the opponent's left shoulder while your left arm extends over the top of the opponent's right arm (see Figure 100).

Wrap up the opponent's right arm with your left by dropping your arm heavily over his arm, grabbing his triceps with your left palm up. Drop your left elbow heavily and squeeze the opponent's right forearm between your left arm and the left side of your torso (be sure to keep your left arm relaxed). As you wrap the opponent's right arm with your left, simultaneously file around his neck with your right arm, stepping across to your left with your right foot toed in (put your right foot down about a foot in front of the opponent's right foot). Wrap the opponent's head tightly and twist his neck, locking his spine down into his hips as you turn your torso to the left (see Figure 101).

Continuing your momentum, shift your weight to your right foot and swing your left foot back until it is parallel to your right foot. Squat a little and thrust your hips past the opponent's right side. As you turn your body to the left, be sure to continue pulling the opponent's right arm toward your left hip, and his head forward, wrapping him around your hips. (see Figure 102).

Continuing, allow the energy stored in your lower torso to spring up out of your feet, extending your legs and bouncing the opponent over your hips as you bend forward from the waist, throwing the opponent to the ground in a forward circle (see Figure 103).

Figure 98

Figure 99

Figure 100

Figure 101

Figure 102

Figure 103

Headlock Hip Throw - Front Choke Defense

Part Three

SPIRALS

(7) REAR HIP SPIRAL

General Description

Spiral throws are divided into two categories; those which cause the opponent to spiral and fall to his front, and those in which he spirals and falls to his rear. The first two throws in this section are examples of rear spirals. Spiral throws are generally very hard to counter and often result in forceful landings, making them efficient throws for combat. As most styles of martial art which include throws seem to favor arcs and circles, and most practitioners have a greater familiarity with these types of throws already, I have included a greater number of spiral throws than throws of the other categories.

The Rear Hip Spiral is the first of the spirals presented. It is one example chosen from a category of various hip spiral techniques, all based on the principle of breaking the opponent's posture to the rear or side and then causing him to rotate around your hip. This same type of throw may also be executed as a front spiral, or as a variation of the basic hip throw. The variation offered below causes the opponent to fall in a rear spiral and is very useful when infighting and in standing grappling situations. When properly set up and executed, the Rear Hip Spiral creates a tremendous amount of momentum and literally accelerates the opponent into the ground. The throw is similar in effect to rear sweeping throws but it allows the thrower to fell his opponent while keeping both feet on the ground, thereby allowing for greater stability during the technique. The flow of the throw breaks the opponent's posture sideways and then spirals him to the ground as if he were sucked backward into a whirlpool.

Method of Application

(1) B stands with his right foot a step ahead of his left. Approach B from the front and grab around his right upper arm with your left hand. Hold his arm gently with soft grip. (see Figure 104).

(2) Pull backward with your left elbow, pulling B's right arm up past your left side, trapping his forearm under your left armpit, your left palm holding his triceps lightly (see Figure 105).

(3) Step out toward your left and slightly forward with your left foot, shifting your weight to your left leg and leaning your torso slightly to your left as well (this will break B's posture by misaligning his hips and shoulders). As you step out with your left foot, slide your right hand up the front of B's chest, then wrap your right arm around his neck from the front (hold B's neck firmly, but leave your right arm relaxed). Your step and weight shift pulls B's right upper arm out and toward his right side, causing him to lean to his right rear (see Figure 106).

(4) Keeping forward pressure on B's neck and the outward pull on his right arm, shift your weight entirely over your left foot and take a step forward with your right foot directly to B's rear, stepping past his right side, placing the foot down toed in (see Figure 107).

(5) Continuing the above momentum, shift the majority of your weight to your left foot as you turn your torso 90 degrees to the left, while pulling B's right elbow and head around toward your left hip. B will spin to his left rear and will fall in a rear spiral (see Figure 108).

Figure 104

Figure 105

Figure 106

Figure 107

Figure 108

Rear Hip Spiral - Method of Application

105

Analysis of Entry

The key to setting up this throw is the wrapping and control of B's right arm. It is important not only to grasp and hold B's arm, it is also important to hold onto his upper arm, above the elbow joint. If you hold below B's elbow, on his forearm or wrist, B will be able to use his arm muscles and bend at the elbow, thereby making the entry into the throw much more difficult. Holding above the elbow not only limits the mobility and strength of B's arm, it also creates a direct connection from your grasp to the opponent's torso, through his humerus bone. The wrapping of B's arm and the wrapping of his head ideally occur in rapid succession, almost simultaneously. If, during actual application, you are able to wrap up an opponent's arm but not his head, you may have to strike or maneuver until you have an opportunity to control the opponent's head or flow into an alternate technique.

When setting up the throw against an opponent in the street, obstructing his blows or moving in to grab his upper arm allows you to connect where there is little or no relative motion. Once you have blended the motion of your torso with the opponent's, his upper arm will be moving very slowly in relation to the potential speed of his hand. In other words, trying to catch the wrist of a rapidly punching hand may be next to impossible, whereas connecting with and catching an arm close to the shoulder (where the arm is moving slower in relation to the hand/wrist) is much easier. When intercepting a punch, the further up the hand from the wrist you connect, the slower the arm is moving relative to points below it.

Once you have control of B's right arm, it is important to keep a steady, outward pulling pressure which continuously pulls his arm out and away from his torso toward his rear angle. Continuation of this sideways pull as you wrap B's head and step allows you to break his posture and leaves him completely set up for the throw itself. Notice that even though you are between B's arms and have locked up with him in a grappling set up, you still move sideways and away from the front of his body, removing yourself from potential attempts at counter attack (from an opponent's knees or left hand). Finally, your intent should be focused on feeling into B's center through the hold you have on his right arm.

Analysis of the Throw

As soon as you have wrapped up B's right arm and have pulled it out to his rear side (taking the slack out), you have a direct connection through his humerus/shoulder into his center (hip area). Pulling B's right arm out toward his rear side will break his posture by misaligning his shoulders and hips. Because of the direct connection you have with B's center and because the angle of the pull to his rear side is almost perpendicular to his baseline, B will be unable to resist your force and his upper body posture will be misaligned. As you step up and out with your left foot and wrap your right arm around B's neck, be sure to shift your weight to your left leg and lean slightly outward. The outward lean allows you to use your body weight to pull B's right arm outward, breaking his posture. If you step and only pull B's right arm with your left arm, you will be forced to use the force of one arm alone. If you hold B's arm under your left arm as if it were part of you and then shift your weight and lean your torso slightly, you will be able to make use of your entire body weight and momentum in breaking B's posture. It is also important to transfer momentum through your hold on B's right arm and not by pushing his neck with your right arm.

Once you have wrapped B's arm and neck and have stepped up and out toward his right rear, you are ready to set up the spiraling momentum which will throw him to the ground. You now shift one hundred percent of your weight over your left leg and step up directly toward B's rear with your right foot. As you shift your weight and take the step with your right, it is very important to keep the outward pulling pressure on B's right arm and the rearward pressure on his neck area. If you release these pressures as you step, B will have an opportunity to right himself (realign his posture). As you put your right foot down toed in and begin to shift some weight to it, turning your torso toward your left, be sure to maintain the outward pull on B's right arm and the squeeze on his neck. This turning action creates a coupling effect along a vertical axis in

B's body (the result of your left arm pulling B's arm backward as your right arm pushes his head toward the rear). The result of this coupling is to create a horizontal, rotational momentum which causes B's left shoulder to turn toward his rear while his right shoulder turns toward his front. Once the horizontal momentum is initiated, bend forward at the hips, allowing the weight of your torso to fall forward as you continue turning your torso toward the left. The horizontal coupling momentum and the downward push of your torso combine to create a downward spiral, the momentum of which sucks B backward toward his right rear as if he were caught in a whirlpool.

As you turn your torso to the left and bend forward, you will shift at least half of your weight over your left leg. As B falls in a rear spiral onto his back, release the hold you have on his neck and allow him to fall. Maintain your hold on B's right arm in preparation for follow up techniques if needed. It is also a good practice to drop your right knee down onto B's right ribs (keeping your left foot flat), allowing your body weight to rest on his ribs which aids in pinning him to the ground. As much as possible, lift B's left arm, pulling it upward and away from his torso (keeping the slack out of the arm). The downward pressure of your right knee on B's ribs together with the upward pull on B's right arm weaken his position and make it hard for him to roll away from you or pull his right arm free.

From this position, the right hand is free to strike down to an opponent's head or throat and his right arm is set up for leverage techniques. Keep your torso more or less upright and be sure to maintain the feeling of your head floating upward. This not only aligns your posture and aids stability, it also allows you to drop a greater percentage of your weight straight down through your right knee into B's ribs. In addition, maintaining good postural alignment in this position allows you to spring back up and move if confronted by another opponent. The flow of your intent is downward and through B which aids in your control of him; even though he is on the ground, you should seek to maintain your control over his center. Be sure to maintain conscious awareness of your surrounding environment as well as as a positional advantage over B.

Analysis of Body Use

The Rear Hip Spiral depends primarily upon utilizing the weight of your torso to unbalance and ultimately throw your opponent. As you will be shifting your weight and leaning to the side and then forward during the course of the technique, it is very important to maintain whole body relaxation and correct alignment, especially in your lower body. When wrapping up B's right arm with your left, you should hold his upper arm lightly and with your intent (soft grip) and wrap his arm up under your armpit by pulling downward and backward with your elbow. This same mechanic holds true for all techniques in which you pull with your arms; try to avoid pulling by lifting your shoulder and elbow and contracting your biceps, as this method of generating pulling force will only succeed in causing tension in your own arm, thereby stifling your power as well as alerting the opponent as to your intentions. A much more powerful method of generating pulling force, and one which an opponent will find harder to resist is the method described above (leaving your arm relaxed, generating pulling force by imagining that your elbow is being pulled to your rear, or that you are elbowing someone behind you). Once you have pulled B's right arm up under your left armpit, hold it firmly in place by leaving your left arm relaxed and gently squeezing his forearm between your torso and upper arm. Be sure to hold B's right arm under his triceps, your palm facing upward.

As you step forward and out to your left (toward B's right rear), extend your right arm over the top of B's left shoulder very close to his neck. Extend your right hand palm down in a circular motion, encircling then squeezing B's neck as if you were trying to grab your own throat. Your right arm should remain relaxed but with a continuous flow of intent which causes your hand to be drawn toward your own throat. As you step and wrap B's neck, shift your weight to your left leg (knees pointing the same direction as the toes) and lean slightly to your left, making sure you are not dependent on B for your balance (this means that if B were to suddenly disappear, you would not lose your balance and fall toward your left). Allow the downward sinking of your weight to propel you

107

forward. As you lean outward, simultaneously lean a bit forward as well, bending from the hips (allow the pull at the crown of your head to lengthen your torso as you bend and lean). You should also take care that your chest does not collapse as you wrap up B's arm and neck.

Now that you have broken B's posture and joined centers with him, you are ready to step forward with your left foot and rotate your torso. It is vital to keep constant pressure on B's right arm and neck as you step up with your right foot past B's right side. If you release the pressure which pulls B's right arm out to his right rear or the pressure your forward leaning torso exerts against his neck, B will have an opportunity to right his posture and escape or counterattack. As you step up with your right foot, be sure your weight is firmly balanced over your left foot, and that you adjust for the step and shift of momentum in your hips, insuring that your weight continuously balances directly over your left foot (cultivating this ability is the goal of Exercise 8 in Chapter Two). As your right foot steps down toed in, shift about 50 percent of your weight to your right foot and continue leaning a little forward as you push B back toward his right rear. As you feel B lose his balance to his rear, immediately turn your torso to the left about 90 degrees, causing B to rotate around your left hip. As you complete the rotation, shift at least half of your weight over your left foot, bending your left knee and extending your right leg. Be sure that your left knee does not extend forward of your ankle and that the knees point in the same direction as the toes.

During the rotation of your torso to the left, and as you shift your weight to your left leg, allow your torso to bend forward at the hips, "falling" forward, its weight and momentum pulling B around your right hip and onto the ground in a rear spiral. Your torso should bend forward smoothly, descending at the speed of gravity until it is angled forward about 45 degrees. Maintain the upward pull at the crown of your head so that your torso lengthens out as it bends forward. Exhale smoothly from the initial step with your left foot through to the completion of the throw. If you wish to maintain control over B as he lands, let go of his head and drop your right knee straight down onto his right ribs. Maintain the hold you

have on his right arm and straighten your torso, aligning your posture so that more of your weight transfers straight down into B's ribs. Straightening your torso also stretches B's right arm upward; this helps to keep the slack out of his right arm and makes it difficult for him to free his arm from your grasp. The upward pull on his arm (initiated by the upward pull at the crown of your head) and the downward pressure of your right knee on his ribs serves to limit B's mobility long enough for you to apply a follow up technique (for example, a strike with the right hand to his throat or nose). Be sure to remain relaxed so that you can adjust as the situation demands.

Combat Applications

The Rear Hip Spiral, like the Headlock Hip Throw, is especially useful when you are caught in between an opponent's arms, or in standing grappling situations. In fact, these two throws may be used in conjunction with the Headlock Hip Throw being applied against an opponent who succeeds in countering the Rear Hip Spiral (as illustrated below). When applied with natural stepping momentum, this technique often results in the opponent's feet leaving the ground as he whips around your hip in a rear spiral. Be careful with this technique in the early stages of practice, adding momentum to the throw only after your partner is familiar with the dynamics of the fall.

Standing Grappling Defense

The opponent closes Safe Distance quickly, and reaches out with both hands in an attempt to grab your head/upper torso area (see Figure 109).

Immediately relax your entire body, sinking your weight and allowing your arms to swing upward and forward. Your arms swing up inside of the opponent's two arms and then move out to the sides, dividing his power. As you swing your arms upward, lift your left foot and begin to step forward and out toward your left at a 45 degree angle off the line of attack (see Figure 110).

Continue moving forward and to the left, shifting your weight to your left foot. As you move forward, extend your left arm over the top of

Figure 109

Figure 110

Figure 111

Figure 112

Figure 113

Figure 114

Rear Hip Spiral - Standing Grappling Defense

the opponent's right arm and then drop your left arm heavily, wrapping his right arm as described above. Simultaneously extend your right hand past the left side of the opponent's neck and then wrap your arm firmly around his neck. As your weight shifts to your left foot, lean slightly out to your left, pulling the opponent's right upper arm out and toward his right rear. Your right arm continues to squeeze and push B's head toward his right rear as well. The opponent's posture is broken (see Figure 111).

Continuing, maintain the pressures on the opponent's arm and neck as you shift your weight completely over your left foot and step up past his right side toward his rear with your right foot, placing the foot down toed in (see Figure 112).

As your right foot touches down, shift about half of your weight over it and begin turning your torso to the left, while leaning forward from the hips. Continue turning left and bending your torso forward, shifting at least half of your weight to your left foot and throwing the opponent around your hip in a rear spiral (see Figure 113).

Release the opponent's head as he falls and maintain control of his right arm. Drop your right knee on his right ribs and and lift your torso, ready to follow up if necessary (see Figure 114).

NOTE: If an opponent grabs you with a front two handed choke hold, the Rear Hip Spiral may be applied as described above.

Lapel Grab and Punch

An opponent grabs your chest lapel with his right hand and cocks his left hand, preparing to punch you in the face (see Figure 115).

Relax and sink your weight as you hook your left hand over the top of the opponent's right elbow crook from outside his arm, letting your elbow hang down heavily. As you hook the opponent's arm, step forward and and to the left with your left foot, moving off the line of attack as you simultaneously extend your right palm straight upward with a palm heel strike under the opponent's chin (besides shocking the opponent with a strike, your right arm serves as a physical barrier between your head and his left punch; see Figure 116).

Now shift your weight to your left foot and extend your right arm past the left side of the opponent's neck, wrapping it firmly inside your arm. As you shift your weight to your left foot, lean out to your left side a little, pulling the opponent to his right rear and breaking his posture (see Figure 117).

Continuing, step up past the opponent's right side with your right foot and shift 50 percent of your weight to it. As you step, bend your torso forward from the hips (see Figure 118).

Turn your torso to the left and shift your weight to your left foot as you continue bending forward from the hips, bend your left leg as you extend your right leg, throwing the opponent around your right hip in a rear spiral (see Figure 119).

You can hold the opponent and follow up as described above.

Rear Hip Spiral to Headlock Hip Throw

Here we have an example of flowing from one throw (which is countered by the opponent) into another with a smooth transition of momentum. Once a practitioner has a good grasp of the principles and applications of various techniques, and is able to apply them smoothly, the next step in training is to cultivate the sensitivity and control necessary to flow from one throw to another. Ideally, we seek to flow from technique to technique without losing our momentum or disconnecting our center from the opponent's center. The sequence below is an example of one throw setting up the next, and the method of linking the two techniques together in one flow of momentum. Of course, the ideal situation is one in which we set up and enter a technique, finishing it directly. However, in real life combat situations, our live opponents will always seek to counter whatever they perceive as a threat. Practicing linking throws together helps the practitioner to prepare mentally as well as physically for the possibility that a single technique will not always end the fight.

Set up the Rear Hip Spiral as described above. As you step up toward the opponent's rear with your right foot, he manages to step back with his right leg, thereby regaining his balance (see Figure 120).

110

Figure 115

Figure 116

Figure 117

Figure 118

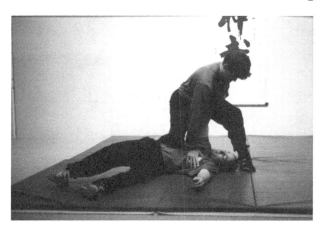

Figure 119

Rear Hip Spiral - Lapel Grab and Punch

Continuing with the above, with your weight on your right foot, swing your left foot back to your right rear, turning your torso to the left. As you step and turn, pull the opponent's right arm around your right side toward your left hip. Simultaneously tighten the hold you have around the opponent's neck and begin pulling his head downward (see Figure 121).

With your feet in a parallel stance, pull the opponent around your right hip. Bend your torso forward at the hips and throw the opponent with a Headlock Hip Throw as described above (see Figure 122).

The transition from the Rear Hip Spiral to the Headlock Hip Throw should occur smoothly and without a break in the overall flow of momentum. When the throws are linked together smoothly, the opponent should find it almost impossible to defend against the second throw.

Figure 120

Figure 121

Figure 122

Rear Hip Spiral - Rear Hip Spiral to Headlock Hip Throw

112

(8) REAR CHIN HOOK

General Description

The Rear Chin Hook is applied from an opponent's side or rear. It may be used in conjunction with or as a follow up to the Rear Head Tilt described above. The throw involves hooking one hand under the opponent's chin and using the hand and forearm as a lever to turn the opponent's head at a 45 degree angle, locking his spine from his head to his hips (much the same as the Headlock Hip Throw). Once we have taken the slack out of the opponent's body, we take him down in a rear spiral. After hooking the opponent's chin, we are able to exert a great amount of control over his entire body, allowing us to throw much larger and heavier opponents. The Rear Chin Hook also sets up the opponent for face down immobilizations (arm bars and shoulder locks).

The overall flow of the Rear Chin Hook involves a double spiraling momentum which first takes the opponent off balance in one direction and then immediately whips him back around in the opposite direction (as if he were caught in a downward spiraling "figure eight" pattern). Double spirals are very useful when attempting to break the posture of or otherwise unbalance much larger and heavier opponents. Because the flow of momentum changes direction so rapidly, the person caught in the throw finds it extremely difficult to recover balance. In fact, by resisting the pull of the initial spiral, the opponent literally throws himself into the second spiral, which completes the throw (this is an example of "borrowing energy" from the opponent and using it to your advantage). Once the dynamics of double spirals are understood, the maneuver may be applied to set up any number of throwing or leverage techniques.

Method of Application

(1) Approach B from his right side. Step up with your right foot toed out, placing it about a foot outside B's right foot. As you step up, gently grab around the front of B's right wrist with your right hand (see Figure 123).
(2) Pull B's right arm up under your right arm and trap it between your upper arm and torso. As

you pull his right arm to you, step around behind B with your left foot, placing the foot down close behind B with your chest touching his back. As you step around with your left foot, swing your left arm around the left side of B's neck. The arm pull, left step and swing of your left arm around B's neck follow one another in smooth succession (see Figure 124).

(3) Continuing with the above momentum, turn your torso to the right about 90 degrees as you step back with your right foot toward your left rear. Hold B's right arm close to your side and allow your rearward step and turn to pull his upper arm out toward his right rear (taking the slack out of B's arm and breaking his posture). As you step back with your right foot and turn, hook the back of your left palm under the right side of B's jaw (see Figure 125. Also see a close up of the chin hook on page 115).

(4) Now suddenly reverse your momentum, and shifting your weight to your right foot, swing your left foot back and around toward your right rear in an arc. As you swing your left foot back, simultaneously drop your left elbow heavily and pry up under B's chin with your left hand, turning B's head to his left and up so that he looks up over his left shoulder. Be sure to keep B close to your chest as you turn, avoid stepping back with your left foot and then attempting to pull B's chin (see Figure 126).

(5) Continue turning to your left about 180 degrees, all the while pulling back and down on B's chin/head. The downward pressure on his chin and the circular momentum create a downward spiral which forces B to spin to his rear and sit in front of you. Maintain the hold you have on his right arm. As B falls onto his rear, squat low behind him and and maintain the opposing pressures which pull his chin toward the left and his right arm toward the right while pressing your left knee into the center of his back (feel as if you want to push B's chest forward; see Figure 127).

(6) Now release the left hand from under B's chin and place your left palm on the back of his right shoulder. Slide you right palm along the inside

Figure 123

Figure 124

Figure 125

Figure 126

Figure 127

Figure 128

Rear Chin Hook - Method of Application

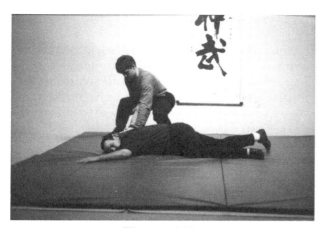

Figure 129

Chin Hook Close-Up

of B's forearm until you catch his wrist. Swing your right leg back around toward your left rear in an arcing step, turning your torso to the right 180 degrees. As you swing your right foot back, simultaneously pull B's right arm around to his right rear (twisting your right palm upward as you pull) and push his right shoulder downward. B will spin to his right 180 degrees and fall forward onto his face. As you turn and push behind B's right shoulder, pull his hand downward (see Figure 128 and 129).

(7) You are now in position to pin B in a variety of ways. One simple method of immobilization is to drop your left knee across the back of B's right shoulder, bringing your weight up over it, pinning B's shoulder to the ground as you simultaneously lift his right arm up and place the top side of his right wrist in the crease of your right hip. Lean forward up toward the top of B's head, pressing your left palm on the back of B's right elbow so that he cannot bend his arm. The pressure brought to bear on B's shoulder coupled with the weight of your body as it kneels on his upper back will hold him immobile. If you do not wish to pin B to the ground, spin him onto his face as described above and then release his arm. The momentum of the spin is quite forceful and the resultant forward fall will cause a great shock to B's body (be careful in practice). An alternative follow up is to apply a rear choke after you have spun B around into the sitting position in step 6 (the choke is automatically set up as your left arm

Pin Close-Up

is already around B's neck; see the Figure above for a close up of the pin).

Analysis of Entry

To set up the Rear Chin Hook you need to enter toward B's rear from his side. When fighting, there is an opportunity to enter the throw directly whenever an opponent throws a straight punch or backfist technique. In order to successfully set up the throw, you need to have control of one of B's arms. It is the antagonistic pull on B's arm and chin which locks his body and allows you to control his center. If you attempt to hook B's chin without controlling his arm, he will simply turn with the pressure on his chin and escape. If while entering to B's rear you lose control of his right arm, the entry (to his rear side) leaves you in a superior position with a safe avenue of escape (toward B's rear).

Once you have control of B's right arm, it is important to hold it close to your torso, which helps you to join centers with B and allows you to lead his torso with the momentum of your own torso, rather than the strength of your arm alone. Although holding B's right wrist with your right hand will also afford you the opportunity to control his torso and enter the throw, when connecting with B's arm it is best to hold and control his upper arm (humerus bone), thereby negating the freedom of movement he will have if you grab below his elbow. Because of its connection at the shoulder, the humerus is a direct link to B's torso. As you step up behind B with your left foot, pull his right arm up between your right upper arm and torso, taking the slack out of his upper arm/shoulder and breaking his posture by misaligning his shoulders and hips.

Once you have control of B's right arm, the left step to B's rear, the shifting of your weight to your left foot, the rear swing of your right foot and right turn of your torso should all occur in one fluid motion. This creates the momentum of the first spiral which breaks B's posture and pulls him into your flow of momentum, allowing you to join centers. You need to practice until you can enter behind B and swing him around toward your right in one smooth flow. B should feel as if he has been caught in a whirlpool which spins him around his center toward his right. Aim your intent into B's centerline from his rear and maintain the alignment of your nose and navel on a vertical line with B's centerline throughout the throw.

Analysis of the Throw

Once you have connected with B, joined centers and have pulled him into the momentum of the first spiral, you can lead him into any number of finishing techniques. It is important to understand that the above entry is not used to set up the Rear Chin Hook exclusively. The connection and spiraling momentum created allow you to lead an opponent into a variety of different throwing or striking techniques. For the purpose of setting up the Rear Chin Hook, however, we want to change directions (from spiral to spiral) almost immediately after we have caught B in the initial spiral. If you spin him too far around to his right, it will be difficult to pull him back in the opposite direction without using brute force or disconnecting your respective centers. As you swing your right foot around in step 3, as soon as you have turned approximately 90 degrees and feel B spinning to his right, immediately reverse the momentum and swing your left foot back, turning left 180 degrees. Pulling B back toward his right rear moves his mass at close to a 90 degree angle to his baseline. This exploits the inherent structural weakness of his base and forces him to turn to his right, as you move him toward his weakest rear angle. As B is pulled around to his right, you have effectively joined centers and made his center subordinate to your own.

As B spins to his right in the first spiral, he is, in reality, "falling" momentarily and will instinctively step to regain his balance. Before B has a chance to step, drop your left elbow and pry up under his right jaw with the back of your hand. This motion creates a first class lever with the point at which your forearm contacts the top of B's left shoulder (trapezius muscle) serving as the fulcrum, your elbow as the point of application of force, the length of your forearm from the fulcrum to the back of your hand acting as the force arm and B's head as the load to be moved. It is important to bend your left hand backward in order to apply pressure to the right side of B's jaw. Leave your left arm relaxed and drop your left elbow heavily. This causes B to look upward and turns his head to his right (he will be looking up over his left shoulder). The net effect is to twist B's head along two axis of movement simultaneously, resulting in the locking of his cervical vertebra.

Continued rotational pressure at the right side of B's jaw twists the slack out of the entire length of his spine, locking into his hips. You now have a connection from the right side of B's jaw directly into his hips. As you pry up under B's chin and lock his upper body into his hips, you swing your left foot back and around to your right rear 180 degrees, turning your torso to the left. As you turn, drop your left elbow heavily and begin to squat so that the overall flow of momentum is downward. The horizontal spin of your body, coupled with the lowering of your hips and the downward pull on B's head creates a downward spiral which will cause B to spin to his left 180 degrees and sit in front of you. Be sure to take the slack out of B's head and spine and turn him to his left before your left foot swings back. Stepping back with your left foot before B's spine is locked will cause your and B's center to disconnect (in actual application, the movements of prying B's chin, stepping back with your left foot and turning left follow one another in smooth succession, without a break between the movements).

Squat as B spins to his left and sits in front of you. You may push one or both knees into B's back to stabilize him momentarily as you move into a follow up technique. Keep the antagonistic pulling pressures on his right arm (pulling it outward and back toward your right rear) and chin (prying down with your left elbow in order to maintain the pull up under his right jaw). These opposite pressures serve to weaken B's posture and divide his attention. B falls because the leverage at the top end of his body pulls him over his base of support. The throw involves a second class lever with B's heels as the fulcrum and his jaw as the point of application of power. We are able to use the entire length of his body as a force arm (from his heels to his jaw), thereby greatly increasing our mechanical advantage. As B begins to spiral to his left rear, we drop our weight by squatting and allowing the weight of our body to pull him down into a sitting position (weight dropping from the rear). It is important not to attempt to hook B's chin and then "yank" him over backwards. The brute strength involved will provide clumsy force against which B may apply resistance, resulting in the use of force against force.

Once you are behind B and have him caught in your momentum flow, transfer your momentum through your entire upper body, rather than through the back of your left hand alone. Try to feel as if your upper torso (especially your chest) is joined to B's upper torso (at his upper back). Relax and spin him as part of your body. Your intent flows forth from your own centerline straight forward into B's centerline, and your respective centers should remained joined for the duration of the throw. After the completion of the second spiral (after B is sitting in front of you), if you choose to put him on his face, a third spiral is involved. Pushing behind B's right shoulder as you pull back on his right wrist creates a coupling effect which forces him to turn toward his right. Twisting your right hand palm up causes B's right arm to twist thumb down; this rotates his forearm bones until they lock into his humerus and causes his right shoulder to rotate forward and downward, forcing B to sprawl forward as you turn. Stepping back with your right foot and pushing downward with your left palm at the same time once again creates a downward spiral which causes B to spin to the right and land on his face. When the throw is followed by the face down pin, three spirals occur in smooth succession.

Analysis of Body Use

As this throw involves turning the body rapidly right and left and the creation of rotational momentums, it is very important to maintain the alignment of the entire body, paying special attention to the vertical alignment of the centerline. If you attempt to spin (and especially if you spin and rapidly reverse directions) and your centerline is not in correct vertical alignment in relation to the earth, you will wobble, just as a spinning top wobbles and eventually topples once the vertical stability of its centerline has been disturbed. As you spin, be sure to maintain complete relaxation and pay attention to keeping your shoulders down as you reach around the opponent's neck with your left arm. It is helpful to focus on the upward pull at the crown of your head as you move through the technique, as this helps to maintain the alignment of your centerline.

As you step up behind B with your left foot and turn your torso to the right, allow the turning momentum to swing your left arm around his neck, so that your arm swings at the speed of gravity. As your left foot touches down, it is toed in slightly so that as you shift your weight to it your leg alignment naturally causes your torso to begin turning to your right (be sure to keep your knee pointing the same direction as your toes). As your left foot touches down, your body weight should shift over it immediately, transferring the forward momentum into rotational momentum. As your body begins to turn to the right, your unweighted right foot comes off the ground a little and the turning momentum swings your right leg toward your left rear. Your right foot should describe an arc as it swings. As you turn right, your right arm and especially the elbow hangs heavily, the weight of the arm pulling B's right arm at a slightly downward angle. As soon as you have turned about 90 degrees, press your right foot down and shift your weight over it, allowing the momentum and weight to compress the leg into the ground. As the stored energy rebounds up through your right leg, use the momentum it creates to turn your body to the left, guiding the movement with your hips. Lift your unweighted left foot and swing it around to the right rear, the foot describing an arc.

As you swing your left foot back, once again consciously relax your arms and use the weight of your left arm to lever B's head as it pulls him downward toward his left rear. As you pull B into a sitting position, squat, using the descending weight of your body to pull him down. As you squat, bend your knees and hips, maintaining the Four Levels and lengthening your torso as it inclines forward. The body turns and weight dropping should all be centered in and guided by the hips. If you choose to take B onto his face and pin, as you swing your right foot around toward your left rear it is important to maintain the forward pressure behind his right shoulder by leaning the weight of your torso forward. Use the weight of your mass pressing through your left arm rather than attempting to shove B down with the strength of your arm alone. During the pin, drop your left knee onto the back of B's right shoulder with your upper leg perpendicular to the ground. Lift your chest as you kneel by allowing the crown of your head to float upward. Keep your right foot flat on the ground, close by B's right side (when pinning or resting the weight of one knee

on a downed opponent, a good rule of thumb is to never allow both heels to come off the ground at the same time. The foot of the kneeling leg will rest on the ball of the foot and while the other foot remains flat on the floor. Kneeling while raising both heels from the ground makes for a very unstable base of support).

Combat Applications

The Rear Chin Hook is set up when you are able to enter outside an opponent's arms, while moving toward his rear. It can also be used as a follow up technique when an opponent succeeds in countering other rear techniques (for example, if you wrap your arm around an opponent's neck from the rear to apply a choke, and he grabs your arm with his hands to counter, you can immediately hook up under his chin and apply the Rear Chin Hook, taking the opponent to the ground and then reapplying the choke or other follow up techniques). The Rear Chin Hook is also a good technique to use when you wish to control another without doing serious harm. When set up and executed correctly, this throw may be applied without striking an opponent at all, as well as leaving the opponent in position for a follow up pinning technique which renders him immobile.

Backfist Defense

You stand facing the opponent at Safe Distance. You are on guard with your hands at your sides. Stand relaxed and focus your intent on the opponent's centerline (upper chest area; see Figure 130).

The opponent suddenly leaps in toward you, swinging his right arm back toward your head in a backfist attack (see FIgure 131).

Immediately lift your left foot and step forward, stepping up and out to your left at about a 45 degree angle, placing your left foot down toed in. Let your right foot slide up a half step behind your left after you step. As you step, swing both hands up and toward the opponent's center, your left forearm warding off his blow behind his elbow as your right forearm checks his hand at the wrist. Sink your weight into your left foot as you

Figure 130

Figure 131

Figure 132

Figure 133

Figure 134

Figure 135

Rear Chin Hook - Backfist Defense

Figure 136   Figure 137

Rear Chin Hook - Backfist Defense (Con't)

check the blow. Your left hand does most of the work intercepting his power close to the source, his shoulder, while your right hand only lightly checks the opponent's hand. The idea is to move in and toward the opponent's rear, intercepting his power early as you move off the line of attack (see Figure 132).

Continuing, grasp the opponent's wrist with your right hand (be sure to leave your hand and arm relaxed and your elbow hanging heavily). As you grab the opponent's wrist, step up behind him with your left foot, placing the foot down toed in just behind his centerline. Move up behind the opponent as you step and slide your left arm around his neck (see Figure 133).

Continuing with the momentum of the left step, turn your torso to the right about 90 degrees as you swing your right foot back toward your left rear. As you turn, pull back with your left elbow, hooking the back of your hand under the right side of the opponent's jaw (see Figure 134).

Immediately shift your weight to your right foot and turn your torso to the left, swinging your left foot back toward your right rear. Turn 180 degrees, squatting and dropping your left elbow heavily as you pry up under the opponent's jaw, which causes him to spin to his left rear and sit in front of you (see Figure 135).

Follow up as described above (see Figure 136 and 137).

Side Headlock Defense

You and the opponent are locked in a standing grappling situation. Remain relaxed and allow your weight to sink into your feet (see Figure 138).

The opponent steps in front of you toward your left with his left foot and reaches around the back of your neck with his left hand, attempting to bend you forward in a side headlock (see Figure 139).

As the opponent steps in and encircles your neck, immediately step up behind him with your right foot and reach around his mid torso with both hands, holding him in a side bear hug. Continue pushing forward and shift your weight to your right foot (you want to push the opponent's weight over his right leg. He will not be able to bend you forward into a secure headlock unless he is able to shift his weight to his left foot in front of you). As you hug the opponent's torso, slide your hands close to his body so that you may catch his right arm under your hands, thus preventing the opponent from punching you in the face or grabbing his own left wrist with his right hand (see Figure 140).

Now whip your hips around to the opponent's rear by hopping in with your left foot and simultaneously lifting your right foot, your left foot landing where the right foot was. Your right foot steps out to the right, past the opponent's right side. Keep the front of your hips pressed

Figure 138

Figure 139

Figure 140

Figure 141

Figure 142

Figure 143

Rear Chin Hook - Side Headlock Defense

Figure 144   Figure 145

Rear Chin Hook - Side Headlock Defense (Con't)

close to the opponent's hips from the rear. You are now holding the opponent from his rear . (see Figure 141).

Reach up with your right hand over the opponent's right shoulder and hook the back of your right hand under the left side of his jaw. Stand up straight and press the front of your hips against the opponent's rear, simultaneously dropping your right elbow heavily as you pry up under his jaw with your right hand. As your hips force the opponent's hips forward, his head is turned so that he looks up over his right shoulder. Now grab the opponent's left wrist with your left hand. The opponent's posture is broken (see Figure 142).

Step back a half step with your left foot and stretch the opponent by pulling his chin to the right and his left arm to the left. Keeping your posture steady and straight, lift the opponent's left arm up and over your head (not shown). As soon as it clears your head, slide your left palm up the inside of the opponent's left forearm, and grab his left biceps. Now drop your left elbow heavily, pulling the opponent's elbow down toward your left hip. Step back with your right right foot turning 180 degrees, pulling the opponent down into a sitting position (see Figure 143).

Pin as described above (Figure 144 and 145).

(9) HEAD TWIST SPIRAL

General Description

The Head Twist is an example of a forward spiral technique. As the name implies, we hold our opponent's head and twist it along two axis at once, locking his spine from his head to his hips which allows us to control his entire body as we throw him. The torque and pressure placed on the opponent's neck and spine in this technique make it inherently more dangerous than most of the other techniques presented in this work. Because of the potential for seriously injuring your partner or opponent, great caution should be exercised during practice and the throw should be applied with restraint in combat situations. In reality, the goal of the Head Twist Spiral is to throw your partner through- the torque applied at his head rather than by attempting to force him to the ground by twisting his neck alone.

There is a saying in the Chinese martial arts that "where the snake's head goes, it's body follows." The Head Twist Spiral illustrates this principle and can be used to great effect on even the strongest of opponents. It can be set up with short strikes to the head area and is very useful in standing grappling situations, especially as a counter to body holds (see the Combat Applications section, front under and over arm Bear Hug Defense below). The Head Twist Spiral can also be used in conjunction with "spot" attacks to vital points on the head and neck and as a prelude to choking techniques.

The overall flow of the throw sucks the opponent down in a forward spiral as if he bent over and caught his head in a whirlpool. It can be done with your hands in various positions on the opponent's head. We will practice a variation in which we hold the back of the opponent's head with one hand and hold his chin with the other. This hand position gives us the leverage to twist the opponent's head to an extreme degree, allowing us to control his entire body.

Method of Application

(1) Approach B from the front. Step up with your right foot and reach up with both hands, your left holding around the back of B's neck and your right cupping under his chin. The thumb of your right hand should be up and the heel of your right palm should press against the right side of B's chin (see figure 146).

(2) Drop your elbows heavily, and pulling B's head toward yourself gently with your left palm, push with your right palm to turn B's head toward his left and slightly upward, so that he looks up over his left shoulder (see Figure 147).

(3) Continue twisting B's head to his left and upward until the slack is taken out of his neck and his body begins to twist toward his left. As B's body begins to twist, pull his head down close to your chest (see Figure 148).

(4) Continuing with the above momentum, hold B's head in its twisted and locked position in front of your chest and sinking your weight, step back with your left foot. Swing your left foot back in an arc toward your right rear and turn your body to the left about 180 degrees. Be sure to keep B's head in front of your chest as you step and turn (see Figure 149).

(5) As you turn and B begins to fall to his front in a forward spiral, squat and bend forward at the hips. B will land in front of you with his head close to your feet (see Figure 150).

(6) You can follow up with a strike or stomp to B's head area, or release his head and return to the upright ready position as you back away from him.

Analysis of Entry

In order to set up this throw you must be very close to B and directly in front of him. The important part of setting up the technique is to obtain a hold on the back of B's neck. This hold can often be set up with a strike to the neck or jaw, or directly during standing grappling situations. The Head Twist Spiral is most often used when you find yourself caught in a disadvantageous position (for example, when an opponent has a solid hold on you or you are off balance), or when you are locked in standing grappling situations and find

123

Figure 146

Figure 147

Figure 148

Figure 149

Figure 150

Figure 151

Head Twist Spiral - Method of Application

it difficult to break the opponent's posture. This throw may also be set up off punch defenses when you are caught inside an opponent's arms, or when space constraints prevent you from maneuvering to a more advantageous angle.

Once you have your left hand in position behind B's neck, you will place your right hand under his chin. In an actual fight, you may strike with the right hand (with a palm strike to an opponent's chin or throat) before you move the hand into position for the throw itself. A knee to the opponent's groin is also an effective set up blow as it will cause an opponent to squat and bend forward, bringing his head toward you where it is very easily grasped. The important point to remember when applying the Head Twist Spiral is that it is usually only applied when you are at a disadvantage, and will very often require a set up strike which diverts the opponent's attention while you set up the throw.

As your intent flows forward into B's centerline from the front, try to feel as if you and B are joined chest to chest. This image will help you maintain the connection between your relative centers as you move through the throw (it is very important to keep B directly in front of you as you step and turn to throw. If you turn your torso first and then attempt to pull B down by the head, you will disconnect centers and will have to rely on brute strength alone to bring B down). It is also important not to attempt to pull B down or initiate the throw with only your left hand in position on the back of B's head. You will be able to pull B forward with one hand at the back of his neck (in a straight line), but you will not be able to twist his head and lock his spine into his hips (with spiral momentum). In the above variation, if you attempt to pull with your left hand only, B will be able to resist the linear force and counter the technique. If you wait to begin applying pressure until both hands are in place, you will be able to generate a spiraling force that is extremely difficult to resist.

Analysis of the Throw

Once you have your hands in position, you are ready to initiate the throw itself. At this point you drop your body weight and relax your arms, squatting a little and allowing the momentum to jerk B's head to his front and down. Use the weight dropping of your entire body to initiate the pull, don't pull with your arms alone (the momentum is transferred from your body through your hands, it is not generated by the arms alone). As soon as B leans slightly to the front, immediately begin to twist his head. The key to taking the slack out of his spine and locking from his head all the way into his hips is to twist his head along two axis at once. The head rotates freely from left to right along its vertical axis. The head also freely tilts forward and backward along its horizontal axis. Turning the head to look right and left (along its vertical axis) or tilting the head to look up and down (along its horizontal axis) are natural movement patterns, and the range of motion is relatively great. If, however, you twist the head to the side and simultaneously upward, you are moving the head along two axes simultaneously, and the range of motion is greatly reduced. The twist on B's head creates a coupling effect which in turn causes a spinning momentum around his upper spine. Twisting the head to look up to the rear at about a 45 degree angle quickly locks the cervical vertebrae, and additional torque at this angle eventually takes the rotational slack out of the whole length of the spine, locking the entire torso from the head into the hips.

Taking the slack out of B's spine allows you to connect the momentum of your respective centers: from your hips, through your connection at B's head down to his hips. In order to keep this connection you need to maintain a constant torquing pressure as you turn and throw. To insure that you keep B locked from head to hips as you turn to throw, turn your body with your arms held stationary in front of our chest, so that B's head stays directly in front of your chest throughout the throw. As stated in the Method of Application section above, if you turn your torso first and then attempt to pull B's head around and down, you will have separated your centers and will have no other option than to rely on brute force. Once you have twisted B's head until the slack is out and his shoulders begin to turn, his posture will be broken as his shoulders and hips are misaligned.

Once you have set up the throw and have taken the slack out of B's torso, swing your left foot back in an arc toward your right rear, turning 180 degrees to the left. You should turn and pull B's head down toward a point that is a few feet forward of the center point of his base. Imagine a line drawn straight from the inside center of one of B's feet to the other. Now draw a line straight out forward from the mid-point of this baseline, at a right angle to it. This is B's weakest forward angle (the angle at which he is least able to resist a force which pushes or pulls him forward). It is toward this angle that you pull B's head, taking full advantage of this inherent structural weakness in his base.

The downward pull makes use of a second class lever. We take B's toes as the fulcrum, his center as the load to be moved, his body as the force arm and his head as the point of application of force. As in previous techniques, pulling at B's head allows us to apply force near the end of the force arm, giving us the greatest possible mechanical advantage. As you swing your left foot back and turn to the left, squat, bending at the knees and hips as you tilt your torso forward a little. Allow you torso to "fall" at the speed of gravity as you squat and pull B down. Moving at the speed of gravity creates a weight dropping effect which makes use of your entire body mass as opposed to squatting and attempting to "yank" B down with the strength of you arms alone.

Twisting B's head at the proper angle and keeping his head in front of your chest as you turn and throw insures that your centers will be joined throughout the technique. B will fall with his head near your feet and his body extended out toward your right side. You should maintain control of B's head as he lands, and should end the throw in a stable squat position. You are in a superior position from which you may immediately apply a follow up technique if necessary. The focus of your gaze should be on B both during and after the throw, while maintaining awareness of your environment through your peripheral vision. If you need to strike B, blows to the head and face area can be applied extremely quickly with one

hand controlling his head as the other strikes. You may also turn B's head so he looks away from you (toward his left) and drop your right knee heavily onto his right jaw or the right side of his head. If you decide not to apply a follow up technique, stand and move around to your left a little until you are directly above B's head and back away from there (standing above B's head is the safest position as it is the furthest from his arms and legs).

Analysis of Body Use

As you set up the Head Twist Spiral, you need to keep both arms relaxed. If you hold the back of B's neck and chin and tense your arms or lift your elbows, you will have no choice but to rely on the power of your arms alone when attempting to throw B. Your shoulders should sink downward and your elbows should hang heavily. If your arms remain relaxed and heavy, the momentum of your entire body will transfer through your hands as you drop your weight and throw. The weight drop and forward pull on B's head should be sudden, with one pulse of energy (be careful not to jerk or twist your partner's head too quickly during practice).

As you twist B's head so that he looks up over his shoulder, connect with him mentally, feeling as if your intent flows straight into B and you are joined front to front. Once the slack is out of B's torso and his head is in position in front of your chest, your arms hold his head stationary in the same relative position as you step back with your left and turn your torso. As you swing your left foot back in an arc toward your right rear, you pivot on your right foot. Be sure to keep your weight balanced directly over your right foot as you turn, and pay attention to the upward pull of your intent at the crown of your head.

As B begins to tilt forward over his toes, begin to lower your body. Bend at the knees and hips and "drop" your weight suddenly. As you squat and drop your weight, it is important to keep the upward flow of intent at the crown of your head. If you allow your upper body posture to collapse as you squat, you will lose the torque on B's head and spine and your posture will become unstable. Your knees point in the same direction as your toes, and as you complete the turn your weight is distributed equally between both feet. As you drop your weight and turn, center the motion in your hips, keeping B's head directly in front of your centerline (chest) until he falls.

In the final position, as B lands on the ground, you are in a half squat position with your torso angled forward from the hips, your head still floating away from your torso without rounding your lower back. Keep the mental extension of energy out through your arms so that you continue to control B as you decide on subsequent action. Exhale in a short burst as you twist B's head and pull it in toward your chest. Exhale smoothly for the remainder of the throw. If you choose to follow up with a knee drop to B's head or jaw, place your left foot just above his head and drop your right knee straight down with the thigh at a right angle to the ground and your torso erect. This position will allow the entire weight of your upper body to pass directly through your right knee into B's head. When dropping your knee, keep your left foot flat on the ground.

Combat Applications

As discussed above, the Head Twist Spiral is most often applied when you find yourself in a disadvantageous position. It is potentially a very dangerous technique and discretion should be used in its application. In the following examples, the Head Twist Spiral is applied when you are at a disadvantage, after the opponent has a hold on you in the first two techniques, and in the third, the opponent is punching you and you are unable to move off the line of attack.

Front Underarm Bear Hug Defense

The opponent grabs you around the waist with both arms and squeezes you tightly (see figure 152).

Immediately relax your entire body and make yourself "heavy". If the opponent attempts to lift you, wrap your left leg around the outside of his right leg, hooking his leg tightly to prevent him from pushing his pelvis forward (if the opponent cannot lean back and thrust his pelvis forward, he will find it very difficult to lift you with the

strength of his arms alone. Wrapping his leg with yours allows you to control his center; see Figure 153).

Hold the back of the opponent's neck with your left palm, and cup your right palm under his chin. If the opponent attempts to bury his face in your chest to prevent your right hand from holding his chin, place your right palm on the left side of his head and press your right thumb into his left eye. The opponent will be forced to lean his head back. Drop your elbows heavily and twist the opponent's head to his left and upward at a 45 degree angle, so that he looks up over his left shoulder (see Figure 154).

Continue twisting the opponent's head and pushing it away from you until he releases the pressure around your torso. Immediately unhook your left foot and swing it around toward your right rear. As you swing your foot, pull the opponent's head in toward your chest suddenly and turn your torso to the left (see Figure 155).

Squat and drop your weight, throwing the opponent as described above (see figures 156 and 157).

Standing Grappling Defense

The opponent grabs the back of your neck with his left hand and your shoulder with his right, locking you in a standing grappling situation (see Figure 158).

Reach up with your left hand and grab the back of the opponent's neck. Continuing, relax and drop your weight a little as you palm straight up under the opponent's chin with the heel of your right palm (see figure 159).

Rotate your right palm thumb up and cup the opponent's chin. Drop your elbows heavily and twist his head toward his left and upward at a 45 degree angle (see Figure 160).

As you feel the torque lock into his hips, pull his head down in front of your chest suddenly and begin to step back toward your right rear with your left foot. Continuing, turn your torso to the left and squat, dropping your weight and throwing the opponent as described above (see figure 161).

You can follow up by dropping your right knee on the opponent's right jaw (see figure 162).

Figure 152

Figure 153

Figure 154

Figure 155

Figure 156

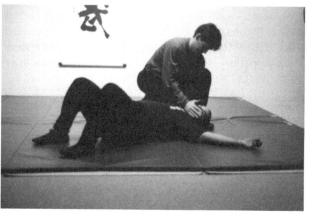

Figure 157

Head Twist Spiral - Front Underarm Bear Hug Defense

Figure 158

Figure 159

Figure 160

Figure 161

Figure 162

Head Twist Spiral - Standing Grappling Defense

Hook Punch Combination Defense

In this scenario, the opponent is driving forward, attacking with hook punches at your head in rapid succession. You are retreating and have either no space or no time to move off the line of attack.

As the opponent steps in with a right hook punch, you are forced to retreat a step (step back with your left foot) and throw up your hands to cover your head (see Figure 163).

The opponent follows up immediately with a left hook punch, shuffle back keeping your right foot forward (try not to step back with the front foot because at the moment your front foot passes your rear foot your base will be very unstable). Swing your right hand outward to cover your head (see Figure 164).

Before the opponent has a chance to cock his arm for another blow, shoot your left hand forward, catching around the back of the opponent's neck and immediately following with a heel of palm strike straight up under the opponent's chin (striking in and upward at about a 45 degree angle will force the opponent's head to tilt back, helping to stop his forward momentum as it stuns him; see Figure 165).

Continuing, rotate your right palm thumb up cupping the palm under the opponent's chin. Drop your arms heavily and twist the opponent's head so that he looks up over his left shoulder (see Figure 166).

Pull the opponent's head down in front of your chest and step back toward your rear right with your left foot, turning left 180 degrees and squatting (see Figure 167).

Throw the opponent with the Head Twist Spiral as described above (see Figure 168).

130

Figure 163

Figure 164

Figure 165

Figure 166

Figure 167

Figure 168

Head Twist Spiral - Hook Punch Combination Defense

131

(10) ARM LIFT HEAD SPIRAL

General Description

Like the Head Twist Spiral, the Arm Lift Head Spiral is an example of a forward spiraling technique. This throw also involves a coupling effect which is created by pushing an opponent's head down while lifting his arm up. The technique can be set up off punching attacks as well as standing grappling situations, and it sets up well from striking attacks to an opponent's head. For a follow up technique, the throw flows directly into an arm break technique which uses the opponent's own body weight to hyperextend his elbow joint.

In the Combat Applications section, two situations in which the Arm Lift Head Spiral is appropriate are presented. In the first situation, the technique is applied as a counter to a front tackle, and in the second situation we use a variation of the Head Twist Spiral to counter a rear overarm bear hug. Both of these attacks are relatively common, and leave the opponent in an extremely advantageous position if not countered immediately. These scenarios are examples of countering linear grappling attacks (one from the front and one from the rear) with spiral throwing techniques.

The overall flow of the throw takes the opponent's head downward in a spiral which spins his body in place, rather than causing him to topple forward as he turns. The throw's momentum causes the opponent to spiral almost 360 degrees and then fall flat on his back. The advantages of this type of tight spiraling momentum are that the throw can be completed in a relatively confined space, and the resultant fall sets up well for an elbow break follow up. Finally, the throw's tight and rapid spin is very disorienting from the opponent's point of view and he will find the momentum hard to counter or escape.

Method of Application

(1) Approach B from the front and hold his left wrist with your right hand (see Figure 169).

(2) Step up with your right foot toward B's right rear, placing the foot down toed in. As you step, turn your torso to the left a little and swing B's left arm up toward his rear (see Figure 170).

(3) Continuing the above momentum, swing your left arm up in a backhand motion and grab the back of B's neck with your right thumb down (see Figure 171).

(4) Push B's left arm up toward his right rear as you sink your weight and begin to pull his head straight forward with your left hand. When the slack is out of B's left arm, he will begin to bend forward and twist toward his left (see figure 172).

(5) Continuing with the above momentum, shift your weight entirely to your right foot and squatting slightly, swing your left foot around toward your right rear in an arc. Continue pulling down on the back of B's neck (pull his head down toward your left hip) as you continue to push his left hand up (push his left hand up toward his right shoulder; see Figure 173).

(6) When B's head is close to your left hip, shift all of your weight to your left foot and turn your torso to the right, stepping back with your right foot. As you step back with your right foot and turn right, push B's head across the front of your waist toward your right side, simultaneously pulling his left hand down toward your right hip (allow B's left wrist to rotate in your right hand as you pull it downward; see Figure 174).

(7) B's body will twist until he is face up at your left side. At this point, allow him to fall straight down on his back (see Figure 175).

(8) The fall sets B up for an elbow break. As he falls, release the back of his neck and hook your left arm up under his left arm, at the back of his elbow joint. Push downward with your right hand on B's wrist and pull upward under his left elbow with your left arm. B's elbow will be locked and the weight of his falling torso will hyperextend his elbow joint (see figure 176). If you choose not to apply the elbow leverage, you may squat with B as he falls and maintain your hold on his left wrist, or release him all together.

Figure 169

Figure 170

Figure 171

Figure 172

Figure 173

Figure 174

Arm Lift Head Spiral - Method of Application

Figure 175

Figure 176

Arm Lift Head Spiral - Method of Application (Con't)

Analysis of Entry

To set up the Arm Lift Head Spiral you must first hold and control B's left wrist with your right hand. Moving B's arm from the wrist gives you the greatest mechanical advantage (as we apply our force at the far end of the force arm, B's wrist, with his left shoulder acting as the fulcrum and his arm is the load to be moved). As soon as you have B's wrist, you should immediately move past his left side and begin swinging his left arm up toward his rear. Hold his wrist with your intent (soft grip) and avoid gripping with brute strength. Attempting to squeeze B's wrist too tightly will alert him as to your intentions and will put tension into your forearm, hindering free movement. Let your right arm "hang" on B's left wrist, the natural weight of your arm pulling the slack out of B's left arm. Swing B's arm up to his rear while gently pulling it away from his shoulder (keeping the slack out) rather than attempting to push his arm up toward his shoulder and force it behind him.

As you swing B's arm up toward his rear, step up with your right foot toward B's left rear, placing the foot down toed in. Toeing in the foot begins to turn the flow of your momentum toward B's center, and as you shift your weight to your right foot, its toed in position naturally causes your torso to turn toward the left. As you step up with your right foot, swing your left hand up and catch behind B's neck, with your left thumb down (in actual application, the grab may be preceded by a

back hammer strike or chop to the opponent's left side of neck or the base of his skull to stun him as you enter). Leave your left arm relaxed and use the right toe in step and left turn of your torso to generate the momentum for the grab (strike).

The flow of your intent should be aimed into B's centerline and his body should remain in front of your chest for the duration of the throw. Be sure to move toward B's rear and initiate the turning of your torso as you lift his arm and pull forward on his head. From the moment you begin the throw until the technique is completed, the pushing and pulling pressures on B's arm and head must not stop, and the momentum generated should be smooth and circular.

Analysis of the Throw

As you enter the throw, the simultaneous lifting of B's left arm upward toward his rear and the forward pull at the back of his neck cause B to bend forward at the waist. As B begins to bend forward, shift your weight to your right foot. Because you have toed in your right foot on the forward step, your torso naturally begins to turn toward the left as you shift your weight to it; this blends the motion of your torso with that of the opponent's, joining your centers. As you begin turning toward the left and your centers join, B's left arm should be extended straight out behind him. Continuing, aim the direction of the push on B's left wrist as if you want to move his left hand directly above his right shoulder. The overall flow of the push should be in a curve, with B's left hand moving from its original position hanging by his side, toward his rear and then curving up and across toward his right shoulder. Moving B's arm along this curved line will initiate a spiral momentum in his torso once his arm locks into his shoulder. Taking the slack out of B's arm and then pushing it across his back toward his right will lock his arm into his shoulder, and subsequent pressure will lock his shoulder into his torso. Once B's arm is locked into his shoulder, you may directly influence his center and transfer the momentum of your mass into his from your hold on his left wrist.

After you have control of B's center and have taken the slack out of his left arm, you begin to turn your waist toward the left as you continue pushing his arm up toward his right shoulder. Simultaneously changing the angle of the pull at the back of B's neck from directly toward his front toward your left hip. Pulling B's head directly toward his front moves his head in the direction of his weakest forward angle (perpendicular to his baseline). Once B has begun to lose his balance forward, you need to change the angle of the pull toward his left front (toward your left hip) in order to induce a spiral momentum (continuing the pull straight forward would result in an arcing momentum which B could easily disrupt by stepping forward with his right foot. Once the momentum changes from an arc to a spiral, B will be unable to step forward and regain his balance). As you continue pushing B's arm upward and pulling his head downward, be sure to turn your body to the left, keeping B directly in front of yourself so that you do not disjoin centers.

The lift on B's left arm and pull at the back of his neck will break his posture by misaligning his hips and shoulders. As you lead B into a forward spiral, his torso will twist and his base will be misaligned as well. When B's head is close to your left hip and his left arm is extended straight up, swing your left foot back toward your right rear, turning your torso 90 degrees. The spiral momentum will cause B to pitch forward over his base toward his left front. B should move as a part of you, feel as if he is an extension of your own center (be sure to keep B directly in front of you

as you turn). At this point, shift all your weight to your left foot and reverse the direction of your turn, swinging your right foot back toward your left rear and turning your torso about 180 degrees to the right. As you turn, change the force you are applying to B's left wrist from an upward push to a downward pull, while simultaneously changing the downward pull at the back of his neck to an upward push toward your right front. The result of your body turn and the directionally opposite pressures applied at B's wrist and neck create a coupling effect which causes his body to spiral past the front of your body and turn face up at your left front.

At this point, B will have no base of support and he will fall backwards. If you do not wish to retain control or apply a follow up leverage technique, now is the time to release his wrist (as B spirals and turns face up, your left hand will naturally release the back of his neck). If you want to take advantage of your position and B's falling momentum to apply the arm leverage/break, step straight forward with your left foot so that you are directly beside B's left shoulder as he falls. Your left arm will be underneath B's left arm after it releases the back of his neck, your left palm up; bend your left arm at the elbow and hook the crook of your elbow under B's right arm, just behind his elbow. Maintain your hold on B's left wrist and rotate his hand palm up (so that his elbow joint is pointing downward), allowing his wrist to rotate in your grip as B spins and falls. As B falls onto his back, squat a little and pulling your left arm up under B's left elbow, push down with your right hand. The weight of B's falling body and downward pressure on his wrist cause a scissoring effect around his elbow (which becomes the fulcrum of the motion at the point your left arm connects with his left elbow). Since the elbow does not bend this way, the scissoring force will cause it to hyperextend or break. The upward pull with your left arm and downward push with your right arm must be timed with B's fall in order to take advantage of his downward momentum. If you choose not to apply the leverage but want to maintain control of B's left arm after he falls, proceed as above but allow your left arm to swing back clear of B's left arm as he falls. Maintain the focus of your intent of B and your awareness of the environment as the throw and/or follow up are completed. Exhale smoothly for the duration of the throw.

Analysis of Body Use

The key to successfully applying the Arm Lift Head Spiral is turning the body in one direction and then reversing the movement, turning in the opposite direction without "cutting" the flow of momentum or disconnecting your center from B's center. In order to make such rapid changes in direction without losing your balance or your control over B, it is vital to maintain the vertical alignment of your centerline. Paying attention to the upward pull of intent at the crown of your head is very helpful in this regard. From the moment you enter the throw until its completion, feel your body continuously lengthening upward. Although this feeling should be a constant in all techniques, it is worthwhile to pay special attention it while practicing this particular throw. If you lean forward or backward during the technique, it will be difficult to rapidly change directions and the momentum which controls B will be interrupted, giving him a chance to escape the throw.

As you enter the throw and push B's left arm up behind his back, shift your weight to your forward right foot. This shifting of the weight allows you to use the power of your legs and the forward momentum of your entire mass to push B's arm up toward his rear, rather than the strength of your right arm alone. Toeing in your right foot on its initial step naturally causes your torso to turn left toward B as you shift your weight forward. Be sure your knee points the same direction as your toes. As soon as your torso begins to turn toward the left, use the momentum to swing your left hand upward to grab (and/or strike) the back of B's neck. Once your entire weight has been transferred to your right foot and you have extended B's left arm up toward the back of his right shoulder, begin to swing your left foot back toward your right rear. Keep your weight directly over your right foot as the left foot moves, and keep B directly in front of you as you turn. Pushing B's left arm upward and pulling his head downward should feel as if you are turning a large wheel, the force of your arms coordinating so that they move at the same

speed. Relax your weight downward as you step and turn to increase your stability in motion.

Once B's head is close to your left hip and his left arm is extended straight up, shift your weight completely to your left foot and step back with your right foot. Once again it is very important to pay attention to keeping your body erect, with your knees and hips slightly bent. Allow the momentum created in the initial left turn to compress your weight into your left leg, and the rebound of force out of your left leg to initiate the right turn of your torso. As B falls, step up beside him with your left foot, and if your decide to apply the elbow break, squat with your torso erect (your head floating upward) and support your left arm (the arm which hooks behind B's left elbow) by placing your left foot directly under it. Bend your left arm as if pinching B's upper arm between your biceps and forearm, keeping your arm close to your body. At the moment B falls, thrust your right arm straight down, dropping your weight simultaneously (be careful not to hyperextend your partner's elbow in practice). As you squat, be sure to bend at the knees and hips, keeping your head and chest up.

Combat Applications

The following situations in which the Arm Lift Head Spiral is appropriate both involve grappling attacks. When defending against a front tackle (more specifically, a double leg tackle in the example below), the key point to remember is to get off the line of attack. If your opponent is a proficient grappler and manages to gain a hold on even one of your legs, the odds are you will be taken down. Attempting to stop an attacker's forward momentum with a strike or counter-push while "holding your ground" is not advisable. Even a much smaller opponent is capable of generating a tremendous amount of momentum when he surges forward with his entire body (which is the basic mechanic of leg tackles). Remember, any technique you attempt is secondary to moving off the line of attack.

The second technique is a defense against a rear bear hug. Examples are given for both under arm (the opponent grabs underneath your arms, leaving your arms free) and over arm (the opponent grabs over your arms, pining them to your sides) variations. Bear hugs can be extremely dangerous holds (as you are vulnerable to being lifted and thrown on your head) and must be countered immediately.

Front Tackle Defense

You face off with the opponent at greater than Safe Distance. Stand relaxed and focus the flow of your intent toward the opponent's center (see Figure 177).

The opponent lowers his body and rushes forward extending his arms to the front, in preparation to grabbing your legs or waist. Immediately step straight out to your right side with your right foot, toeing the foot in. As you step, begin to bend forward from the hips and lower your body (bend a little at the knees).   At the same time, begin to extend your own arms toward the opponent, keeping your intent focused on his center (see Figure 178).

As the opponent continues his forward rush, shift your weight to your right foot and swing your left foot back toward your right rear in an arc (your body turns toward the left). As your left foot swings, extend your right arm forward and down, connecting inside the opponent's left arm near his biceps. Simultaneously, your left hand reaches for the back of the opponent's neck (see Figure 179).

Continuing with the above momentum, pull on the back of the opponent's neck with your left hand, pulling his head down and toward your left hip. As you pull his head down, simultaneously turn your right hand palm up and bend the your arm at the elbow, hooking around the opponent's left arm (squeeze his arm between your biceps and forearm; see Figure 180).

As the opponent's head moves past your left hip, take a half step forward with your left foot and shift your weight to it, then swing your right foot back in an arc toward your left rear, turning your body toward the right. As you step and turn, push the opponent's head upward with your left hand as your right hand pulls his left arm toward your right (see Figure 181).

The opponent will fall onto his back at your left side. If you want to apply the elbow break, slide your right hand along the inside of the opponent's left arm and grab his wrist as he falls. Step up with your left foot and squat as you hook up under the opponent's left elbow with your left arm, and apply the leverage as described above (see Figures 182 and 183).

Bear Hug Defense
(Over Arm)

The opponent approaches from your rear and reaches around your arms, holding you tightly (see Figure 184).

As soon as you are aware of the hold, spread your legs out to the sides (widen your base) and drop your body, bending at the knees. As you squat, simultaneously thrust your rear back forcefully into the opponent's hip/pubic area, bending forward at the hips (see Figure 185).

Keep your weight down and "make yourself heavy." Squatting and thrusting your hips back momentarily prevents the opponent from pushing his pelvis forward and arching you backward, into a lift. As you squat, bring both hands up in front of your chest with the palms facing one another, as if you were holding a small ball (see Figure 186).

Drop your rear straight downward as you straighten your torso and squat a little lower. As you squat, rotate your your arms until the backs of your hands face your chest. This rotation causes your elbows to lift out to the sides. As you rotate your arms and lift the elbows, do not drop your hands, rotate the "ball" in the same relative position in space (in front of your chest). The dropping of your body together with the rotation of your arms will allow you to slide out of the opponent's grip. As soon as you feel your arms free of the opponent's hold, immediately grab his left wrist with your right hand (this prevents the opponent from choking or striking you in the face; see Figure 187).

Now turn your torso to the left and strike back with your left elbow into the opponent's left lower rib area. The shock of the blow should allow you a moment to pull the opponent's left arm straight out to the front (taking the slack out of his arm; see Figure 188).

Immediately strike back with your left elbow again, this time to the left side of the opponent's head or neck (see Figure 189).

Figure 177

Figure 178

Figure 179

Figure 180

Figure 181

Figure 182

Arm Lift Head Spiral - Front Tackle Defense

Figure 183
Arm Lift Head Spiral - Front Tackle Defense (Con't)

Continuing, and without withdrawing your left arm, drop your left hand onto the back of the opponent's neck and step around toward him with your right foot, turning your body to the left (see Figure 190).

As you step and turn, push the opponent's left arm up toward his rear. The opponent is now set up for the throw. Shift your weight to your right leg and swing your left foot back around toward your right rear, turning your body to the left. As you step and turn, continue pulling his head down toward your left hip as you push his left arm up toward his rear shoulder (see Figure 191).

As the opponent's head passes your left hip, shift your weight to your left foot and swing your right foot back toward your left rear, turning your body toward the right. Push the opponent's head up in front of you as you pull his right arm down toward your right hip (see Figure 192).

Follow up as described above (see Figure 193).

Figure 184

Figure 185

Arm Lift Head Spiral - Bear Hug Defense (Over Arm)

139

Figure 186

Figure 187

Figure 188

Figure 189

Figure 190

Figure 191

Arm Lift Head Spiral - Bear Hug Defense (Over Arm) - Continued

Figure 192

Figure 193

Arm Lift Head Spiral - Bear Hug Defense (Over Arm) - Continued

Bear Hug Defense
(Under Arm)

The opponent approaches from your rear and reaches around your waist or chest, holding you with his arms under your arms (see Figure 194).

Immediately spread your legs and squat, thrusting your hips back into the opponent's hip/pubic area. Bend forward from the hips and sink your weight, making yourself "heavy" (see Figure 195).

The opponent has his left hand on the outside of his right. Grab the opponent's left wrist with your left hand and hook the four fingers of your right hand around the opponent's left little finger (see Figure 196).

Bend the opponent's little finger back until he loosens his grip. As soon as you feel his grip loosen, thrust your rear back again and jerk his hands apart (see Figure 197).

Continuing, grab the opponent's left wrist with your right hand and turn your torso to the left, striking back with your left elbow to the left side of the opponent's head or neck. Pull the opponent's left arm straight out in front of you as you strike. Be sure to hang onto the opponent's left wrist with your left hand until you have a firm grip on it with your right hand. (see Figure 198).

After the strike, drop your left hand onto the back of the opponent's neck as you step around toward the left with your right foot. As you step, push the opponent's left arm up behind him toward his right shoulder (see Figure 199).

Continue with the throw as in the variation described above (see Figures 200 through 201).

Figure 194

Figure 195

Arm Lift Head Spiral - Bear Hug Defense (Under Arm)

Figure 196

Figure 197

Figure 198

Figure 199

Figure 200

Figure 201

Arm Lift Head Spiral - Bear Hug Defense (Under Arm)

(11) LEG BAR SPIRAL

General Description

This technique involves a leverage which locks the opponent's leg into his hip, in preparation for either a front or rear spiral throw (depending upon whether we lock his leg from the inside or the outside). Although the technique may be set up with a leg pick up during grappling, it is most efficiently applied as a kick defense. Very often when sparring or fighting, it is possible to catch an opponent's kicking foot. Throwing down an opponent once you have captured his foot seems like a simple affair (and very often just lifting his leg higher will suffice to throw him onto his back). However, with a skilled opponent, capturing a kicking foot only allows you a split second in which you must control and throw him, otherwise, you may find that he has already freed his foot, or has hopped in and obtained a hold on (or has struck) your head.

One simple and oft times effective technique commonly seen in many martial arts is to first catch an incoming kick, and then to step up close to the opponent and apply a leg sweep, sweeping away the opponent's supporting leg. While this is a sound technique and is often fairly easy to apply, a skilled fighter will take advantage of your advance to strike and grab you. And if you continue with your sweep you may find that the opponent is able to take you to the ground with him. The Leg Bar Spiral is a technique which allows you to throw a kicking opponent to the ground with great force once his foot has been captured, without moving in close enough for him to grab or strike you. It is, therefore, much safer to apply than techniques which involve close body leg sweeps.

The technique is described as applied when you catch an opponent's kick on the inside of his leg (throwing him in a rear spiral), and when you catch his leg on the outside (throwing him in a front spiral). As the Leg Bar Spiral is designed to deal with kicking attacks specifically, its variations as presented as they are applied against a direct attack (combining the Method of Application and Combat Application sections). Please note that all of the relevant principles apply exactly to leverages and throws which involve an opponent's legs as apply to those which involve his arms.

Method of Application
(Inside Leg Rear Spiral)

(1) You and B square off at greater than Safe Distance. You are standing relaxed with your vision focused on B's upper chest, and your intent flowing into his centerline (see Figure 202).

(2) B crosses Safe Distance and launches a right front kick toward your abdomen. As B moves in, take a small step out to your right with the right foot, placing the foot down toed in. Shift your weight to your right foot and begin to step back with your left foot, turning your body to the left and raising your hands (move off the line of attack; see Figure 203).

(3) As B's kick extends toward you, pull your hips in a little and drop both hands downward, covering your mid-section (keep your elbows hanging down heavily). Deflect his kick outward (toward your left) with your right forearm as you left forearm drops on top of his ankle. You can also strike the opponent in the face with your right palm (see Figure 204).

(4) Continuing, wrap your left arm around B's ankle (his forward kicking momentum will be spent as you have employed the principle of avoiding force if late). Your right forearm presses just above his knee. Your left foot has now completed a full step back and slightly toward your right rear. Stand up straight and balanced. Shift your weight over your right foot, and lean forward and downward a little, applying pressure to the top of B's leg just above his knee. As you do, continue pulling B's right foot away from his body, thereby taking the slack out of his leg (be careful to lean forward only slightly, do not bend so far that B can reach your head; see Figure 205).

(6) As soon as your weight is over your right leg, swing your left foot back toward your right rear in an arc. Your body will naturally turn to the left. As you turn, maintain the downward pressure on B's leg with your right hand, keeping his right foot close to your left hip (see Figure 206).

(7) Turn your body about 180 degrees, bending forward slightly as you do. B will swing around with you as the centrifugal force and downward

Figure 202

Figure 203

Figure 204

Figure 205

Figure 206

Figure 207

Leg Bar Spiral - Method of Application (Inside Leg Rear Spiral)

pressure on his leg cause him to fall in a rear spiral (see Figure 207).

You can either let go of B's leg as he falls and remain clear of him or maintain your hold and apply a follow up technique. From this position, B is vulnerable to strikes to the leg or groin and leg and ankle locks.

(Outside Leg Front Spiral)

(1) You and B square off at greater that Safe Distance. Stand relaxed with your vision focused on B's upper chest and your intent flowing in toward his centerline (see Figure 208).

(2) B lunges toward you with a left front kick aimed at your mid-section. As soon as B initiates his forward momentum, step out to your right with your right foot a half step, toeing the foot in. As you step out with your right foot, raise your hands and lower your hips a little (see Figure 209).

(3) Continuing with the above momentum, shift your weight to your right leg and begin to swing your left foot back in an arcing step toward your right rear, moving off the line of attack, your body naturally turning toward the left. As you step, pull your hips back away from the kick and drop your arms, your right forearm pushing outside of B's lower leg near his knee (push his leg away from your body) as your left forearm drops on top of B's ankle (be sure to keep your elbows hanging heavily). B's foot will pass by your left side as you avoid his force (see Figure 210).

(4) Wrap your left arm around B's ankle from the top, holding his heel with your left palm, close to your left hip. Simultaneously slide your right forearm up until it presses above B's knee (on the outside of his leg; see Figure 211).

(5) Continue turning your body toward the left, stopping the rear swing of your left foot after it has moved through a 90 degree arc. After your left foot has stopped, shift your weight to it and lean forward slightly, pressing your right forearm into B's left leg. As you lean forward and press into B's leg with your right forearm, continue turning your body toward the left until it has turned a full

180 degrees. As you turn, your right hip will press behind B's left hip and the centrifugal force and downward pressure on B's leg will cause him to fall in a forward spiral (you can extend your right leg in front of B's right leg by taking a small step forward, see Figure 212).

B will pitch forward and fall onto his face. As he falls, you can release his left leg and return to the upright ready position. Be careful with this throw in practice and go slowly until your partner is familiar with the forward fall.

Analysis of Entry

As a general rule, it is always advisable to move off the line of attack as soon as possible when confronted with a kicking attack. Kicks are extremely powerful and if you attempt to stand your ground and block with your hands, the force of impact may result in serious injury to your arms. As the reach of a kick is quite long, and a competent kicker can extend his leg very quickly, maintaining Safe Distance is the best first line of defense against leg attacks. Once an opponent raises his foot or otherwise makes an aggressive advance, you should immediately begin to move out of the way (off the line of attack). If you allow an aggressor to come within Safe Distance even slightly, although you are just out of range of hand techniques he may be able to kick your lower body before you are able to respond.

As B begins to raise his foot and lunge forward, immediately move to one side or the other. If you choose to step to the right side as in the techniques described above, step first with the right foot. Take a small step and toe the foot in. This initial step begins to move your torso off the line of attack and allows you to generate momentum for your body turn and evasion. Toeing the foot in as you set it down begins to turn your body toward B's leg. As soon as your right foot makes its initial step, shift your weight to it and begin turning your body to the left as your left foot starts to swing back toward your right rear. Create the momentum for the body turn and left step by relaxing and sinking your weight into your right foot. As you begin to turn left, pulling in your hips a little stabilizes your posture and also helps to move your torso off the path of B's kick. During the initial right

Figure 208

Figure 209

Figure 210

Figure 211

Figure 212

Leg Bar Spiral - Method of Application (Outside Leg Front Spiral)

step you raise your hands to cover your body in preparation for catching B's leg. Leave your arms relaxed and heavy, and keep the elbows well bent and your palms facing outward. Curve the fingers a little and keep the hands above B's kick. DO NOT attempt to block B's kick with your hands, doing so would expose your fragile fingers and wrists to the force of the kick.

As you move off the line of attack, you can use your forearms to push B's leg away from your body (push outward with the elbows, keeping your hands up). As B's kick extends past your left side, you immediately catch his leg, wrapping around his ankle with your left arm as your right forearm slides into position above his knee. You have now avoided the incoming force and have made a physical connection with B. Throughout the entry your intent should continue flowing in toward B's centerline, feeling as though you are connected to him energetically chest to chest.

Analysis of the Throw

Once you have entered the throw and have a hold of B's leg, it is very important to allow his forward momentum to continue. Throughout the technique, continuously pull B's leg out and away from his body. This keeps the slack out of his leg, helps to "disconnect" his leg from its source of power (his body) and gives you a direct connection to B's center. Shifting your weight to your right foot after you take the initial toed in step will naturally cause your body to turn toward the left, blending the motions of your and B's torso. As you continue to pull B's leg forward and away from his body, the slack is taken out of his leg and you obtain a direct connection to B's center. Hold B's foot near your left hip so that you can brace his leg close to your body, thereby stabilizing your hold on his leg.

Now that you have control of B's leg and a direct connection to his hips through his leg, you swing your left foot back and continue turning your body toward the left. It is important to note that it is the momentum of your body which transfers into B's body through the hold you have on his leg which ultimately causes him to fall, and not the strength of your arms alone. Your arms should remain relaxed and heavy for the duration of the

technique. As you step back with your left foot and turn your body to the left, you lean forward slightly and press above B's knee with your right forearm. When applied during the Inside Leg Rear Spiral variation, the pressure on B's leg creates a third class lever effect which causes B's hips to move downward. A third class lever has the point of application of force (in this case, the area just above B's knee) in between the fulcrum (B's kicking foot which is held next to your left hip) and the load to be moved (B's hips). The leverage applied to B's leg which lowers his hips combined with the centrifugal force caused by the left turn of your body results in a downward spiral which swings B to the ground. It is interesting to note that the centrifugal force created serves to pull B's body away from the center of the spin (your body), making it even more difficult for B to grab or strike you as you throw him. The leverage and momentum created during the throw serve to misalign B's base as his hips are pulled forward. The continued rotation of B's body pulls his hips away from his base of support (which is only the area of one foot) and B falls.

As you turn and apply leverage to B's leg, relax downward and drop your weight. Lower yourself at the hips and bend your knees slightly so that your torso does not lean too far forward. If you bend forward too far, you jeopardize your balance and may bring your head into range of B's arms. When executing the Outside Leg Front Spiral variation, the leverage on B's leg and spiral momentum are the same as the previous variation, however, in the Front Spiral technique we also bring our right hip into direct contact with the back of B's left hip. We use our right hip to reinforce the pressure of our right arm as well as using our right leg as a barrier which "trips" B's right leg as he spirals forward. Using the right hip and leg directly against B results in a very sudden and forceful fall (face first).

The flow of the Leg Bar Spiral is very much like the game of "crack the whip," with you rotating at the center of the circle, causing your partner to spin around you at a much greater speed. The overall rhythm allows you to turn fairly slowly as B whips about you at great speed. Once B is caught in your momentum flow, his center becomes subordinate to yours and he has no choice but to follow your motion. You may release B at any time during the spiral and back away, the momentum of the throw carrying B away from you and leaving you with a safe avenue of escape. If you decide to maintain control of B's leg as he lands, squat a little, bending at the knees and hips with your head lengthening up from the crown. You will be standing in a stable and superior position from which you can strike or apply leverage to B's captured leg. From the moment B launches his kick through to the end of the throw, keep the aim of your gaze on B's upper torso, and keep his body directly in front of yours. Maintain the connection from your center to B's center and move him as a part of yourself.

Analysis of Body Use

The key to the Leg Bar Spiral is to rotate your body around a central point, while keeping B's center subordinate to your own. In order to spin quickly and smoothly, it is important to maintain the alignment of your torso, and center the rotation about your hips. Maintain a steady forward flow of intent toward B from the initial right step as you move off the line of attack until B falls. At no time during the technique should you lean back. Leaning back even slightly will release the pressure you are applying to B's leg, affording him a chance to counter or escape.

Your right foot is the point around which your body will spin during the throw. As you swing your left foot around toward your right rear, pivot on the ball of your right foot. Be sure not to let your right leg bend too much, and keep

your right knee directly above your right ankle. When moving your left foot, it is important to swing the foot back in an arcing step, with the foot lightly skimming the ground rather than lifting the foot up and stepping back in a straight line. The impetus for your body's left turn comes from the sinking of your entire body weight into your right foot, and using the rebound of force from that foot to move your torso. Your hips direct the turning motion (be sure to keep your shoulders and hips in alignment, and bend at the hips without rounding your lower back or collapsing your chest in order to maintain the integrity of the Four Levels).

As you spin and swing B around you, it is helpful to consciously direct the crown of your head to lift upward (away from your torso). Keep this feeling of lengthening your torso as you bend forward at the hips to press your right arm down on the top of B's leg. You need to bend forward at the hips in order to use the weight of your torso to put pressure on B's leg, rather than attempting to remain perfectly upright and push on his leg with the strength of your arm alone. If you release B as he begins to fall, you can immediately return to the upright ready posture and move away. If you choose to maintain control of B's leg as he falls, squat a little, bending at the knees and hips and lower your body at the speed of B's fall, bending forward slightly as you do. If you attempt to hold B's leg and stand upright or lean away from him, the weight of B's descent may jerk you forward and off balance. As B lands, your intent is still focused on his center. Exhale smoothly for the duration of the throw.

Part Four

SACRIFICE THROWS

In this final section, an example of a sacrifice throw from each of the categories of throws (arcs, circles and spirals) will be covered. Although sacrifice throws necessitate going to the ground yourself in order to execute the technique, they are very useful in certain circumstances, and are sometimes one's only practical option. The throws presented below are among the more practical, and the situations offered in the Combat Applications section are those more likely to occur in a real fight. In addition, I have taken into consideration that you will most likely be falling on a hard surface in the street. The following throws are among those which result in a minimal amount of shock for the thrower upon impact with the ground.

Besides the practical aspects of being competent at sacrifice throwing, the following techniques are offered as a means of illustrating the fact that the same principles which apply to standing throws also apply to sacrifice throws. In fact, many of the basic principles presented previously are all the more obvious when applied to sacrifice throws (for example, there is no more obvious example of weight dropping than actually falling bodily to the floor in order to execute a throw). For practitioners of arts which include sacrifice throws (judoka and wrestlers for example), seeing the principles of throwing and body use as they apply to these types of throws may be especially helpful in clarifying the ideas I have attempted to present. For practitioners unfamiliar with sacrifice throws, the following techniques will hopefully serve to introduce a new area of practical technique.

ARCS

(12) ARM AND LEG SCISSOR THROW

General Description

The Arm and Leg Scissor Throw involves sweeping with your legs in one direction as your arm pulls in the opposite direction, creating a scissoring effect along the length of the opponent's lower body. More specifically, the opponent's feet are blocked at the heels as rearward pressure is applied at the front of his waist; since the opponent is unable to step back, he is forced to fall in a rear arc. This throw is especially useful as a counter to holds and leverages which force you to bend forward, as well as a follow up technique to leg takedowns which are countered by the opponent. The mechanics of the throw itself are very similar to those of a basic side breakfall; you attach yourself to the opponent's waist and lay down onto your side.

Before attempting the throw itself, it is important to point out that sacrifice throws must be performed at full speed (the speed of a fall, that is, the speed of gravity). It is impossible to "fall" slowly when learning the technique. It may be helpful to go through the motions of the techniques in this section without actually attempting to throw your partner before you execute the techniques "for real." Make sure your partner knows what to expect in advance, and be sure you have a clear idea of the mechanics involved so that you are clear of your partner as you both land.

Method of Application

(1) Approach B from his right side, stepping up with your right foot just to the side of B's right foot (see Figure 213).

(2) Step up with your left foot behind B and bend forward at the hips, placing your right hand down on the ground close to the inside of your right foot (hold your right arm almost straight). At the same time, extend your left arm across the front of B's hips, grabbing around the front of his left hip with your thumb down (see Figure 214).

(3) Support your weight with your right hand as you lift both feet off the ground, extending your legs toward B's left side while swinging both legs forward into the backs of B's heels. As you extend your legs, push your body into B's right side (you fall into rather than away from B; see Figure 215.

(4) As you fall onto your right hip, your legs are extended behind B's heels, with your left leg on top of your right. As you fall, simultaneously begin turning your body to the left, pulling back and down across B's hips (see Figure 216).

(5) B will fall in a rear arc onto his back. Continue your turning momentum and come up into a sitting position. Leave your left arm across the front of B's hips. You may now stand up and move away from B, or control and follow up. One method of control is as follows: In order to check any potential kicking attack from B, reach underneath both of his legs with your right arm and squeeze his knees together, holding them firmly against your chest. As you hug B's legs, scissor your legs so that your right leg extends toward your left side, and your left leg extends toward your right side. Lean your weight onto your left arm (pressing down on B's hips to control him as you do) and bring your left knee up close beside B's right side, close to his right armpit. As you come up into the kneeling position, bring your right knee up, placing your right foot close behind B's rear as you rock his knees up toward his face (see Figure 217).

Keeping your weight down and heavy, you can strike with your left arm into B's throat or head area. You may also push B's legs toward his left, causing him to turn his back toward you as you escape or strike him from behind (see figure 218).

Analysis of Entry

In order to set up the Arm and Leg Scissor throw, you need to enter from B's side. This throw is most often set up as a counter to head holds or arm leverages, and provides a means by which you may escape a disadvantageous situation and obtain a dominant position. In the examples presented in the Combat Applications section

Figure 213

Figure 215

Figure 216

Figure 214

Figure 217

Figure 218

Arm and Leg Scissor Throw - Method of Application

151

below, the technique is entered by flowing with the opponent's force once he gains the advantage, and directing his own momentum into a counter throw. This throw may also be set up actively whenever you enter from an opponent's side, and is especially useful as a follow up to attacks to the lower body or legs.

It is very important to move into B during the set up phase of the throw. As you reach across B's hips with your left arm, press the left side of your body into B's right hip and leg, making contact with as much surface area as possible. Your intent flows into B's center region (the area of his hips and pelvis) as if you want to wrap yourself around him. It should be noted that if you attempt the throw by falling away from B as you wrap his hips and extend your legs, you may end up in a much worse position than you were in originally. Enter the throw with the intent of literally sweeping B off his feet.

Analysis of the Throw

As you enter the throw and swing your legs behind B's feet, your left side will press into the side of B's right hip. It is at this point that you join centers with B. The back of your left arm and your left side should make contact with B with as much surface area as possible. Push off your right leg and feel as if your left hip is being pulled upward slightly as you extend your legs in the air. Don't jump up as your legs leave the ground, rather lift from the hips and drop your legs into position behind B's feet. Once your legs are in the air and extending toward B's left side, they should close together and swing forward, toward the backs of B's legs. Be sure your legs are together with the left leg stacked on top of the right. If your left leg is opened out and extended behind B, he may fall on and injure your leg.

Once you move into B and make contact with his hips, your point of contact becomes the center point around which your body rotates as you swing your legs into position. As you land, the backward and downward pressure applied at B's hips creates a second class lever, with B's heels as the fulcrum, his center as the load to be moved and the place your left arm pulls his hips as the point of application of force. There are a couple

of details which should be noted. First, be sure to drop your right leg all the way to the ground, touching the backs of B's heels. In this position, your leg blocks B's legs at the furthest point from which you apply force (his hips), thereby taking advantage of the longest possible force arm (the entire length of B's legs). Second, be sure to wrap your left arm around the top of B's hips (just below his navel) so that the load (B's center) is between the fulcrum and the point of application of force (your left arm).

Because B is standing in a more or less parallel stance, the direction of your left arm's pull should lead B's hips straight back at a right angle to his base (pull evenly with your left arm across the length of the front of B's lower abdomen, rather than with unequal force at one of his hips or the other). The angle of the pressure your left arm applies should be downward and toward B's rear at about a 45 degree angle. Since your legs block B's feet and he is unable to step back to maintain his balance, his lower body is misaligned and his center of gravity moves to point outside of his base. B has no recourse but to fall in a rear arc. One other point to consider is that although your legs swing into the backs of B's heels, you do not have to swing them with such force that they knock B's feet out from under him. As long as your legs are pressed against the backs of B's heels, you are in position for the throw.

To take full advantage of the weight dropping effect of your body weight (the primary impetus of momentum for all sacrifice throws is weight dropping), it is important to extend your legs and swing them into position behind B's legs as you move in against his right hip. Now allow yourself to fall onto your right side, your right foot touching the ground just outside B's left foot a moment before your right hip lands. As you fall, begin turning your body toward the left and pulling at a downward angle with your left arm. Do not fall to the ground and then attempt to pull B over your legs. Although this may be possible, you will have to rely on the strength of your left arm alone as your falling momentum will be spent. Your left arm is only the connection through which you transfer the momentum of your falling body to B's. First join centers with B as you swing your legs behind his and then fall as one body. When correctly set up and executed, it should require no more effort to take B down than it does to fall onto your side alone.

If you choose to follow up as described in the Method of Application section above, reach behind B's knees and hug his legs to your chest. Holding behind B's knees gives you more control than attempting to hold onto his feet. As you bring your left knee up beside B's right side, rest the entire weight of your body on your left forearm, which presses across B's hips (your left arm remains in the same position it was in during the throw). Pressing across B's hips helps to hold him down and restricts his movement as you move into a more advantageous position. If you release the pressure on B's hips and attempt to get up, he is completely free to turn toward you and strike or kick. As you come up on your left knee, keep the knee very close to B's right side, not leaving him space to turn toward you or slide away from you. Your right knee presses against B's rear as you rock his knees up over his head. Once B's hips are off the ground, his power and mobility will be severely limited. You are now in a dominant position from which to strike or escape. It is best to push B's legs toward his left so that his back is to you before you stand upright. If you choose to stand up as soon as you have thrown B, in order to protect yourself from his feet and knees you should grab the outside of his right knee with your right hand as soon as you hit the ground. Continuing, scissor your legs as described in the Method of Application section above and sit up, pushing B's knees away from you (toward his left) as you come to your knees below B's rear. From here, you can safely stand and move away from B.

Analysis of Body Use

The overall flow of the Arm and Leg Scissor Throw involves your legs swinging in one direction and then transferring the momentum of the swing into your upper torso, which turns in the opposite direction. As with all sacrifice throws, you transfer the momentum of your falling body into the opponent's, which causes him to fall to the ground with you. The principle dynamic is weight dropping which involves the entire body mass. Postural considerations are most important during the set up and follow up phases of the technique. Once you "attach" yourself to the opponent in the correct manner, you need only let yourself fall passively to the ground. The key to techniques such as these is to fall at such an angle that the opponent is unable to support your weight, and is pulled to the ground.

In the Arm and Leg Scissor Throw in particular, it is important to bring your center of mass (your hip and pelvis area) directly underneath B's center and transfer the momentum of your falling body into his center, but at an angle which takes B's center of gravity outside the rear perimeter of his base. In practical terms, this means you must move into B as you swing your legs into the fall. This is the key determinant of success or failure in the throw. In order to get close enough to drop your weight under B, you need to place your right hand down close to his right foot. As you bend forward and put your right arm on the ground, it is important not to bend the arm too much. Bending the right arm too far causes your torso to be lower than B's hips; if your torso is below B's hips you will not be able to move the mass of your body directly into B's hips and will be forced to rely on the power of your left arm alone when pulling him down. In addition, bending your right arm to too great an angle ruins the alignment of your humerus and forearm bones, forcing you to use brute force in your arm in order to support your weight as you lift and extend your legs behind B. Placing the right arm down with only a slight bend at the elbow aligns the upper and lower arm in the strongest position, the alignment which requires the least amount of effort to support your body weight.

As your left arm reaches across the front of B's hips, wrap your left hand around the front of his left hip and feel as if you are squeezing B's hips into your left side. Make contact with as much surface area as possible along the entire length of your left arm and armpit area. As you bend forward and begin to swing your legs behind B's heels, consciously lift from the crown of your head in order to "lighten" your torso and make it easier to lift your feet. As your legs swing through the air and drop into place, extend them straight out and close them together. Your intent should extend out through the bottoms of your feet.

As soon as the outside of your right foot makes contact with the ground (just outside B's left foot), drop your right hip onto the ground. As you drop your hip, begin to turn your torso to the left, pushing across the front of B's hips. It is important to feel the proper rhythm in the drop and turn. Don't try to turn your upper body to the left before your right foot touches the ground, neither should you begin turning left after your right hip has already landed. Begin to turn your body just after your right foot makes contact with the ground, but before your right hip lands. Most importantly, feel as if your torso moves into B as you fall. You should end the throw in a sitting position and not laying flat on your back. As you turn your torso to the left into B's hips, you should maintain the alignment of your hips and shoulders as always. In addition, maintain the upward flow of energy at the crown of your head throughout the throw. After you land, your torso is still lengthening upward. If you continue with the follow up technique described above, lead the motion of coming up to your knees with the lifting at the crown of your head. Exhale smoothly for the duration of the technique.

Combat Applications

The following examples of situations in which the Arm and Leg Scissor Throw is appropriate both involve escaping positions in which you are at a serious disadvantage. In a real life confrontation on the street, it is usually not advisable to take the fight to the ground if you can resolve the conflict standing up. However, there are certain situations in which going to the ground is unavoidable, and executing a sacrifice throw may well be the only alternative which allows you to turn a disadvantageous situation into one in which you are in control. In the following examples, we are presupposing you have been caught in a hold and are at least partially controlled by your opponent. Of course, in a real fighting situation, you would attempt to counter these techniques long before they reach this point. In the following situations, the Arm and Leg Scissor Throw is presented as a "back up" technique in case the opponent manages to obtain such an advantageous position.

Arm Bar Counter

The opponent holds you in an arm bar, holding your arm between his legs and torso. There is considerable pressure on your elbow joint and it is not possible to stand up or pull your arm free. It is important to counter the hold immediately before the opponent hyperextends your elbow or presses you face down on the ground (see Figure 219).

Relax your weight downward and place your right palm on the floor next to the opponent's right foot, at the same time, hook your left palm around the outside of the opponent's left hip (see Figure 220).

Raise your hips a little and lift your feet off the ground, extending them toward the opponent's left side (see Figure 221).

As your right foot touches the ground, drop onto your right hip and begin turning your body toward the left (see Figure 222).

Push the opponent's hips back and downward at a 45 degree angle toward his rear. The opponent falls onto his back in a rear arc (see Figure 223).

You may follow up as described above.

Counter to Side Headlock Attempt

The opponent approaches from your left side and reaches around the back of your neck with his right arm (see Figure 224).

Continuing, the opponent steps in front of you with his right foot and begins pulling your head forward and down into a side headlock. As he pulls you down, extend your left arm across the front of his hips before he tightens the hold (see Figure 225).

Bend forward at the waist and place your right hand on the ground beside the opponent's right foot as you wrap your left hand around the opponent's left hip (see Figure 226).

Raise your hips a little and lift your feet off the ground, extending them toward the opponent's left side (see Figure 227).

As your right foot touches the ground, drop onto your right hip and begin turning your body toward the left (see Figure 228).

Push the opponent's hips back and downward at a 45 degree angle toward his rear. The opponent falls onto his back in a rear arc (see Figure 229).

You may follow up as described above.

Figure 219

Figure 220

Figure 221

Figure 222

Figure 223

Arm and Leg Scissor Throw - Arm Bar Counter

155

Figure 224

Figure 225

Figure 226

Figure 227

Figure 228

Figure 229

Arm and Leg Scissor Throw - Counter to Side Headlock Attempt

(13) HEADLOCK BACKROLL THROW

General Description

The Headlock Backroll is a sacrifice throw which involves wrapping the opponent's head in a front headlock choke (popularly called the "guillotine") and then falling backwards, throwing the opponent completely over your body in a forward circle. As a follow up technique, you can continue your backward momentum and roll over on top of the opponent's chest, from where you may choke him into submission. This throw is particularly useful as a follow up technique to standing chokes when your opponent manages to push you back and off balance, as well as in standing grappling situations when an opponent rushes into you and attempts a front tackle. If you are unable to move off the line of attack, you may be forced to flow with the incoming momentum and transform the force of an opponent's rush into a sacrifice throw.

The feeling of the throw is as if you and the opponent unite as two halves of a single sphere, and roll together as one entity. You join with the opponent both above and below with your arm wrapping his neck and your foot hooking inside one of his legs. The throw is potentially very dangerous in that there is a strong possibility that an unsuspecting opponent without breakfall experience will land on the top of his head. Be careful in practice and use restraint in actual application (the thrower may control the throw to insure the opponent clears his head and lands on his back. If the opponent is not incapacitated from the fall, the thrower may apply a choke which will quickly render the opponent unconscious).

Method of Application

(1) Approach B from the front, stepping up with your right foot just inside B's right foot (see Figure 230).

(2) Reach up with your right arm and wrap it around the back of B's neck from his right side. Pull his head forward and down until the radial (thumb side) of your right wrist is pressing into B's windpipe. As you wrap B's neck, grab the back of B's right upper arm with your left hand (see Figure 231).

(3) Begin to sit straight down, holding B's head firmly under your right arm and pulling his right arm into your chest as you descend. As your weight begins to drop, lift your right foot and hook the top of your ankle inside B's right knee, with the top of your foot pressing into the back of his knee joint (see Figure 232).

(3) Let your weight drop straight down as you lean your upper body backward, pulling B's body over the top of your body. Simultaneously begin to lift inside B's right leg with your right leg (see Figure 233).

(4) Continue rolling backward as your rear touches the ground. Round your body by tucking your chin in toward your chest and curling your pelvis upward. Your back should be curved and you should roll up the length of your back smoothly, as if you were a ball. Continue lifting B's right leg up and over your body with your right leg. Hold B close to you as you fall and roll. B will pass over the top of your body. If you do not wish to roll over onto B and apply the choke, as soon as he hits the ground turn your body toward your right and come up into a kneeling position facing B. From this position, you may strike B's head area or return to the upright standing position. If you choose to mount B and apply the choke, continue with the backward rolling momentum of the throw, staying connected with him as you roll back over him. As you roll over, turn your head to the right and roll over your right shoulder (see Figure 234).

(8) You will land on top of B's chest, with your knees on either side of his torso (land on the balls of your feet). Maintain your hold on B's neck as you roll back and lift your head, straighten your torso and lift your chest, which pulls B's shoulders and upper back up off the mat. As you lift your torso and pull B's head up off the mat, bring your right knee up and put the sole of your right foot down at B's right side in order to stabilize you base. You may grab your right wrist with your

Figure 230

Figure 231

Figure 232

Figure 233

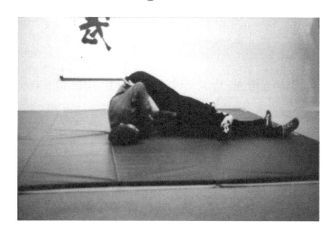

Figure 234

Figure 235

Headlock Backroll Throw - Method of Application

left hand to reinforce the hold, or put your left hand on the mat for support. Lift your chest and pull straight upward with your right wrist into B's throat. The pressure will choke B (the partner being choked should 'tap out' by slapping the person applying the choke as soon as the pressure becomes uncomfortable. As soon as the partner applying the choke hears or feels the tap, he or she should immediately release the pressure; see Figure 235).

Analysis of Entry

The Headlock Backroll Throw may be set up from a striking attack or from a standing grappling situation. Regardless of the situation in which you enter, it is advisable to control B's right arm with your left hand as you wrap your right arm around the back of his neck. Holding B's right arm adds a degree of control as well as preventing B from striking you as you move in. As you wrap your right arm around the back of B's neck, grab his right triceps with your left hand and pull his right arm into yourself so that his biceps is pressed against your chest. Holding B's right arm in this manner allows you to control the mobility of his torso as you limit B's ability to turn his shoulders. You have now made a connection with B's upper body. In actual application, you may strike the opponent on the right side of his neck with your right elbow to stun him as you wrap your right arm around his neck. It is important to take the slack out of your hold and make a direct connection with B's center before you fall back into the throw.

Hold B's head firmly with your right arm and lift your chest a little until you feel you have taken all of the slack out of B's neck. Once the slack is taken out of B's neck (that is, you have pulled his head forward and away from his torso with the pressure applied as your armpit presses downward at the back of B's head), you will have a direct connection with his center. As you lift your chest, pull upward with your right wrist into B's throat which initiates the choking pressure you will intensify on the ground. Be sure that the right side of B's head is pressed firmly against the right side of your ribs, leaving no space for him to pull his head free.

Analysis of the Throw

Once you have control of B's head and right arm, you are ready to apply the throw itself. The overall feeling of the technique is as if you and B are two halves of the same sphere. It is vital that you think of falling together, as one unit, rather than you falling first and then attempting to pull B over you. When you sit and begin to drop your weight, be sure to sit straight down. If you fall backward your and B's center will disconnect and at best he will end up falling on top of you. Sit straight down so that your center (your hip and pelvis area) is directly below B's center as his upper body rocks forward.

As you sit, hook your right foot around the inside of B's right knee, your right leg well bent. The contact you make with your foot and ankle reinforces the overall spherical shape of your respective bodies, as it joins you below as well as above. In addition, your right leg plays an important part in helping to lift and throw B over your body. It is preferable to hook your foot inside B's knee as opposed to the inside of his ankle. Lifting with your foot from his knee area applies pressure directly to his femur, which, in turn, is directly connected to B's center. If you hook B's ankle and attempt to lift his leg, B may escape the force by bending his right leg at the knee.

As you sit and begin to roll backward, you should fall directly in front of B, so that the momentum of your fall pulls B directly forward at a right angle to his baseline. Pulling B directly forward takes advantage of the inherent structural weakness of his stance. The momentum of your weight dropping which pulls B's upper body downward combined with the force of your leg which lifts his legs upward result in a coupling force which causes B to rotate around his center in a full circle. In order to create this coupling force it is important to harmonize the opposing momentums so that they may combine to create a rotational force. Therefore, the timing of the throw is critical to executing a technique which requires very little effort. The proper timing is to begin lifting inside B's right leg with your own leg as soon as you begin to sit into the throw. Keeping the downward pull at B's head and the upward lift at his leg equal and simultaneous is the key to a smooth coupling movement and effortless throw. Once again, feeling as though you and B are two halves of the same sphere is most important. You should imagine that there is one circuit of dynamic energy which flows around your connected bodies.

When you sit and pull B's upper body forward and down, his hips and shoulders will be misaligned and his center of gravity will move outside the forward perimeter of his base. Because you fall almost directly under B's center, the sharp angle at which his upper body bends forward and down makes it impossible for him to step forward to reestablish his base of support. B has no choice but to pitch forward head first toward the ground. If you choose to roll over on top of B and apply the choke, continue the lifting energy of your legs and maintain the connection of your respective centers, allowing B's momentum to pull you over on top of him. As you roll over backward, you need to turn your head so that you look toward your right shoulder. Turning your head in this manner lets you support the weight of your rolling body with your shoulder and not with your head and neck.

As you come up on top of B's chest, spread your legs a little so that the balls of your feet touch down on either side of his torso. Immediately sit on B's chest and lift your head and chest upward so that B's shoulders leave the ground. As you lift, bring your right knee up and put your right foot on the ground near B's left side. Let your weight sink down into B's chest as you lift upward with your right wrist, which cuts up into B's throat. Arch your back slightly as you do to increase the downward pressure of your armpit at the back of B's head. The pressure of your body weight holding B's torso to the mat, combined with the upward force at his throat and the downward force at the back of his head result in a tremendous pressure which pinches B's windpipe, shutting off his supply of air (practice the choke very slowly and release the pressure as soon as your partner taps either you or the mat). In actual application, maintain your awareness of the environment as you choke. Because you have already placed your right foot flat on the ground, upon releasing the opponent's neck you may quickly return to the upright ready position

Analysis of Body Use

As you wrap B's neck with your right hand, his head should be held firmly between your right forearm and armpit. Be sure that your arm remains relaxed, and that you hold B's neck with the weight of your arm and your intent alone. After you pull B's right upper arm against your chest with your left, allow your left elbow to hang heavily and feel as if B's head and arm have become a part of your own body. Throughout the entire process of set up and entry, be sure to remain relaxed, use the natural weight of your arms to set up and connect with B, and hold him firmly, yet without tensing your arms or upper body.

When you begin to sit into the throw itself, first bend your knees and hips and feel the weight of your lower torso and hips pulling you straight downward. If you have made a firm connection with B's neck and right arm, it will not be necessary to actively pull B forward and down, you only need to fall yourself and B will move as a part of your body. Feel as if you are sitting forward a little toward your right foot so that your center moves directly under B's center. At no time should you loosen your hold on B's neck. Allow your weight to fall naturally and as you drop downward, begin to curl your body by tucking your chin in toward your chest as your pelvis curls upward slightly. By the time your rear has made contact with the ground, your right foot should already be hooked inside B's right knee.

You will, of course, drop to the ground at the speed of gravity. Once you have landed, it is very important to translate the falling momentum into a backward rolling momentum by continuing to curl your pelvis upward and lifting with your feet. Your body should be rounded and should roll on the ground like a ball. As B passes over your head, your right foot should still be connected to B's right leg, feeling as though B is "pulling" you back over on top of him. As you feel your body rock back onto your shoulders, turn your head to the right, looking in the direction of your right shoulder. This allows you to roll over your shoulder and not your head. Maintain the roundness of your body as you separate your legs and let the balls of your feet touch down on either side of B's torso. You should still feel as if you are tightly connected to

B (the hold you have with your right arm around B's neck should still be very firm). Exhale as you sit and throw.

As you land on B's chest, immediately lift your torso, leading the movement with the pull of intent at the crown of your head. As your torso moves into the upright position, bring your right knee up and put the sole of your right foot on the floor next to B's left side for increased stability. Continuing your upward flow of energy, inhale and lift your chest as you arch your back slightly, simultaneously pulling straight upward with the radial side of your wrist directly into B's windpipe. As you lift and pull upward, relax your body weight downward onto the top of B's chest. Your weight will hold B's body down as you apply the choke. You can either maintain your hold on the back of B's right arm with your left hand, or you can grab underneath your right hand with your left in order to reinforce the upward pull and choke. Be sure to place your right foot on the floor ahead of you so that your right shin is perpendicular to the ground. Inhale as you lift and choke. Once you have completed the choke, lift from the crown of your head and stand up into the upright ready position. In actual application, remain aware of the downed opponent and step away from his body as soon as you stand.

Combat Applications

The Headlock Backroll Throw is useful when you are caught in between an opponent's arms, or in face to face standing grappling situations. The hold on an opponent's neck is easier to obtain with an opponent who is shorter than yourself. If an opponent is much taller, it is often necessary to induce a reaction which causes him to bend forward (such a reaction may result from a kick to the groin or a punch to the solar plexus). As mentioned above, striking back into the side of the opponent's neck with your elbow before you wrap your arm around the back of his neck is also an effective way of setting the opponent up for the throw. A final cautionary note: be sure that your partner is familiar with the throw before you practice it all the way through. Be careful also with the choke. When practicing choking techniques, always apply pressure slowly and release the pressure as soon as your partner signals discomfort by tapping either you or the mat.

Hook Punch Defense

You and the opponent face off at Safe Distance. The opponent cocks his right arm in preparation for a hook punch (see Figure 236).

Immediately begin to move forward, stepping up and slightly out to the right with your right foot, placing the foot down toed in. As you step forward, turn your waist to the left a little and swing both arms up and out toward your left side, both arms curved with your wrists crossed, the right wrist inside and touching the left wrist. Your arms should remain relaxed, and should be extended without completely locking the elbow joints, about a foot or so from your head. The forward step, turn of the waist and raising of the arms should be one smooth motion, the momentum of which is initiated from the forward movement of your body. Your body and arms remain relaxed and your gaze is directed toward the opponent's upper chest area (see Figure 237).

The rotation of your body and the angle of your arms deflects the opponent's blow around your left side (the goal of the movement is not to "block" the incoming punch, it is to redirect the momentum around you by intercepting it early). Now shift your weight to your right foot as you turn your waist toward the right and strike back with your right elbow into the right side of the opponent's neck. The blow will stun the opponent and will divide his attention long enough for you to set up the throw (see Figure 238).

Continuing with the above momentum, wrap your right arm around the back of the opponent's neck as you slide your left hand over his right arm and grab his right triceps. Sink your body weight and pull the opponent's head forward and down until it is wrapped tightly under your right arm and the radial side of your right wrist is pressing into his windpipe. Simultaneously pull the opponent's right arm firmly against your chest (see Figure 239).

Bend at the knees and hips and begin to sit downward and a little forward, pulling B down and to his front (see Figure 240).

Figure 236

Figure 237

Figure 238

Figure 239

Figure 240

Figure 241

Headlock Backroll Throw - Hook Punch Defense

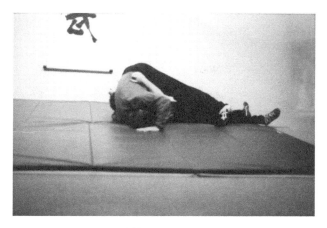

Figure 242

Figure 243

Headlock Backroll Throw - Hook Punch Defense (Con't)

As you fall, bring your right knee up, hooking the top of your foot inside the opponent's right knee. Curl your chin toward your chest and begin to tilt your pelvis forward and upward as you round your back (see Figure 241).

Rock backward and throw the opponent over your body, lifting inside his right leg with your own right leg (see Figure 242).

Continue rolling back until you are sitting on top of the opponent's chest. Lift and choke him as described above (see Figure 243).

Front Tackle Defense

You are facing the opponent at greater than minimum Safe Distance. He suddenly lunges forward lowering his head while reaching forward with both arms in an attempt to tackle you (see Figure 244).

If you are caught by surprise and it is too late to either intercept early or move off the line of attack, step back with your right foot and lower your body as you "catch" the opponent by wrapping your right arm around the back of his neck. Simultaneously grab behind his right arm with your left hand and pull his arm firmly into your chest (see Figure 245).

If you find the opponent's forward momentum too great to resist, bend your knees and hips and begin to sit downward and a little forward, rounding your back by tucking your chin and pelvis as you hook your right foot around the inside of the opponent's right knee (you may need to retreat by shuffling backward before you sit and throw) (see Figure 246).

Rock backward and throw the opponent over your body, lifting inside his right leg with your own right leg (see Figure 247).

Continue rolling back and land on the balls of your feet, then slide your knees up and sit on the opponent's chest. Lift and choke him as described above (see Figures 248 and 249).

Figure 244

Figure 245

Figure 246

Figure 247

Figure 248

Figure 249

Headlock Backroll Throw - Front Tackle Defense

(14) FOREARM HOOK SPIRAL

General Description

The Forearm Hook Spiral is a sacrifice throw which involves attaching to an opponent's arm and then falling to his front, pulling him over you in a forward spiral. This technique is useful when you catch and control another's arm from the outside, and wish to take the fight to the ground. The throw is often used as a follow up technique in situations in which an opponent attempts to resist standing joint locks (such as arm bars), or off low punches when it is too late for you to move completely off the line off attack. The resultant fall is quite hard and the opponent is left vulnerable to follow up joint locking techniques (one of which will be included below).

The basic flow of the throw makes the opponent feel as if he was caught in a rapidly spinning whirlpool, his body diving and rotating in a tight spiral. The Forearm Hook Spiral is especially useful when an opponent resist you by attempting to push you away. This provides a good opportunity to turn his own force against him and lead him into the technique. In actuality, you need only lead his force in the correct direction, and the opponent will throw himself. Once the throw is completed, you will be flat on your back. As this is a vulnerable position you need to make a quick decision either to follow up from the ground or immediately return to the standing position. Because of the vulnerable position in which you must end in order to complete the throw, this technique is best executed as a follow up to other techniques from which an opponent is about to escape, or when you have either been caught or forced off balance and a sacrifice throw is your last alternative.

Method of Application

(1) Approach B from his front left side and grab his left wrist with your right hand, your palm pressing against the inside of his wrist, your thumb hooked around his radial bone and your four fingers wrapped around the ulna side of his wrist (see Figure 250).

(2) Pull B's left arm, extending it forward as you drop your elbow over his arm, trapping his forearm under your right armpit. Hold B's arm firmly by squeezing his forearm between your right upper arm and ribs, with B's thumb pointing upward (see Figure 251).

(3) Step up with your left foot, placing the foot down toed in directly in front of B's centerline (your foot should be lined up with the mid-point of B's baseline, about two feet in front of B). After you step with your left foot, begin shifting your weight to it and turn your body to the right, pulling the slack out of B's left arm (his left arm should be fully stretched out to his front center; see Figure 252).

(4) Continuing with the momentum of the weight shift and turn, keep turning your body to the right, and holding B's left arm firmly against your body, begin to fall backwards (see Figure 253).

(5) B will be pulled forward and his body will begin to rotate toward his right. Continue turning toward your right as you fall until you land on your back. The weight of your falling body coupled with the pull on B's left arm will cause him to spiral forward over your body and land on his back at your right side (see Figure 254).

(6) If you choose to stand up immediately, throw B's left arm across his chest and roll away toward your left, coming up onto your feet as you do. If you choose to follow up from the ground, there are several options for striking or joint locking techniques. From the ground, you may hold onto B's left wrist with your left hand and immediately strike back to his head or face area with your right elbow (see Figure 255).

(7) Continuing from the elbow strike, you may apply a joint lock submission technique as follows: pull B's left arm down across your chest with your left hand until his arm is stretched straight, his hand close to your left hip, palm up. Continuing, wrap your right arm over the top of B's left biceps, and insert your forearm underneath B's forearm, grabbing your left wrist with your right hand. Be

Figure 250

Figure 251

Figure 252

Figure 253

Figure 254

Figure 255

Forearm Hook Spiral - Method of Application

Figure 256

Forearm Hook Spiral - Method of Application (Con't)

sure that your right forearm is above the back of B's left elbow joint. From this position, pull downward on B's left wrist as you inhale and lift your chest, pressing up behind B's elbow and causing it to hyperextend (you may also lay your right leg across B's hips to limit his mobility and prevent him from sitting up). In practice, apply the pressure slowly and release as soon as B signals discomfort by tapping either you or the mat (see Figure 256).

Analysis of Entry

In actual application, the Forearm Hook Spiral is most often used as a counter to pushing pressure or as a follow up throw when an opponent resists an initial joint locking technique, such as an arm bar. The throw may be set up any time you are outside an opponent's arm and have control of his wrist, or your forward arm is over an opponent's extended arm. Although the set up calls for you to step up directly in front of your opponent, you are still leading from a safe angle because you are moving the opponent's arm ahead of your body, which leaves you always toward his rear. In practice, the key to successfully setting up the throw is to obtain a secure hold on B's left forearm by tucking it firmly under your own right arm, then stretching his arm forward until all the slack has been taken out of his arm/shoulder connection. If B's arm slips down and out from under your arm,

it will impossible to complete the throw as the slack created will allow B enough time to readjust his posture and escape. The throw may also be set up off low line punching attacks (see the Practical Application section below) in which you have moved off the line of attack outside the attacking arm, while allowing the opponent to extend his punching arm as much as possible.

When leading B into the throw it is important to continuously encourage him to move forward. Ideally, we want the person we are throwing to give us forward momentum which we absorb and redirect into a downward spiral. If B's forward momentum is sufficient, he will literally throw himself as we guide his force in the appropriate direction. As we connect with B and begin to lead him forward, our intent flows back into his center as we begin to turn toward him. It is important to feel a connection from our hold on B's arm all the way into his center, before we begin to fall. Try to lead B forward and be sure all of the slack is taken out of his arm before you begin to fall into the throw.

Analysis of the Throw

Once you have a firm hold on B's arm and have stepped forward with your left foot, you begin to turn your body to the right. Since B's arm is already stretched out forward to its natural limit, the winding action of your body turning will result

167

in the slack being taken out of your hold on B's arm, pulling the slack out of your connection all the way to his center. You have now effectively joined centers through your hold on his arm. It is also very important to step up with your left foot directly ahead of B, placing your left foot down a couple of feet in front of the mid-point of his baseline. The baseline is represented by drawing a line between the centers of B's feet, your left foot should end up directly in front of the mid-point of this line, so that a straight line drawn from your left foot toward B would bisect the mid-point of his baseline at a right angle. Placing your left foot down in approximately the right spot is much facilitated by visual reference to B's center. Simply step up with your left foot and put it down directly in front of B's centerline. Toe in your left foot so that when you shift your weight to it you will automatically begin turning toward your right, the winding action created will take up any slack in your hold.

Now that you have a direct connection to B's center, you should immediately fall into the throw itself. You need to fall backwards as you continue rotating your body toward the right, in order to create a spiral momentum. Because of the rotation of your body, your head moves toward B's right side. For the duration of the throw, it is important to hold B's left arm firmly under your own right arm as if his arm is a part of your body. As you fall and turn, feel as though you are pulling toward your rear with your right elbow. The angle of the fall and the turning of your body result in your pulling B's left elbow down toward a point directly in front of the mid-point of his baseline (his left elbow should pass directly over the point at which you originally placed your left foot). Pulling B's left upper arm toward this point moves his body toward his weakest forward angle, which is perpendicular to his baseline. The more accurate you are in guiding B's left upper arm toward this point, the less he will be able to resist, thereby taking advantage of this inherent structural weakness in B's stance.

As your falling weight pulls B's left arm forward and downward, his left shoulder will move forward very rapidly, misaligning his shoulders and hips. As your body lands on the ground, B's upper body will have been pulled forward of the front perimeter of his base, and he will have no choice but to pitch forward and fall in a forward spiral. The weight dropping created by your falling body creates the force which acts on B as a second class lever, with B's toes as the fulcrum, his center as the load to be moved and his body as the force arm. The effect created by the weight dropping in this particular throw is interesting in that the rotational motion of your body as it falls creates leverage which occurs in the overall momentum of a spiral.

As you land and B passes over the top of your body, maintain your firm hold on his left arm as he lands so that he may not roll away nor strike you with his left elbow should the fall be insufficient to incapacitate him. If you wish to apply the follow up described above, immediately upon landing grab B's left wrist with your left hand. Don't release B's wrist with your right hand until you have grabbed it with your left. Now release your right hand and strike back directly into the left side of B's head, throat or neck with your right elbow. As your right elbow strikes, pull B's left arm across your body toward your left hip, taking the slack out of his arm. Rotate his hand palm up as you pull. Continuing, lift B's arm away from your chest a little (keep pulling his arm away from his body) and wrap your right arm over the top of B's left biceps and bending your arm at the elbow, insert your forearm underneath B's left forearm and grab your own wrist. Your right forearm must be positioned above the back of B's elbow joint. If B's arm is so long that you cannot reach your own wrist with your right hand in this position, you may also reach up and grab your own shirt or lapel on the left side of your upper chest. Pull down with your left arm, hyperextending B's left elbow.

The elbow bar leverage involves a second class lever. The fulcrum is the point at which B's upper arm makes contact with your right forearm, the point of application of power is B's left wrist and the load to be moved is B's elbow. Since the length of B's forearm serves as the force arm, the further toward his hand you apply pressure, the greater the mechanical advantage. Therefore, hold his wrist with your left hand as close to his hand as possible for the most leverage. Laying your right leg across B's hips adds a measure of control as its downward pressure limits the mobility of his center. Be sure to maintain awareness of your surrounding environment after you land. If there is the possibility of attack by others, you may wish to stand up immediately after completing the throw.

Analysis of Body Use

When setting up the throw, it is important to obtain a good hold on B's left arm. Your right hand should hold his wrist with soft grip, using your intent to grip as if your hand and his arm were one unit. When you trap B's forearm between your right arm and body, be sure not to raise your right shoulder, and let your right elbow hang heavily. Feel as if your right arm is very heavy and is glued to your right side. As you step up with your left foot, toe the foot in turning the entire leg from the hip, with the knee pointing the same direction as the toes. Your left knee should be directly above the ankle. Shift your weight to your left leg without allowing the knee or hip to move forward; your body weight should pass straight down through your left leg into the ground. Because of the toed in alignment of your left foot, as you shift your weight to it your torso naturally begins to turn toward the right, at this point, your body should still be upright, with your head floating upward from the crown. It is vital at this juncture to keep a firm hold on B's left arm, pulling it with you as if it were part of your body. This allows you to move B with the momentum and the power of your entire body. If you step and turn first and then attempt to pull B toward yourself, you will be forced to use the strength of your right arm alone.

As you shift your weight to your left foot and begin turning to the right, B will be pulled forward and his own body will begin rotating toward his right. At this point you begin to fall, making sure that you fall back and away- from B, continuing to turn your torso toward the right as you drop. To insure you fall back and away from B at the correct angle, do not allow your left leg to collapse as you begin to drop, rather feel as if you are compressing into and consequently rebounding out of your left foot, the force of the rebound propelling you backward into the fall. Again, it is very important to maintain your hold on B's left arm without

allowing any slack to develop as you fall. During the fall, maintain the alignment of your shoulders and hips, turning your body as a coherent unit. Falling as a unit makes it possible to use the entire mass of your body falling at the speed of gravity to throw B, and prevents you from sitting down first and then attempting to pull B down with the strength of your right arm alone.

The resistance of B's body weight will act to break the momentum of your fall, so that you land on the ground without a jarring impact. Because you continue the rotation of your body toward the right as you fall, you will land flat on your back. It is helpful to look at B's face from the time you step up with your left foot, through the fall and continue to look toward him as he lands on the ground. Focusing your gaze in this manner helps to match the rhythms of your respective bodies and the connection of your centers. Exhale for the duration of the throw. If you follow up with the right elbow to B's head, strike by dropping the weight of your arm alone. Avoid raising your upper body off the ground in an attempt to generate more power in the strike, as this may give B an opportunity to sit up with you and escape. If you apply the elbow bar follow up and lay your right leg across B's hips, feel as though your hips are pushing down into the ground heavily, and that your right foot seeks to press into the ground outside B's right hip.

Combat Applications

The Forearm Hook Spiral is most often used as a last resort technique, and is applied most efficiently when borrowing an opponent's force and using it against him. The situations in which this technique may be appropriately applied are those which find you at a disadvantage (for example, you are being pushed backward, or your opponent resists an initial technique in which you have control of his arm). Most styles of martial art include some variation of the standing arm bar. Because this leverage is very common, I have included an example of the Forearm Hook Spiral as a follow up to an attempted arm bar which the opponent counters by bending his arm and pushing you away. As discussed above, the throw is best set up and executed when your opponent provides

Figure 257

Figure 258

Figure 259

Figure 260

Figure 261

Figure 262

Forearm Hook Spiral - Body Punch Defense

forward momentum, and you should develop the sense of yielding to, rather than resisting his forward pressure as you set up the technique.

Body Punch Defense

You and the opponent face off at Safe Distance. The opponent lunges forward suddenly with a left straight punch toward your solar plexus area. You are too close to either intercept early or completely move off the line of attack (see Figure 257).

Slide your left foot back and pull your hips back away from the incoming blow, turning your body toward the left. As you retreat and turn, hollow your chest and quickly close both arms in front of your torso, your right forearm deflecting the opponent's left forearm toward your left. The retreat and cover serves to absorb and deflect the force of the opponent's blow (see Figure 258).

Continuing with the above, try to grab the opponent's left wrist with your left hand and hold his arm close to the front of your body. The opponent continues moving in and attempts to push you back before you have a chance to counter attack. Yield to the opponent's forward pressure by stepping back and to the left with your left foot, placing the foot down toed in in front of the opponent's centerline. As you yield and step, grab inside the opponent's left wrist with your right hand and drop your right elbow over his forearm, trapping his forearm between your right arm and body (see Figure 259).

Still yielding to the opponent's forward pressure, begin shifting your weight to your left foot and turning your torso toward the right. The opponent's body will begin to turn as his shoulders and hips are misaligned and he begins to tilt forward (see figure 260).

Fall back as you continue turning you body toward the right. The opponent falls over you and lands by your right side (see Figure 261).

Follow up with the elbow strike and leverage as described above (see Figure 262).

Follow up to an Arm Bar Counter

You are attempting to bend the opponent forward in a standard arm bar (see Figure 263).

Before you are able to lock the opponent down, he counters by bending his arm at the elbow and pushing his forearm into your chest, in an attempt to push you away (see Figure 264).

At this point, it is futile to continue trying to apply the arm bar (and further attempts to complete the leverage will invariably result in the use of force against force, placing you at a disadvantage if the opponent is stronger than you). In order to take advantage of the situation and maintain a superior position, yield to the opponent's forward pressure and step back and toward the left with your left foot, placing the foot down toed in front of the opponent's centerline. As you step, slide your right hand over the top of the opponent's forearm and grab the inside of his wrist, trapping his right arm between your right arm and body. Still yielding to the opponent's forward pressure, shift your weight to your left foot and begin turning your body toward the right (see figure 265).

Begin to fall back as the opponent's body tilts forward, throwing him over your body in a front spiral (see figures 266 and 267).

After the opponent lands by your right side, apply the elbow strike and leverage as described above (see figure 268).

171

Figure 263

Figure 264

Figure 265

Figure 266

Figure 267

Figure 268

Forearm Hook Spiral - Follow Up to an Arm Bar Counter

Appendix

INTRODUCTION

In the following sections I have commented on both the concepts and terminology used in the main chapters of this book, as well as relating the ideas presented herein with the relevant principles found in the classic theories of martial art, as espoused in classic texts (Chinese and Japanese) on the arts of unarmed personal combat. The following information is really a collection of essays on single topics. My hope is that this information will help clarify the concepts and principles discussed in Chapters One and Two, as well as relating these principles to classical theory (actually, I have attempted to define and explain these ancient concepts within the context of the principles of application and body use as I understand them).

It is my sincere wish that the following essays will help explain the basic principles of unarmed martial art in terms which are straightforward and logical, thereby demystifying concepts which are often discussed in such abstract and nebulous terms that the student is never able to form a clear and workable understanding of their meaning. Of course, the following ideas are my own interpretation of the principles of martial art, based on my own research and experience. It is the responsibility of each individual to come to his or her own conclusions based on one's own experiences. As far as martial theory is concerned, the ultimate test of "truth" is whether or not the views you hold help to make you a more efficient fighter.

THE ESSENCE OF MARTIAL ART: AN OVERVIEW

Everyone possesses an inborn ability to fight; it is a natural reaction to threat or stress and requires no formal training. What, then, distinguishes these random patterns of attack and defense which arise spontaneously in the untrained from the actions and reactions of a trained martial artist? The answer to this question lies in the trained fighter's application of certain principles to the movements and strategies of unarmed combat. These principles form the basis or "essence" of martial art. It is because these principles are utilized that fighting is elevated to the level of "art." In fact, it is the understanding and application of basic natural principles which allows mankind as a whole to continuously improve and refine capabilities in any endeavor. Such knowledge is made manifest in technique; technique, in turn, is based on the understanding of natural principles. Technical application of natural principles makes it possible for construction workers to build houses, doctors to treat diseases and the weaker to overcome the stronger in a fight.

Without formal training, the larger and stronger naturally defeat the smaller and weaker. Therefore, a basic premise of training to fight as an "art" must be that the methods employed should make it possible for the smaller and weaker to defeat (or at least successfully defend against) the larger and stronger. As we have observed, it is not necessary to create techniques for the stronger to defeat the weaker, as this occurs without formal training. So it is logical that the basic premise of creating fighting techniques which qualify as "art" must, at least theoretically, be designed so that a smaller and weaker combatant can apply them successfully against a larger and stronger opponent. Now that we have a definition of martial art, the next logical question to ask is what type of techniques will allow the weaker fighter to defend him or herself against the stronger.

Which techniques will be effective against larger and stronger opponents? Common sense tells us that techniques based on brute strength will never allow the weaker to defeat the stronger (the stronger opponent by definition possesses more brute strength than the weaker, so a technique based on brute force is doomed to fail the weaker fighter because in a contest of force against force, the stronger force invariably prevails). Once techniques of brute force (that is, techniques which require the use of force against force) have been disqualified as fitting our definition of martial art, upon what shall we base our techniques? The logical answer is to base martial techniques upon principles which allow us to use our strengths against an opponent's weaknesses, thereby circumventing superior force and applying our own force where it will have the greatest effect. Another way of describing the techniques of martial art is to say such techniques are based upon maximum efficiency in obtaining the desired result. What is efficient technique? In a violent encounter there is a real possibility for injury, and the longer the fight lasts the greater the chances of you being hurt. Therefore, efficient technique should allow one to end the encounter as quickly as possible. This means that an efficient technique should either disable an opponent or afford one an opportunity to escape in the shortest possible span of time.

Now that we have a definition of martial art (techniques of combat based upon principles which allow a fighter to use his or her strengths against an opponent's weaknesses) and have defined the parameters within which we want these techniques to operate (maximum efficiency in ending the threat to one's person in the shortest possible time), we need to discover which principles are relevant to creating efficient martial technique. A logical place to start is with ourselves. We should begin by discovering which principles of body use will allow us to use our minds and bodies most efficiently, thereby maximizing our abilities to move in a free and coordinated manner as we generate power appropriately. These principles of maximum efficient use of ourselves must be universal (as there can be only one "best" way to use ourselves), and will apply to movements in any physical endeavor. These are the principles which underlie all efficient motion. It is these same principles which are included and discussed in the various martial classics (both ancient and modern).

The cardinal principle of efficient movement is balance. This includes an internal balance which

unifies the mind and body as well as the actual physical balance of the body itself. Balance is a dynamic state, one which involves constant adjustment even when standing still. When the body is in a state of true balance (that is, aligned with gravity and completely free of excess tension), it is poised to move and work (generate force) most efficiently. The mind and body have innate mechanisms which act to maintain the alignment and balance of the body, in motion and at rest. Allowing these mechanisms to function as they should, free of subconscious bad habit as well as unnatural posturing under conscious control is the first step toward creating efficient martial techniques. In fact, all martial techniques must be structured around the innate reflexes and natural design of the body if they are to be truly efficient. In short, using the body as it was designed to be used will always prove more efficient than using it in contradiction to its natural design.

Since balance is paramount to efficient movement in general and efficient martial technique in particular, it follows that postures and patterns of movement which interfere with the continued dynamic balance of the body should be avoided. Improper skeletal alignment and excess muscular tension are the causes of loss of true balance (although you may not fall to the ground if you have bad posture or tense muscles, you are no longer in the state of full and natural balance as dictated by the design and nature of the human body. When the physical structure is misaligned, you are not balanced in the gravitational field, and are literally forced to "hold" yourself up by expending constant effort). When true balance is maintained in stillness and motion, one is capable of utilizing and focusing his or her entire physical potential. In this state of balance, we work with the innate design of the body which allows full access to all our inherent strengths, as well as harmonizing our movements with the great natural forces to which we are subject. The force which we are capable of generating when completely relaxed and aligned with gravity I refer to as "natural power". "Natural" because it is generated without undue effort or strain, and because it is power created in harmony with the body's design. If the above holds true then the basic movements of martial technique must be based upon the principles of true balance and natural power.

Now that we have a definition of martial art (techniques which allow us to use our strengths against an opponent's weaknesses and are designed to remove us from the threat of physical harm as quickly as possible) as well as a set of guidelines for which types of body motions will be most efficient (those based on true balance and natural power), the next task is to actually create techniques which adhere to the principles of body use and fit the definition of martial art. Care must be taken to continually balance the requisites of body use with the demands of efficient technique. This means that not only should a technique be based on true balance and natural power, it must also meet the requirements of maximum efficiency in application. Within these parameters there is still room for great variety in technique. Martial techniques which are based on the correct use of the body and are designed around maximum efficiency in application, no matter how diverse, all qualify as martial art.

The next logical question, now that we have created a system of true martial technique, should address how to practice these techniques so that the martial artist may apply them successfully in actual combat. It is obvious that an intellectual understanding of a technique is no guarantee that it will spontaneously manifest in a fight. In order for techniques to be useful, they have to be practiced until they are "internalized," that is, until the practitioner applies the appropriate technique without conscious deliberation over individual movements (that is not to say one cannot consciously choose a certain technique to be applied, it means that the physical manifestation of the technique should occur with as little gap in time between the conscious decision to apply it and its actual application. Internalization of a technique also implies that the various movements and flow of the technique, once the martial artist makes the decision to use it, occur as spontaneously as a reflex). Another consideration when choosing a set of techniques to internalize deals with their "universality" in application. Obviously, one cannot practice and internalize a separate technique for every possible situation which may occur in a fight. It is important, therefore, to

design and practice techniques which have a broad range of potential applicability. Unfortunately, there is no single technique, nor collection of a few techniques which will be sufficient to deal with the vast spectrum of randomness within which fights occur. Fortunately, it is possible to internalize a basic number of carefully chosen movement patterns and techniques (chosen for their relative universality in application) which the subconscious mind will modify and combine, providing the trained martial artist with constructive responses to practically every situation likely to occur in a fight. But the question of how to practice in order to internalize martial technique remains.

It is a fact known to every student that the amount of information absorbed and retained through focused awareness is far greater than the amount absorbed through mindless repetition. I'm sure you have had the experience of reading a page in a book while thinking of something else, only to realize as you turned the page that you had no idea what you just read (although you "read" every word). No matter how many times you read the same page without focused awareness, you will still not absorb and retain the information contained therein. So it is with the practice of martial technique. Mindless repetition of technical movements may qualify as exercise, but the vast majority of time spent in practice of this type is wasted as far as internalizing useful patterns of movement is concerned. On the other hand, focused awareness on the practice at hand maximizes the time spent in practice, allowing one to internalize techniques in the shortest amount of time, as well as guarding against the negligent acquisition of unwanted habits. In short, the most efficient method of training for internalizing martial technique involves mind and body unity, with the mind (intent) actively aware of and guiding the movement of the body. The goal is to maintain conscious awareness of the thought process (the mind in the brain) as well as the kinesthetic sense (the mind in the body). The key is "awareness." Focusing this awareness on what we are doing is the method of efficient practice.

In summary, it is important to remember that an almost unlimited number of efficient martial techniques (those based on true balance and natural power, which allow us to use our strengths against an opponent's weaknesses and remove us from the threat of physical harm as quickly as possible) are created and developed from a relatively small number of basic principles of body use and technical application. It may be helpful to think of techniques (including the methods of body use as well as martial applications) as being physical manifestations of underlying principles. The principles of body use and application are the unchanging foundations of unlimited technical expression. And the focused awareness of mind and body unity in practice is the method through which martial movements and techniques become internalized, and therefore useful. These principles and their method of internalization form the essence of martial art.

ON MIND/BODY UNITY

Among the various martial disciplines it is often repeated that the strongest state of being is one in which the mind and body are unified. This refers to focusing one's total being, both mental and physical, on the task at hand. We discussed in the section above the importance and ultimate efficiency of studying and practicing with the mind and body in unification. Although there are different methods of cultivating mind and body unity, the essence of this unification boils down to one factor, and that is awareness. Once your intent (that part of your mind which is under conscious control) becomes aware of your mental and physical state, your mind and body are unified. Acquisition and internalization of martial technique and the development of martial ability is a very slow and difficult process in the absence of mind and body unity. Without awareness, we never know that bad habits exist, and are helpless to inhibit them. Without awareness, practice is inefficient at best and often times mindless practice (practice in the absence of awareness) is ultimately counterproductive. It is interesting to note that although the unification of the mind and body requires absolutely no effort, only awareness (effort here actually precludes true mind/body unity), the consistent unification of the mind and body proves to be a most elusive discipline.

Martial techniques are based on conditioned patterns of movement and the trained sensitivity (both visual and tactile) which allows one to apply the appropriate technique at the appropriate time. Conditioned patterns of movement are created by repetitious practice. There is no way to internalize specific patterns of movement without physical practice. Awareness of the event of "practicing" as it occurs provides accurate feedback as to the quality and feeling of the movements practiced. The old axiom that "practice doesn't make perfect, perfect practice makes perfect" holds true for the acquisition of any skill. How does one practices "perfectly," or at least maximize the the results of the time spent in practice? The answer lies, at least in part, with the awareness of a unified mind and body, with the mind controlling the physical actions. This is often referred to in the martial classics as "using the intent and not force."

Use of the appropriate muscles without residual or antagonistic tension is the key to efficient movement in any task. It makes sense, therefore, to begin from a state of correct postural alignment and complete relaxation. Beginning this way we may be sure that there is no unwanted tension or stress anywhere in the body. If we begin moving without awareness, it will be very difficult to maintain this original state of relaxation and balance, and without awareness the practitioner is incapable of processing feedback from the kinesthetic sense. During motion, the only way to move and consistently monitor and maintain balance and relaxation (the keys to unlocking the full potential of one's physicality) is to lead the movements of the body with the intent (which is another way of describing the awareness of a unified mind and body). You "will" it done and it is done; this is the source of natural power and movement without effort.

Finally, it is the mental state which is the primary determinant of one's ultimate performance. The most skilled exponent of any discipline is doomed to failure if he or she lacks the "heart" or "spirit" to act. "All things being equal," the stronger individual invariably defeats the weaker, but all things are rarely equal in real life. And the phenomena of the weaker and less skilled defeating the stronger and technically superior is often repeated in real world encounters. As all things are relative, if the spirit and determination of the seemingly inferior exponent is stronger than that of the superior, the former becomes relatively more powerful than the latter. Just as even the strongest and most skilled fighter in the world is doomed to defeat if he loses the will to fight, the weakest novice is potentially lethal if he focuses himself with single minded determination on victory. Cultivation of the proper mind set during training is a key factor in the ability to utilize one's full potential. And although performing at full potential is no guarantee that you will always win, it insures you have the best chance possible under the circumstances.

ON POSTURAL ALIGNMENT AND GRAVITY

In most discussions of movement and exercise, the role of gravity is oddly overlooked. This is a strange omission as the pull of gravity is the predominant natural force acting (incessantly) upon our bodies, both in movement and at rest. Without gravity things have mass but no weight, and without weight muscles have nothing to exert against. Whether any specific movement is efficient or not is primarily determined by its relative harmony with the force of gravity. The human body's systems of muscle-machines moving bone-levers are what allow us to generate force and move through space. And the pull of gravity is the most basic force against which we move. So, when devising exercises or task specific movement patterns (like martial techniques), a primary consideration should be the quality of the movement with respect to gravity. Efficient movements are those which accomplish the task for which they are designed while harmonizing with and utilizing the force of gravity in concert with the natural design of the body itself. Since all movement is in relation to gravity, freedom of movement (or the lack thereof) is determined to a large degree by one's poise in the gravitational field. To remain truly balanced (aligned with gravity without excess tension), the body must make continuous anatomical adjustments in response to its relative position in the gravitational field. A balanced body requires a minimum of effort to move (the T'ai Chi Ch'uan Classics advise us to "stand poised like a balanced scale"). Maintaining true balance also provides maximum stability as well as the freedom to move and adjust the balance in response to outside influences (the Classics also state that a properly balanced body is "so sensitive that the weight of a fly will set it in motion"). Correct skeletal alignment is a prerequisite for complete relaxation. While it is possible to stand in correct alignment and be tense, it is not possible to truly relax if the alignment is off. Once the skeleton is misaligned, the constant downward pull of gravity necessitates excess tension in some muscles to keep the misaligned body from falling to the ground. So correct skeletal alignment is the first consideration when dealing with the maximum efficient use of our physical selves (gravity demands it). Besides maintaining alignment with gravity relative to our physical structure, we also need to move at the speed gravity dictates in order to utilize the natural power of the body and harness the tremendous force inherent in gravity's pull. Since moving either faster or slower than gravity dictates necessitates the use of excess muscle tension, coordinating the movement flow of our entire body with the force of gravity allows us to make full use of the natural power of our bodies as well as take advantage of the gravitational force, allowing us to channel it appropriately. As we are organisms designed to resonate within the gravitational field of the Earth, natural power (referring to the potential power inherent in our mental and physical design) and the use of gravity as an ally in generating force (primarily through weight dropping) are inseparably connected. When the body is correctly aligned, the force of gravity is transferred through the skeletal structure into the ground, there is no need for excess muscle tension to keep the body from falling. The body in true balance functions with the postural muscles in correct tone, neither too slack nor too tense. This is the state of dynamic relaxation that is the source of natural power. Maintaining this state of balance is a natural function of the body. Problems occur because we lose our awareness of ourselves over time, and bad habits come to replace the natural state of relaxed alignment. Moving the misaligned body with its attendant tension is analogous to driving a car with the emergency brake on, there is always a degree of internal struggle. Naturally, in this state optimal performance of any physical task becomes an impossibility. Our innate strengths and natural power are only completely uninhibited when we are not fighting against gravity but are aligned with it. This is the basis of true balance and the root of complete relaxation.

ON RELAXATION

Besides correct anatomical alignment, true balance and the ability to utilize all of one's inherent (natural) power is dependent upon complete relaxation of the muscles. The term "relaxation" refers to the state in which muscles are held in proper tone, neither too tense nor too slack. The tonus of complete relaxation gives the muscles an "elastic" quality, the same elasticity naturally present in small children (you will notice that all small children have perfect posture as well). Only when muscles are completely relaxed can the body move and function as a coherent unit, free of the restrictions of tension. Only when the muscles are completely relaxed will the individual muscle groups come into play as needed, generating the correct amount of force for the movement task at hand. Only when the muscles are completely relaxed can one harmonize with and take full advantage of the force of gravity. And only when the muscles are completely relaxed can one become sensitive, both to the body's own internal, kinesthetic sense a well as to pressures applied from the environment.

It is important to understand that correct muscle tone is maintained without any conscious effort or conscious imposition of tension whatsoever. All that is necessary to insure correct muscle tone is to remain aligned with gravity (and any other externally imposed force) and constantly relax as much as you can. Correct alignment and movement is perceived as the most comfortable and relaxed state. When generating power from this state you will feel momentum, but no exertion. Completing the task at hand with the least amount of effort is another test of one's relative state of relaxation. If you feel the force you are exerting with any one part of your body exceeds the force generated by the rest of your body, you are probably too tense and will not be using the power of the body as a coherent unit.

If one accepts the premise that the mind and body are inseparable, then it logically follows there cannot be true and proper physical relaxation without mental "relaxation." In the Asian martial classics the advice given is to relax the body and calm the mind. The correct mental state is referred to as one of "quietude," referring to a mind free of internal conflict (which is very different than attempting to "empty" the mind. Besides being impossible, attempting to stop the flow of thought is unnatural, as it is the natural function of the mind to think). A quiet mind is sensitive to itself, with the intent focused on the task at hand. Since the mind and body are inseparably linked, the relative state of one has a profound influence on the state of the other. In order for the mind and body to work in harmony (without the conflict which causes tension), the movements of the body must be directed by the intent/awareness of the mind, while the mind needs to be sensitive to feedback from the body. The mental direction referred to implies spontaneity and flow as opposed to calculation and coercion. Awareness and acceptance of things as they are automatically removes resistance, and without resistance there is no need to use force (that is, results are obtained without effort). This is the key to maximum efficiency (although this does not always guarantee victory, it does mean you will perform at your full potential). Practicing martial art with a relaxed body/quiet mind allows the body to function in accordance with its design, insuring true balance and natural power.

It is obvious that any posture or movement other than lying still on the ground requires the use of muscle force. It is also true that "effort" is primarily a subjunctive evaluation of exertion, with identical movements perceived as requiring more or less effort depending on the person performing them. Obviously, the amount of weight a champion powerlifter moves "effortlessly" will be perceived as extremely heavy to the average untrained man. Similarly, the conditioned marathon runner may jog several miles without breaking a sweat while the sedentary individual might become short of breath while walking a short distance. In actuality, it is not really possible to to set a "standard" of exertion below which movement is effortless and above which movement is stressful. What is perceived as effortless action or stressful exertion is a subjunctive evaluation which varies from individual to individual.

How then do we know when we are relaxed physically? A basic guideline would be to use the minimum amount of force necessary for any given task. At any moment, one can "tune into"

the kinesthetic sense and consciously relax the working muscles as much as possible, reducing exertion to the minimum necessary for the task at hand (this also includes adjusting one's relative position in space, one's posture, as well as technique or method in order to maximize efficiency and reduce effort). Understanding and making use of the principles of correct and efficient body use are the keys to maintaining relaxation in any situation. And the foundation of correct body use is once again found in the maintenance of postural alignment in respect to gravity. Maintaining awareness of the body, directing movement with the intent and organizing all movement around correct anatomical alignment while relaxing the muscles as much as possible insures a calm mind and relaxed body. The result of the unification of a calm mind and relaxed body is true balance and natural power.

When one moves in accordance with the natural design of the body in harmony with gravity, the movement should feel light and comfortable. In fact, one good indicator as to whether a movement is performed "correctly" or not is how easy it feels. The easier a movement or technique feels, the closer you are to maximum efficiency. Although, in general, the judgment as to whether a movement or the application of force is effortless or not remains relative, with respect to the techniques of martial art (as defined above), there is a standard by which their degree of effort may be judged. Simply put, when a movement or technique applied to another has the intended effect, and the movement or technique as applied requires no more effort than the movement done in the air in the most relaxed manner possible (as in a "form"), then the technique may be judged "effortless." When you can throw an opponent with the minimum amount of effort it takes to move your own body through space, your technique has reached the level of maximum efficiency.

ON INNATE AND ACQUIRED ABILITY

The automatic functions of the human body are innate, that is, they manifest without conscious intention. In order to "internalize" martial movements and reactions so that they become spontaneous and powerful, the movements chosen should be in harmony with the natural functions and reactions already present in the body's design. Martial skills must be practiced until they become reflexive. "Reflexive" here refers to action which manifests automatically, without having to "think" about it, with awareness and response occurring almost simultaneously. Although one may understand a certain technique intellectually, unless it has become internalized (a reflex), the time it takes to consciously retrieve it from memory precludes its practicality in most real life fighting situations.

Reactions must be reflexive (which means as soon as the intent to apply a technique occurs, the body reacts without further conscious deliberation) as there is very little time to weigh alternatives in a fight. Once a movement or technique has become internalized (part of one's physical self), it transcends mere intellectual understanding and acquires true usefulness. With continued practice and the internalization of a broad range of movements and techniques, the subconscious mind will reach the point where it is able to modify and combine basic patterns, allowing the martial artist a degree of spontaneity free of the constraints of conscious deliberation. Reflex martial skill is what separates the veteran from the novice. True spontaneity is what separates the master from the veteran.

Although the ultimate goal is the ability to react spontaneously and appropriately as the situation demands, skill must be acquired through practice. The most expeditious method of training is one which makes use of the body's innate abilities, strengths and natural reactions as a foundation upon which to build martial ability. Practicing movement patterns and techniques in harmony with our physical design is most efficient because they work in harmony with one's nature, with what is already there, as opposed to attempting to impose unnatural patterns of movement on the neuromuscular system. By definition, "innate" abilities are those which are already present. We are already "good" at them. Practicing martial movements which take advantage of innate abilities and the body's design (i.e. the kinesthetic sense, the potential power in pre-stretched muscles, the elasticity of soft tissue, the strength of the properly aligned bones, reflex reactions, mass etc.) allows the practitioner to build upon what is already there, in accordance with his or her nature (putting a round peg in a round hole, so to speak). The key to unlocking and developing the great potential power inherent in the mind and body is to harmonize with one's innate nature and train in accordance with the body's design.

A final consideration when practicing martial skills is the problem of previously acquired bad habits. A habit by its very nature is something one does automatically, without conscious decision. It is self evident that if we wish to internalize certain movement patterns and physical abilities into our neuromuscular system and brain, any existing bad habits of posture or movement will interfere in our training. Without careful, conscious awareness as we train, the unconscious presence of bad habits will distort our perceptions of what we are actually doing. When left unchecked, bad habits will taint our perceptions of what is occurring; what we think we are doing and what we are actually doing may be two very different things. It is logical, therefore, to begin training by tuning our awareness to things as they are, being careful to remain impartial as we begin working at the most basic level (primarily with posture and our ability to differentiate between various states of muscle tension) while constantly reminding ourselves that as feedback is interpreted through the distorted perception of our bad habits, what we think is occurring and what is actually taking place may not be the same thing. Habits cannot be changed, they can only be replaced. In the early stages of training, it is most important to employ a method which allows you to check and inhibit bad habits until they are no more, so that your innate abilities and reactions may once again function free of negative conditioning. Once the body is free of bad habits, the practitioner is able to internalize martial skills and acquire ability in concert with the body's own nature and design.

ON STABILITY VS. MOBILITY

There are two ways to increase the stability of an object; the first is to lower its center of gravity and the second is to widen is base of support. Bottom heavy objects with wide bases of support are inherently very stable (pyramids, for example). The stability of a human may also be increased by lengthening/widening the stance and lowering the body (which lowers the center of gravity). Many martial artists believe stability and mobility have an inverse relationship, that is, increased stability means decreased mobility and vice-versa. But where the stances and footwork of the martial arts are involved, the relationship between stability and mobility is not as simple as it appears. With relation to the human body, a third variable influencing stability is flexibility, or perhaps more appropriately, elasticity. If you push toward the center of mass of a solid, rigid object with sufficient force, it can be toppled, even if it is wide based and bottom heavy. But imagine a similar object that is not rigid, but pliable. You would have to aim your push very carefully, because the slightest deviation in the direction of your push away from the objects center of mass would cause its center to change location relative to your push, thereby neutralizing your force. Applying this principle to the human body one can see that a stiff, rigid body is easier to unbalance than one which is yielding and pliable (all other variables, including depth of stance and area of base being equal. This is another reason the martial classics advocate complete physical relaxation). So, considerations of stability and mobility in the martial arts must include not only the area and depth of stance, but also the relative flexibility/rigidity of the body as a whole.

Another variable which further complicates the question of stability/mobility is that the human body is not only capable of varying its states of tension (from extreme rigidity to extreme pliability), its movement is based on a system of levers. Raising and lowering the center of gravity as well as adjusting the size of the base may be accomplished in more ways than one. If fact, contrary to what simple physics implies, lowering the center of gravity and enlarging the area of the base without attention to correct alignment will actually make the body less stable. For example, when bending the knees and lowering the center of gravity, a reciprocal bend at the hips must take place or the body will become stiff, thereby decreasing stability. In addition, the placement of the feet, momentum, outside influences (gravity, terrain, the force applied by another), the position of the arms and head, the focus of the vision, the flow of intent, the degree of awareness and the nature of the movement task at hand all influence the relative stability/mobility of the body.

With regards to martial technique, the question of stability and mobility must be analyzed within the context of the goal one is attempting to achieve. For the martial artist, the primary concern is the ability to maintain balance while retaining the freedom to move about and generate force without time consuming adjustments in posture, as well as the ability to translate incoming pressure (from gravity or an opponent) through the skeletal structure directly into the ground. Taking into consideration all of the relevant variables of physics, design and efficiency, in the vast majority of movements and techniques the optimal stance ("stance" refers to the depth and area of the base while stationary or in motion) has certain parameters which may be applied to a great variety of positions and steps. In general, the distance between the two feet should not exceed the length of the individual's normal walking step. Regardless of the distribution of the weight or the placement of the feet, stability and mobility both are jeopardized when the distance between the feet exceeds the length of a normal step. In regards to depth of stance, the knees should be bent slightly at all times ("locking" the knees involves contracting the thighs which inhibits mobility), and except for rare exceptions (going to the ground for example) the bend at the knees should not exceed about a 30 degree angle. Squatting below a 30 degree angle causes tension in the legs and hips which hinders one's ability to move the body and adjust to external pressures. Finally, the body must bend at the hips to compensate for a bend at the knees, in order to maintain correct alignment. This is another reason why it is so important to maintain the lumbar curve and not allow the pelvis to rotate out of alignment. Tilting the pelvis out of its natural alignment and flattening the lower back destroys the "connection" between the upper and lower body, thereby compromising both stability and mobility. The importance of the relative alignment of the hips and legs is referred to repeatedly in the martial classics of both China and Japan. The concept of the waist and hip area as the center of one's physical self and the area around which motion is organized is universally held by all the major martial traditions of Asia. The correct alignment of the hips and legs is vital to the stability and mobility of the entire body.

Very long and low stances are not as stable as the more upright, natural stance. The unavoidable muscle tension and rigidity inherent in very deep stances inhibits free movement (mobility) as well as the flexibility necessary to neutralize incoming force (resulting in less stability). Freedom of movement is necessary in order to create momentum, so the relative immobility of very extended and deep stances limits one to the use of muscle force alone when generating power. When the situation or technique requires lowering the body to a greater degree (when attacking an opponent's legs for example), it is preferable to widen the stance and bend the knees to a slightly greater angle while increasing the bend at the hips rather than leaving the stance relatively narrow and bending the knees to a deep angle. Once the bend at the knees becomes greater than 90 degree, it is preferable to drop onto one knee in order to maintain alignment and reduce muscle tension.

The relative states of stability and mobility should not be viewed as a duality in which one is sacrificed for the other. When the principles of design and environment are taken into consideration, aligning the body correctly and the maintenance of complete relaxation (true balance) will automatically dictate the parameters within which optimal states of stability and mobility will coincide. Either lowering the center of gravity or increasing the area of the base so far that tension results will disturb the body's balance, and therefore both stability and mobility will be compromised. Although the above guidelines dictate the parameters within which stability and mobility may be maximized, it should be noted that the "ideal stance" will differ with individual variations in height, weight, body structure, flexibility and strength. Martial artists should not force themselves (or be forced to) "conform" to exact, preset dimensions of what stances and footwork should be. Of course, the practitioner needs a model or prototype form upon which to pattern movement, but the "fine tuning" of stance and footwork must be left up to the individual as he or she works within the parameters of true balance.

ON SEEKING STILLNESS IN MOTION

The Martial Classics make reference several times to the concept of "seeking stillness in motion." The usual interpretation of this statement is that while externally, one is physically in motion, one should maintain a mental calmness internally (stillness). Although remaining calm while in motion is certainly very important (physical relaxation is impossible without mental calm), this is only a partial explanation of the stillness in motion concept. The concept goes much deeper than a quiet mind in a moving body, it refers also to a dynamic physical state in which the body, although in motion, is perceived by the mind to be "motionless." And this perception of stillness in motion is primarily the result of moving in true balance while coordinating the movements of the parts into one harmonious flow.

Here we should distinguish between two different states of kinesthetic perception, tension and momentum. Imagine for a moment that you are falling through space. You can remain perfectly still (that is, you can fall completely free of tension, without actively moving a muscle), but the momentum of your mass moving through space you will perceive as motion. You are falling (motion) without actively exerting any force (stillness). When moving in balance with the individual movements of each part coordinated into a coherent flow (that is, with rhythm), there is a "stillness in motion" effect similar to the falling through space example above. Moving out of balance, in an uncoordinated manner or with excess tension disturbs the stillness that would otherwise occur in the absence of these things.

The perception of motion is relative. If I hold my arm out in front of my chest and then begin turning circles, my hand will appear to be motionless in relation to the center of my body (that is my hand will always remain in the same position relative to my center). In reality, however, my hand is moving through space at a fairly rapid rate, much faster than my center. Because I am turning my body in a unit, I will experience a sensation of "stillness" even as I move. When you are riding a merry-go-round, everyone and everything on it appears to remain still, relative to yourself. In truth, every part of the revolving disc moves at a different speed. Because all parts are coordinated around the movement of the center, there is a sensation of stillness in motion.

A similar principle may be applied to the movements of the human body in order to coordinate motion and maintain stillness (and therefore true balance) in motion. Here again the concepts of centering movement in the hips and maintaining the alignment of the centerline become paramount. Any part of the body that does not move in concert with the whole will be moving out of rhythm with the whole and, in effect, will be moving in a different direction. In this state the uncoordinated part of the body is perceived as having "motion" in relation to the rest; excess tension is inevitable and the quality of stillness in motion is lost. The key to maintaining stillness in motion is to coordinate the movements of the limbs with the movement of the torso. The movement of the torso around its central axis or as a unit through space provides the impetus for and must constantly adjust to the movements of the arms and legs. As the arms and legs are not moving "independently" of the torso, they are not perceived as "in motion" relative to the rest of the body (the torso and head). This is the state perceived as stillness in motion, the feeling of which may be used to gauge the quality of one's movement.

ON MOVING IN A UNIT AND WAVES OF FORCE

In order to make full use of inherent strengths and maintain balance, the body must be moved as a coherent unit. This is closely related to the concept of "stillness in motion" and implies the overall body rhythm which is basic in generating whole body power. The motion of any part of the body which does not move in concert with and contribute to the overall flow of momentum in the body as a whole becomes "disconnected" from the rest and results in a fragmentation of power. Fragmented movement results in a kind of "partial" balance (which requires undue effort to maintain) and detracts from maximum efficient movement. Fragmented motion will never be as powerful as unified motion, as the power of the entire mass working in concert will be much more powerful than the force of isolated parts. The obvious advantage unified motion confers is that it is the means by which one's full physical potential may be achieved, allowing the ultimate expression of natural power.

It is important to clarify what is meant here by the term "unit." In fact, there is more than one way to move the body as a unified entity. One method would be to hold the various parts of the body in alignment through excessive muscular tension. Holding oneself in a unit this way is relatively easy, just tense the muscles until it is impossible to move, and you are have forged yourself into an inflexible unit. Of course, when applied in the martial context the "freezing" of your muscle structure should only take place at the moment you impact with an opponent (in percussive techniques) or when aligning oneself to resist incoming force from a single angle (freezing the body into a rigid unit at any other time makes it impossible to move). When this method of unifying the body is employed in anatomically correct alignment, it is possible to generate a considerable force, especially if the practitioner is physically very strong and heavy. One drawback to generating force with this type of rigid unit is that it is impossible to make full use of momentum or the force of gravity (as tension in the muscles acts to inhibit momentum's flow). Another consideration is that the body in this state will be relatively slow to change and therefore succeptable to counter attack. Finally, it is relatively easy to disturb the balance of the body held in a rigid unit as pressure applied at any one point will directly influence the center.

Another, more flexible type of unitary whole body power may be achieved by maintaining correct anatomical alignment while relaxing the muscles completely. This body state allows one to generate power with momentum and align with the force of gravity. Maximum efficiency in technique becomes possible because the body is free to move, and balance is less easily disturbed as the relaxed body is capable of making instantaneous adjustments in relation to incoming forces. Here we have a body state which is capable of generating power much the same as a whip or bow. It is the inherent elasticity and "relaxed" nature of the whip and bow which give them their potential power. Maintaining a state of true balance with the body completely free of excess tension is the prerequisite for this type of whole body power.

The T'ai Chi Ch'uan Classics make several references to this type of power in various passages which advise the practitioner to "stand balanced like a scale" and "feel as if the body is `threaded' in a flexible unit (like a string of beads)." One is also advised to issue force "as a bow shooting an arrow." Utilizing the type of elastic power inherent in a balanced and relaxed body is the cornerstone of the Chinese "internal" martial arts as well as the the traditional Ju Jitsu arts of Japan (the character "ju" literally translates as "soft, pliant or supple").

In order to use the body as a coherent unit it is necessary to remain completely relaxed. Excess muscle tension inhibits the flow of momentum and serves to "disconnect" the tense area from the rest of the body. For example, if you shift your weight and turn your waist to generate momentum for a punch, and then tense or raise the shoulder of the punching arm, the momentum of the body as a whole is unable to pass through the rigid tissue of the shoulder and is greatly reduced. With balance and relaxation it becomes possible to move each part of the body in a coordinated rhythm, with each part of the body contributing to the movement of the whole in the right sequence and at the right

time (which is also the basis of "timing" one's movements correctly). Proper rhythm is the key to utilizing the full physical potential of the body in most forms of athletics. It is often quoted that a weapon (knife, stick etc.) is an extension of the hand. What is often overlooked is that the hand is an extension of the body. In order to generate and transfer momentum smoothly through the body as a whole, and manifest the power in the hands, balance and relaxation must be maintained. Involving the entire mass of the body in each movement will allow the practitioner to make use of his or her full potential, and will always prove more powerful than the limited power of fragmented parts. In the Chinese martial classics, the correct method of moving the body in a unit and generating a wave of force is described as "rooting in the feet, generate momentum with the legs, guide the momentum with the waist, allowing it to pass through the torso and transfer out through the hands."

ON DOUBLE WEIGHTING

The T'ai Chi Ch'uan Classics refer to the condition of double weighting as an "illness," and go on to state that even after years of training those practitioners who have not yet overcome this fault may be readily defeated by others. It is clear that the masters of old considered double weighting to be a serious problem. Double weighting is usually defined as the condition of standing with the weight evenly distributed between both feet (as in the classic "horse" stance). This, however, is not necessarily the case. Whether or not double weighting occurs is not determined directly by the relative distribution of weight between an individual's feet, but rather by whether or not one has joined centers with the opponent.

For example, if an opponent pushes against me with sufficient force to threaten my balance, and I tense up my body and resist directly into his force, his center and my center are two separate entities, or two separate "weights" resisting one another. If, on the other hand, I yield to the opponent's push and pull him into my momentum flow, joining centers with him, there is is only one common center for both our bodies. In the second example, the opponent and I are joined as one homogeneous weight. Now I may control the opponent as if he were an appendage and lead him into my technique without the use of force against force. It is in this condition that the application of technique becomes effortless.

It is important to note that after contact double weighting does not occur until the antagonistic pressure between your body and the opponent's body becomes so great that your state of relaxation and balance is threatened. As long as the force you are applying to an opponent does not clash directly with his, you are not double weighted. Whether throwing, applying joint locks or striking, maximum efficiency depends upon the avoidance of double weighting. When setting up a throw, the most efficient technique is the one which allows you to join and subsequently control an opponent's center in the shortest possible time, preferably immediately upon contact. When applying a percussive technique you are double weighted when your strike is angled such that its force is returned (at least partially) back into your own body. The most successful strikes (in terms of the amount of force the person receiving the strike absorbs) are those which enter at such an angle that the opponent is unable to resist the incoming force and must absorb it completely.

Once you have made a physical connection with an opponent, the immediate goal is to join centers and move him as a part of your own body. If at any point the opponent resists into the direction of your force, you must yield and change in order to avoid double weighting. Since force can only be applied against resistance, yielding to and circumventing an opponent's force guarantees the condition of double weighting will not occur. Once you resist into another's force, you must be physically stronger in order to prevail. Of course, the condition of double weighting can only occur when in contact with another. When confronted with an opponent, before actual contact is made, seeking an advantageous position from which to make a connection is very helpful. Connecting with another from an advantageous angle greatly facilitates joining and controlling another's center in the shortest possible time. In light of this fact, it becomes apparent why maintaining the correct distance from an opponent, the position of your body relative to his, the focus of your intent and the flow of your respective movements are all important variables which influence the relative ease or difficulty with which a technique may be set up and executed.

Finally, it may be helpful to realize that there is really only one angle at which you are double weighted, and that is the angle at which your force clashes directly with the force of another. Applying force to an opponent at any other angle allows you to avoid the fault of double weighting. This means that when in contact with another, the number of angles at which you are not double weighted is infinity minus one. Although this is the case, oddly enough most of us require a considerable amount of training before we do not react to incoming force by direct resistance. And no matter how powerful we are or how many techniques we know, our power or technique cannot be applied within the context of martial "art" until we understand and have rid ourselves of the illness of double weighting.

ON THE MECHANICS OF FORCE

Any martial art technique requires one to generate and apply force. We could even go so far as to say that the entire process of martial art training can be summed up as the process of learning how to generate force (solo training) and developing the ability to apply force to another (technique practice). In the Asian martial traditions, there is a distinction made between brute force (the application of which requires no training) and coordinated force (which is the result of systematic practice). The power inherent in true martial art technique is derived from the latter type of coordinated force. When training your body to generate force, several variables should be considered. These variables include how quickly the force may be generated, the parameters of applicability of the force generated (whether or not the same force may be applied to different techniques), the maintenance of balance while generating and applying force, the degree of continuity possible while generating force (whether or not force may be generated continuously or requires a period to build up momentum between applications), and whether or not the methods of generating force allow for maximum efficiency in body use as well as in application to another.

In light of the above variables, certain parameters should be set when devising methods of generating and applying force. The primary consideration should be the maintenance of balance. Techniques which generate a considerable amount of force but leave one off balance and vulnerable to counter attack are inferior to comparable techniques which allow one to maintain balance and the freedom to change which balance confers. Methods which allow one to generate force with a minimum of preliminary movements (i.e. "winding up") are superior to methods which require preliminary movements in order to generate force (as the ability to generate force without a wind up requires less time and gives an opponent less time to counter or escape). Methods which allow force to be generated in a continuous flow are superior to methods which require time intervals to build momentum between waves of force. Force which is generated and supported by the whole body is superior to force generated by isolated parts. Methods which allow one to generate force in a "non-specific" manner (force which may be applied to a variety of techniques) is superior to methods which generate force which is specific to a single application. If we accept the above value judgments concerning the generation and application of force to be true, then training (both solo and technical) should be structured around them, and the only body state which will allow the practitioner to adhere to the above criteria requires correct anatomical alignment and complete relaxation.

We have already discussed at great length the importance of maintaining correct anatomical alignment and complete relaxation (true balance). In order to remain relaxed and balanced, so that we might take full advantage of our inherent strengths and the natural forces of our environment (producing natural power), we need to generate momentum without undue tension anywhere in the body. Tension is the condition of exerting force against ourselves, of pitting the force of one muscle against another. Tension only serves to inhibit momentum and reduce one's potential power. We should remain aligned and relaxed so that momentum may pass through our bodies as a wave passes through water (waves of momentum will not pass through steam, as steam has no structure. Neither will waves of momentum pass through ice, as ice is too "tense."). And momentum properly generated and applied will overcome brute force every time.

In the Asian martial traditions, there is a clear distinction between coordinated power and brute force. The Chinese even use separate words for the two types of power, referring to the coordinated force of the whole body as "Jing," while brute force is referred to as "Li". The type of coordinated force which powers martial arts technique, and which is predicated upon true balance and natural power, makes use of momentum to produce waves of force through the entire body. This type of force insures that the power of the whole body is behind every move, and that one wave of force may be applied from any and every part (along its direction of flow). Since waves of force are generated primarily by the movement of the center and gravity, they pass through the relaxed body unobstructed and will not cause undue tension which would inhibit natural power, mobility, stability or balance. And because the body is always held aligned and in a state of relaxed readiness, there is no need to adjust the posture or relax before moving, so waves of force may be generated in continuous succession without the need for repositioning or preliminary movements. There is always potential force stored in a correctly aligned and balanced body.

ON THE MECHANICS OF POWER: FORMS AND STYLES

It is important to realize that all of the movements of martial arts were originally created around sets of underlying principles. The various creators of martial "styles," through diligent practice and trial and error in combat, came to understand the principles of effective methods of offense and defense, and attempted to organize these methods into coherent systems. In general, the founders of the ancient martial styles were very successful at personal combat, as proven by the fact that they survived to pass their methods on to others. The "natural selection" which weeded out less skilled combatants served to insure that only effective methods and techniques survived. As the prevalence of hand to hand combat gave way to modern warfare, it became possible to practice and teach a "martial art" without ever having to subject one's skills to the acid test of a real fight. Unfortunately, in many cases the basic principles upon which effective systems were founded were misunderstood or forgotten, leaving sets of movements which were faithfully taught and practiced but which were devoid of substance and which no longer served the purpose for which they were created (the purpose of imparting real martial ability). Under these conditions, forms were handed down from teacher to student as a "tradition," or out of a sense of obligation to persons long since dead. And although "going through the motions" of forms and techniques might qualify as a form of exercise, or even a form of "self cultivation," without the underlying principles upon which they were based, they no longer qualify as martial art.

The core and essence of the martial arts lies not in which style or form or technique is superior to another, or how many techniques a martial artist "knows," but whether or not the practitioner understands and practices according to the principles which underlie and form the basis of these arts. When executed in alignment with the correct principles of body use, any motion is inherently powerful. All of the great masters of old understood these principles (if not consciously, then intuitively) and the variation in the "styles" which they created were merely reflections of their personal bias and background. In fact, with a firm understanding of core principles, variations in movement and technique are practically endless. The attentive student will notice that all the movements and techniques of any particular martial art will all have the same "flavor," which reflects the bias (personal, ethical, experiential, physical, etc.) of that styles creator. This underlying consistency is indicative of the relatively small number of principles upon which the style was based, and which dictate the parameters within which effective technique may be expressed.

Although some degree of martial skill and power may be acquired through practice which is not in accord with the correct principles of body use and application, the fact remains that the same time spent in training would yield far greater results if it were structured around these principles. A big, strong, tense man can throw a powerful punch, but the blow will never be as powerful as the one thrown by an equally big, strong and relaxed man. As forms of movement and techniques were passed down without an understanding of the principles upon which they were based, students mastered the movements of a style only to discover when attempting to apply them "for real" that their techniques didn't work as expected. Incorrect body use and a lack of knowledge of the correct methods of application gave way to an emphasis on brute force. Without an understanding of the principles of correct body use and methods of application, the failure of a technique to produce the desired result is naturally blamed on a lack of strength.

The ill informed student now turns to the increased use of brute force in an attempt to make a technique "work." The result is a collection of techniques which can only be applied against weaker individuals, and which consequently are no longer deserving of the title of "art" (of course, it is always better to be stronger than weaker, and a certain amount of strength is always required. The point is true martial technique is based on the most efficient application of one's entire body against an opponent's weaknesses, and not the use of force against force. Although it is true that "all things being equal the stronger always wins," correct body use and true technique are the only means whereby the smaller and weaker may "unequalize" things in their favor). In the Chinese Martial Classics there is a passage which reads "When a man in his eighties is able to defeat several young men, how can this be due to strength or speed?" Basing martial training and technique on brute strength is ultimately self defeating, as after a certain point in life it inevitably begins to decline. Although it is good to be strong, being strong and being able to utilize one's strength most efficiently are two different things. And no matter how strong you are, in order to reach your full physical potential and maximum efficiency in technique you must use your body in harmony with its design and apply your strengths against an opponent's weaknesses. It is for this purpose that the various martial disciplines were created.

ABOUT THE AUTHOR:

Tim Cartmell began his martial arts training in in the art of Kung Fu San Soo in 1972. After receiving his Master's degree (eighth degree black belt) in 1984, he moved to the Republic of China to continue his training.

During the ten years Tim lived in China, he had the opportunity to study various martial arts (focusing on the "Internal" arts of Hsing Yi Ch'uan, T'ai Chi Ch'uan and Pa Kua Chang) with a number of outstanding teachers both in Taiwan and Mainland China.

Besides his martial arts training, Tim studied Chinese language and literature at the Taiwan Normal University full time for five years.

Tim is an Asian full contact tournament champion, with first place victories in both the light-heavyweight and middle-weight divisions.   In 1995 Tim returned to the States, where he divides his time between training, studying, teaching martial arts, writing and translating.

FOR FURTHER INFORMATION, PLEASE CONTACT:

Shen Wu School of Martial Arts
P.O. Box 4054
Westminster, CA
92684

The Author would like to thank Terry Spaulding, Todd Everhart, and Glen Rosenzweig for their help with the photo illustrations in this book.

From left to right, Terry Spaulding, Todd Everhart, Glen Rosenzweig, and Tim Cartmell

4635 McEwen Road, Dallas TX 75244
Tel: 239-280-2380
www.beckettmedia.com